Malaŵi
Wildlife, Parks and Reserves

Judy Carter

MACMILLAN

First published 1987
Reprinted 1989, 1990

Published by MACMILLAN EDUCATION LTD
London and Basingstoke
Associated companies and representatives in Accra, Auckland, Delhi, Dublin, Gaborone, Hamburg, Harare, Hong Kong, Kuala Lumpur, Lagos, Manzini, Melbourne, Mexico City, Nairobi, New York, Singapore, Tokyo

in association with
The Central Bookshop Ltd, Blantyre, Malaŵi

Printed in Hong Kong

British Library Cataloguing in Publication Data
Carter, Judy
  Malawi: wildlife, parks and reserves.
  1. Malawi — Description and travel —
  Guide-books
  I. Title
  916.897'044   DT858.2

ISBN 0–333–43987–2   Pbk
ISBN 0–333–43349–1

To my husband James, whom I met in Malaŵi.

Contents

Preface

I was fortunate enough to have the opportunity to live and work in Malaŵi for a couple of years, during which time I made many lasting friendships and travelled throughout the country. In the course of my work I saw much of Malaŵi's varied wildlife and scenery, and in the company of my friends and colleagues I visited many of the remoter and wilder areas of the national parks, game reserves and forest reserves. It was an experience I value greatly and I hope that this book will give similar pleasure to others, besides stimulating interest in Malaŵi's admirable wildlife conservation programme.

Introduction

For the general reader who does not know Malaŵi this book is designed to give an introduction to her wildlife, spectacular scenery and conservation programme. Those fortunate enough to be planning a visit to Malaŵi, or already resident there, will find that *Malaŵi: Wildlife, Parks and Reserves* provides detailed practical information for planning trips to the many national parks and game reserves. The book also covers a variety of natural history topics and indicates sources of further information for those with specialised interests.

As far as possible the text has been written in a non-technical manner, although it does attempt to explain the ecology of the country in some detail. The first chapter provides an overview of Malaŵi and her position in the African rift valley. It then reviews the history of the country with special emphasis on how human activities have influenced wildlife, and outlines the development of the national parks and game reserves. Subsequent chapters cover each main landscape type, and describe in detail the parks and reserves there.

For ease of reference there is a box containing basic information on each national park and game reserve. Boxes are located next to maps of the areas, at the beginning of the sections on individual parks and reserves. It is hoped that this feature will be of use to visitors planning their itineraries. Once in a park or reserve the book is designed to be used as a guide. Symbols illustrate the various facilities and possible activities in each area; a guide to the symbols is given below.

Facilities

1. Accommodation

 Rest camp

 Lodge

H Hotel

Hostel

▲ Camping

△ Tented camp

2. General

 Picnic area

Restaurant and bar

Self-catering cooking

S Shop

Swimming pool

I Information room

Game-viewing hide

3. Transport

Access for 2-wheel-drive vehicles — normally all year, (but check Access section)

Access for 2-wheel-drive vehicles — dry season only

Access for 4-wheel-drive vehicles — all year (in some cases internal roads are closed during the rains)

Petrol

Airstrip

Boat

Activities

 Game-viewing

 Bird-watching

 Fish-viewing

 Wild flowers

 Historical site

 Outstanding scenery

 Walking

 Angling

 Water sports

 Beach

Additional information is contained in the appendices. These cover general information; useful addresses; places to visit for special interests; scientific names of indigenous plants and animals; and a list of further recommended reading.

Where information has been obtained from other sources these are indicated by numbers in the text; references are listed by number after the last chapter.

The tourism information is based on the situation in 1985/6.

Nether Falla, Eddleston, Scotland   August 1986

Acknowledgements

I should like to thank the following people for all their assistance in the preparation of this book:

Richard Bell, John Burlison, John McCracken, Charlotte Randall Page, Luke Masimbe, Richard White, Tom McShane, Digby Lewis, Denis Tweddle, John Pallot, Alison Burlison and Frank Johnston for commenting on all or part of the manuscript, and in some cases supplying further information. I should like to emphasise that the opinions expressed in the book are ultimately mine, and may not always reflect the views of the above-named.

Bob Dowsett and Françoise Dowsett-Lemaire for supplying information on fauna and flora of the evergreen forests and Lengwe thickets, and on rinderpest; and for assistance with scientific nomenclature;

Gordon Scott, University of Edinburgh, John McKracken and Frank Ansell, for assistance with rinderpest research;

Nick van der Merwe, University of Cape Town, for permission to use unpublished information on iron smelting;

Brian Sherry, for permission to use unpublished information on the Majete elephant;

Malcolm Douglas and David Elias, for assistance with plant identification;

Caroline Crawford, for assistance with the map of Kasungu Park;

all former colleagues in the Department of National Parks and Wildlife for sharing their knowledge of Malaŵi's wildlife with me, and for their company on field-trips: sadly they are too many to name, but my special thanks to Richard Bell, David Elias, Matthew Matemba, Tom McShane, Francis Mkanda, John Mphande, Humphrey Nzima and Leonard Sefu;

staff of the National Library of Scotland for assistance during historical research;

my parents, Christopher and Susan Carter, for hospitality and tolerance during the initial stages of writing;

and finally my husband James Oglethorpe for much assistance, advice and encouragement during all stages of preparation of the book.

The author and publishers wish to acknowledge with thanks permission granted by Messrs Chatto and Windus (Hogarth Press) to quote from *Venture to the Interior* by Laurens van der Post.

Photographic acknowledgements

From *Narrative of an Expedition to the Zambezi*, David and Charles Livingstone, John Murray, 1865. Courtesy of The Royal Commonwealth Society. (page 13)
From *The Last Journals of David Livingstone*, H. Waller, John Murray, 1874. Courtesy of The Royal Commonwealth Society. (page 15)
From *British Central Africa*, H.H. Johnston, Methuen, 1897. Courtesy of The Royal Commonwealth Society. (page 17)
Courtesy of The Royal Commonwealth Society. (page 17)
From *British Central Africa*, H.H. Johnston, Methuen, 1897. Courtesy of The Royal Commonwealth Society. (page 18)
From *The Last Journals of David Livingstone*, H. Waller, John Murray, 1874. Courtesy of The Royal Commonwealth Society. (page 57)
From *Travels and Researches among the Lakes and Mountains of East and Central Africa*, J.F. Elton, John Murray, 1879. Courtesy of the Royal Commonwealth Society. (page 113)
From *Cape Maclear*, P.A. Cole-King, Department of Antiquities Publication Number 4, Malaŵi. Courtesy of the Royal Commonwealth Society. (page 114)
Cover photograph *Pel's fishing owl* courtesy of LIZ and TONY BOMFORD, SURVIVAL ANGLIA.
Back cover photograph courtesy of James Oglethorpe.

Chapter One

Malaŵi

Malaŵi is a small country by African standards, little known on the international safari circuits but harbouring a great wealth of scenery, landscapes and wildlife. It lies, landlocked, along the western side of part of the great African rift valley. A long, deep lake in its trough covers almost a fifth of the area of the country, and spectacular escarpments, plateaux and high mountains rise above the floor of the valley to give a wide range of scenery, climatic conditions and habitats for a variety of wild animal communities. Altitudes range from just above sea level in the south of the rift valley to 3002 m on top of the Mulanje Massif. In a short space of time one can travel from viewing the highly territorial, brightly coloured cichlid fish in the sparkling waters of Lake Malaŵi, passing foaming waterfalls on the steep escarpments, to the high mountain areas where herds of reedbuck graze and white-necked ravens drift overhead.

Not only is Malaŵi rich in natural phenomena: the country has an interesting and varied history, involving diverse peoples and cultures over the centuries. The result today is a friendly and courteous people who take great pride in their country and heritage. Visitors are welcomed in a genuinely friendly manner: Malaŵi truly is the warm heart of Africa, and a visit there is a never-to-be-forgotten experience.

To understand why the country has such a wealth of natural features it is necessary to look at its position in the African continent as a whole, and events which took place in the past, some of them millions of years ago in the geological timescale. These produced the wide range of landscape types and strongly influenced their plant and animal communities.

Local fishermen on the Elephant Marsh. The Marsh lies in the trough of the rift valley, overlooked by the rift escarpment and, beyond, the Mulanje Massif. OBERHOLSTER/SARTOC

The African rift valley

The African continent is one of the oldest in the world: much of it has been a land area since Pre-Cambrian times, more than 600 million years ago. Like other continents it has been affected by great, deep-seated forces within the earth which cause the phenomenon of continental drift. Three hundred million years ago Africa formed the core of the great continent of Pangaea. Due to the forces of convection within the magma deep beneath the earth's surface, the crustal plates of South America, Antarctica, the Indian sub-continent and Australasia broke away, and continue to drift slowly apart today (see figure 1.1). The mid-Atlantic ridge is a great rift valley system with mountain ranges and volcanoes, but deep beneath the Atlantic Ocean, formed at the margin of two of the crustal plates. The rift valley of Africa is the largest crack on the land surface of the earth, and it marks the early stages of a further splitting up of the continent. Perhaps one day far in the future much of Malaŵi, instead of being a landlocked country, will lie along the eastern side of a smaller African continent. The process of geological faulting which has given rise to the African rift valley is illustrated in figure 1.2.

The rift valley system of East Africa extends from the Zambezi River in the south, through Africa to the Red Sea and Jordan Valley in the north, as shown on map 1.1. It covers a distance of nearly 3000 km, more than one sixth of the earth's circumference. The system consists of a series of valleys; there is no single, continuous valley running the full length from north to south.

As the African continent is tilted, rising up in the east and south to high plateau surfaces of 1400 m and more, the rift valley is particularly impressive having formed within this high plateau. In addition, on either side of the rift valley and along its length mountain ranges have been formed, and these are very well illustrated in Malaŵi. Further north,

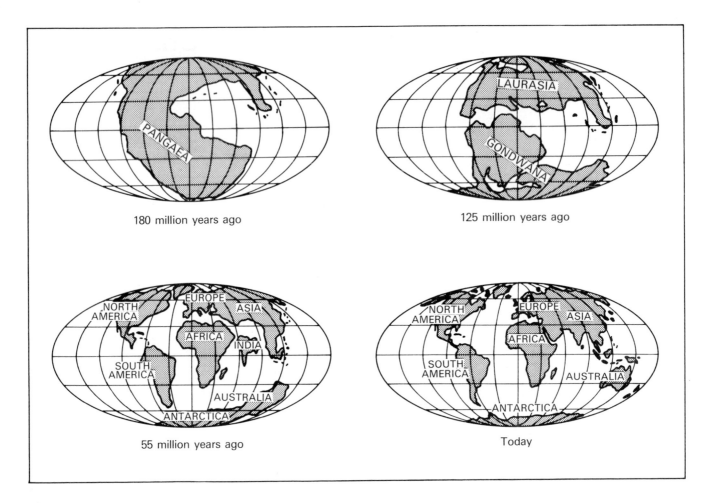

Fig 1.1   The process of continental drift

mainly in Ethiopia and Kenya, extensive and numerous layers of lava have formed within and around the valley adding further to the height of the land.

In many parts of the rift valley there are signs of activity within the earth's crust. Extinct volcanoes are common in Kenya, Tanzania, Uganda and Zaïre, and O1 Doinyo Lengai in Tanzania and a couple of volcanoes in Zaïre are still active, having erupted on

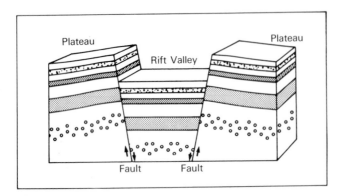

Fig 1.2   Rift valley formation

various occasions this century. Hot springs boil and bubble at various locations in the valley floors including Malaŵi, emitting a strong smell of sulphur. Some of the rift valley lakes are strongly alkaline because of the hot springs, and flocks of thousands of flamingos feed on the highly productive algal growth of the warm alkaline waters. Lake Magadi in Kenya is an important commercial source of soda. In parts of the rift valley volcanic activity has given rise to highly fertile soils. Elsewhere, as in Malaŵi, soils of the valley have formed from the deposition of large amounts of sediment resulting from natural erosion of the Pre-Cambrian rocks of the adjacent plateaux and escarpment walls. They are often more fertile than the soils of the plateaux on either side. (Geological information:[1,2])

Uplifting, rifting, volcanic activity and the deposition of sediments in the valleys have had a large impact on drainage patterns in the region, causing the diversion of many river courses and giving rise to various characteristically long, narrow and often very deep lakes (map 1.1). The longest of these is Lake Tanganyika, 650 km in length with an average width of 50 km and a depth of 1470 m at the deepest point[3].

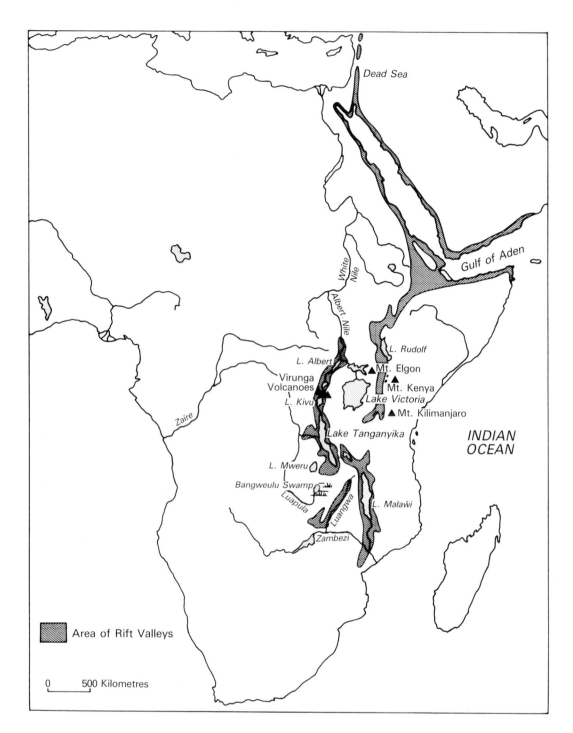

Map 1.1   The rift valley system of East Africa

Lake Malaŵi is 570 km in length, and is the second longest rift valley lake after Lake Tanganyika.

The development of these lakes and other changes in the drainage patterns created a great variety of new habitats for the widespread aquatic fauna existing in the region. In the most isolated basins such as those of Lakes Tanganyika and Malaŵi a great evolution of new aquatic species took place with a wide divergence from the previously occurring fauna, and these two lakes are now each thought to contain more species of fish than any other freshwater lake in the world. Over 500 species of fish are thought to occur in Lake Malaŵi; the total number is not yet certain as many have not yet been named and described — more continue to be discovered each year. The great majority of them are cichlids, and in this group 98% of known species are endemic (ie occur nowhere else in the world)[4]. Of particular interest are the brightly coloured *mbuna* cichlids, favourites amongst aquarists throughout the world.

Hot spring by Lake Bogoria in the Kenyan Rift Valley.
JAMES OGLETHORPE

Making a fish trap near the Elephant Marsh. Seventy per cent of the nation's animal protein is obtained from fish, caught by a variety of traditional and modern methods.   LIZ and TONY BOMFORD, *SURVIVAL ANGLIA*

Terrestrial parts of the rift valley floor often support vegetation types and animal populations which are very different from those found on the nearby escarpments and surrounding plateaux. Apart from variations in soil fertility, this is sometimes due to marked climatic differences. The floor of the valley may lie 500 m or more below the plateaux, consequently experiencing warmer weather. Such a temperature difference may create locally unstable atmospheric conditions in the region. Rainfall is often greater over the higher areas on the plateaux than in the valleys. Thus, vegetation and animal communities found on the Central African Plateau differ from those found along the valleys, which are more typical of lowland Africa.

Malaŵi

The southern section of the rift valley which passes through Malaŵi starts to the north of the country with two relatively short forks consisting of the Ruaha and Rukwa Valleys in Tanzania, the former containing the Ruaha National Park. These merge at the head of the section of the rift containing Lake Malaŵi; at this point volcanic activity has created mountains in the valley, and the higher ground separates the drainage basin of Lake Malaŵi from the others. The rift then runs southwards along the line of the lake to another series of forks round the Chiripa Hills at the southern end of the lake, and the Shire Highlands. A long fork to the east of the Shire Highlands incorporates Lakes Chiuta and Chilwa and the Ruo Valley, extending north-north-east to the Lugenda Valley in Mozambique. This branch of the rift, however, has been obscured by subsequent warping of the land surface. The major rift valley passes to the west of the Shire Highlands, and along it flows the Shire River which drains from Lake Malaŵi. Further south, outside Malaŵi territory, the Shire reaches its confluence with the Zambezi River while the rift continues a short distance south of the Zambezi into the Urema basin and Gorongosa National Park in Mozambique.[5]

Malaŵi's international boundary follows Lake Malaŵi for much of its length in the east, while in the west it lies on high ground along the watershed between the catchment areas of the Shire River/

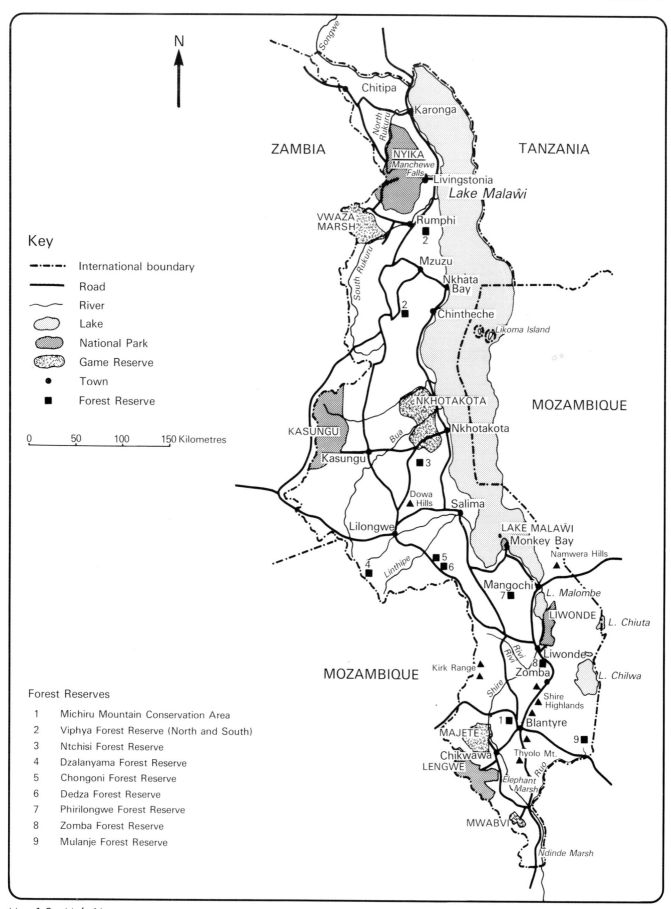

Forest Reserves

1   Michiru Mountain Conservation Area
2   Viphya Forest Reserve (North and South)
3   Ntchisi Forest Reserve
4   Dzalanyama Forest Reserve
5   Chongoni Forest Reserve
6   Dedza Forest Reserve
7   Phirilongwe Forest Reserve
8   Zomba Forest Reserve
9   Mulanje Forest Reserve

Map 1.2   Malaŵi

Lake Malaŵi and the Zambezi. In the south Malaŵi territory includes the south-eastern shores of Lake Malaŵi; Lake Chilwa and part of Lake Chiuta; the Shire Highlands and much of the Shire Valley, as shown on map 1.2. As a country, therefore, Malaŵi covers a wide range of altitudes and landscape types, each with its characteristic climate, scenery, soils, vegetation, animal life and land-uses.

Climate

The overall pattern of Malaŵi's climate is similar to that of most of the rest of Southern Africa. There is a wet season which starts in November or December and lasts until April, followed by a cool dry season from May to August and a hot dry season from September until the onset of the next rains. The rains usually start and finish earlier in the south of the country than in the north. Rainfall varies from about 600 mm to over 2400 mm, being greatest on high areas and steep slopes exposed to the prevailing south-east winds, and least in low areas lying in the rain-shadow of hills. Temperatures vary with altitude, the hottest areas being in the trough of the rift valley and the coolest on the high mountains and plateaux. During November the mean maximum temperature in the former may be greater than 35°C, whilst on the highest areas it is less than 27°C. Medium level areas have intermediate temperatures. The cool season temperatures are much lower, being pleasantly cool in the low areas and cold in the high mountains where frost may even occur at night in July. The cooler temperatures at this time of year are usually accompanied by clear skies and brilliant sunshine. Occasionally this weather is interrupted for a few days when much of southern and central Malaŵi experiences cold weather and light rain with mist over high ground: this is known as *chiperoni*.[5,6]

Landscape types

The main landscape types in Malaŵi are: the high mountains and plateaux; plains and undulating areas below them, some of which are part of the main Central African Plateau; the steep escarpments of the rift valley; Lake Malaŵi and the lakeshore plains; and the Shire Valley. They are shown on map 1.3 and illustrated diagrammatically in figure 1.3.

High mountains and plateaux

The high mountains and plateaux rise in isolation from the relatively flat plains below. Many occur

near the lip of the rift valley and others lie on the country's western border; they add interest to the scenery of the surrounding areas. The most extensive is Nyika Plateau in the north, but perhaps the most

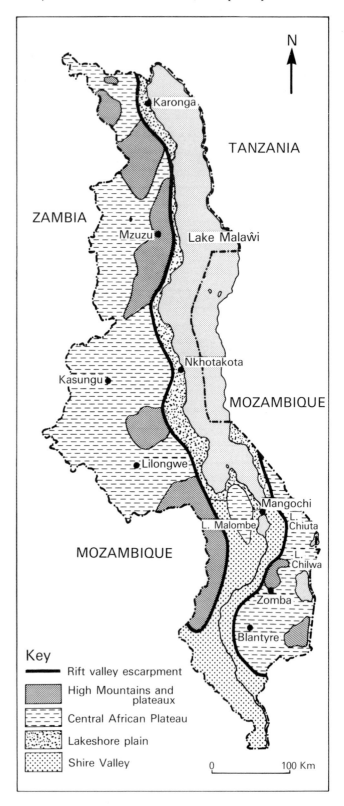

Key

— Rift valley escarpment

High Mountains and plateaux

Central African Plateau

Lakeshore plain

Shire Valley

0   100 Km

Map 1.3 Major landscape types of Malaŵi

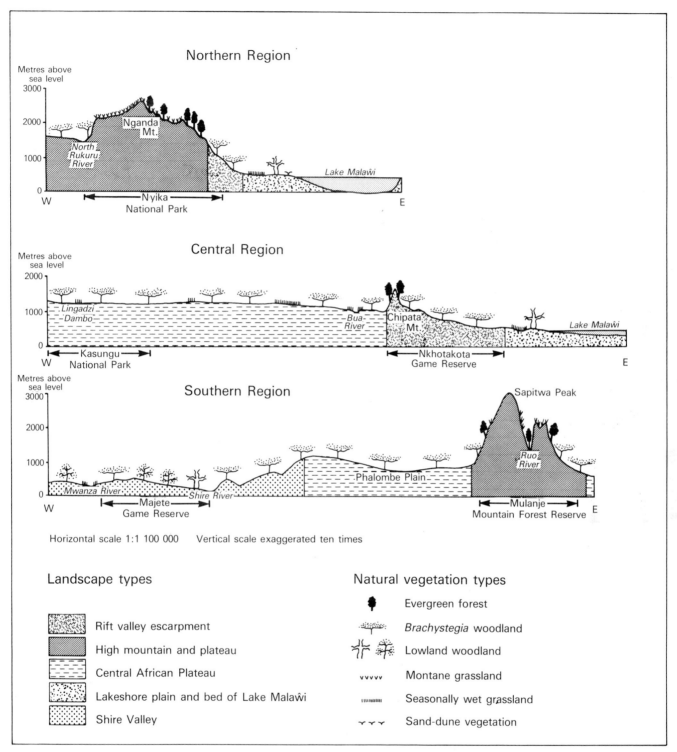

Northern Region

Metres above sea level

3000

2000 — Nganda Mt.

North Rukuru River

1000

Lake Malaŵi

0

W   Nyika National Park   E

Central Region

Metres above sea level

2000

Lingadzi Dambo

1000

Bua River   Chipata Mt.   Lake Malaŵi

0

W   Kasungu National Park   Nkhotakota Game Reserve   E

Southern Region

Metres above sea level

3000   Sapitwa Peak

2000

1000   Phalombe Plain   Ruo River

Mwanza River   Shire River

0

W   Majete Game Reserve   Mulanje Mountain Forest Reserve   E

Horizontal scale 1:1 100 000   Vertical scale exaggerated ten times

Landscape types

- Rift valley escarpment
- High mountain and plateau
- Central African Plateau
- Lakeshore plain and bed of Lake Malaŵi
- Shire Valley

Natural vegetation types

- Evergreen forest
- *Brachystegia* woodland
- Lowland woodland
- Montane grassland
- Seasonally wet grassland
- Sand-dune vegetation

Fig 1.3   Malaŵi's major landscape and vegetation types East-west cross-sectional diagrams through a selection of protected areas

spectacular is Mulanje Massif in the south, rising almost sheer for 2000 m above the Phalombe Plain, ringed with verdant tea estates at its base.

The high areas were mainly formed from intrusions of magma giving rise to hard rocks such as granite and gneiss. These have withstood weathering and erosion whilst softer surrounding materials were worn away, leaving isolated inselbergs, mountains and high plateaux standing above the present-day surface of the Central African Plateau.[2,5] Although many of these features appear at first sight to be extinct volcanoes there has in fact been very little volcanic activity in Malaŵi. Some of the mountains are very old: for example igneous rocks on Nyika are

The Mulanje Massif, its tallest peaks rising 2000 m above the plain below.   FRANK JOHNSON

estimated to be 1300 million years old. Mulanje on the other hand is much younger, about 125 million years old.[7]

Ascending these mountains, the woodland of the plains gradually gives way to natural heaths, montane grassland and often patches of evergreen forest as the climate becomes colder and wetter. Clear, fast streams flow and the air is fresh and cool while the plains below shimmer with heat. Views from these high areas are spectacular, sometimes extending for hundreds of kilometres. Wild animals include the klipspringer and dassie, agile on rock outcrops. Some of the high plateaux have been planted in commercial forestry operations though the wilder, less accessible areas remain much as they have been for hundreds of years. Tea and coffee plantations have been developed in places on the lower slopes of Mulanje, the hills of the Shire Highlands and some of the northern hills.

Inselbergs rising above the Central African Plateau south of Lilongwe.   JUDY CARTER

Central African Plateau

Below these high areas lie plains, most of which are part of the old Central African Plateau. They are flat to undulating areas, often traversed by broad, meandering drainage lines. Where the vegetation has not been cleared for agriculture or timber and firewood production they are usually covered with *Brachystegia*, *Combretum* or *Acacia* woodland. Drainage lines are often flanked by broad strips of grassland known as *dambo*, where interesting flowers including orchids grow. In the north a large wetland occurs, the Vwaza Marsh, which is protected in a game reserve.

Much of the plains area is cultivated, maize and tobacco being the main crops: tobacco is Malaŵi's most important export. Firewood and timber plantations also occur in the area, the former being used both for domestic purposes by the majority of people living in the area, and for the processing of flue-cured tobacco. Cattle, goats and sheep are grazed on the *dambos*.

Rift valley escarpments

At the edges of the rift valley the land falls steeply away from the Central African Plateau, often in a tortuous jumble of hills and ridges, towards the trough of the rift. Rivers plunge down steep drops, and foam through rocky gorges and steep valleys on their way down the rift valley escarpments. The few roads which descend the escarpments wind and turn round hairpin bends and across narrow bridges, with the occasional breathtaking glimpse of the valley below. Most of the slopes are covered with *Brachystegia* woodland though there is some evergreen forest in a high rainfall area by Nkhata Bay. Near here there are coffee and tea estates and a rubber plantation, the only one in the country. Otherwise, the main cultivation on the escarpments

The narrow lakeshore plain nestling below the rift valley escarpment near Chiweta in northern Malaŵi, with the mouth of the South Rukuru River in the distance. Across Lake Malaŵi are the hills of Tanzania. DENIS TWEDDLE

consists of timber and firewood plantations, and subsistence crops such as maize, groundnuts and bananas. The escarpments are generally not highly populated; a few small isolated villages perch precariously on top of narrow hills. In some places, soil erosion resulting from clearance and cultivation leaves deep red scars on the landscape.

Lake Malaŵi and the lakeshore plains

Below the escarpments lies the floor of the rift valley which ranges in width from about 40 to 90 km.

The lower Shire Valley near Chikwawa.   LIZ and TONY BOMFORD, *SURVIVAL ANGLIA*

Much of it is occupied by Lake Malaŵi, 570 km long and 80 km across at the widest point (more easily memorised as being approximately 365 miles by 52 miles, the figures being the same as the number of days and weeks in the year). At its deepest, north of Nkhata Bay, the water depth is greater than 700 m and the lake bed at this point lies below sea-level. It is in the shallower parts of the south, however, that fish productivity is highest. Many people living along the lakeshore depend on fishing for their livelihood, and fish protein is a very significant part of the Malaŵian diet. The lakeshore comprises rocky faces, shallow reedy areas and sandy beaches. Some of the latter have been developed for tourism, the lake being the most important attraction in Malaŵi.

Many of the lakeshore plains are very fertile and have been developed for large-scale agricultural projects such as sugar, rice and cotton, as well as subsistence agriculture. Where the natural vegetation remains it comprises floodplains, grassy *dambos* and lowland woodland, the latter including trees such as the baobab with its strange, swollen trunk, and the yellow-barked fever tree in areas of high water table.

The Shire Valley

At its southern end Lake Malaŵi is drained by the majestic Shire River, the only outlet from the lake. It follows the line of the rift valley, flowing into Lake Malombe and resuming its course on the south side through Liwonde National Park, to descend a series of spectacular rapids before slowing and spreading into the huge Elephant Marsh. This is a complex maze of islands, channels, papyrus and other reed beds, a haven for fish, water birds, crocodile and hippo.

The fertile parts of the Shire Valley to either side of the watercourse are used for the cultivation of sugar, rice and cotton, as well as subsistence crops. Livestock are grazed in less fertile areas and valuable timber is obtained from natural and plantation forests. Vegetation of undisturbed areas consists of *Brachystegia*, *Combretum*, *Sterculia* and mopane woodland, thickets and grassy floodplain areas.

So, in a comparatively small area, Malaŵi contains a great diversity of landscapes and scenery. Whilst travelling, there is always some new feature of interest round the next corner. One rarely senses the boredom of the 'miles and miles of b... Africa' syndrome experienced in other parts of the continent, where flat, featureless areas can seem very monotonous and directionless. It is a place where many different southern and east African habitat types and animal communities may be seen within a short distance, and in relative comfort. Malaŵi is also rich in history, having been inhabited successively by hunter-gatherers of the Stone Age and cultivators of the Iron Age; been at the crossroads of major trade routes, first for ivory and then slaves; witnessed much tribal warfare; been 'discovered' by missionaries and explorers; briefly been a British Protectorate; and finally emerged as an independent modern African state. The story of Malaŵi's history is interesting and varied, and it is outlined below as it enhances the understanding of the country and its wildlife as they are today.

History of Malaŵi[5,8,9]

Stone Age

It is not known when man first inhabited the land which is now Malaŵi. Some of the oldest known vertebrate fossil remains are of wild animals which lived two million years ago; these were discovered in the 1960s by an archaeological team from the University of California, in sediments at the northwest end of Lake Malaŵi in Karonga District. The fauna included several different types of elephant, black and white rhino, giraffe, several kinds of pig, many bovids, gazelles, three-toed horses and ostrich, indicating that the vegetation was then more open than it is today. In the lake at that time hippo (large and pygmy), crocodile, water tortoises and fish occurred. These records are of special interest as Karonga is the most northerly known site for the occurrence of certain Southern African genera and species at that time, and the most southerly known limit for some East African forms. This pattern continues today in Malaŵi, lying as it does on the edge of these major zoo-geographical regions.

Parts of present-day Malaŵi offered a favourable environment for hunter-gatherer people with a reasonable abundance of wild animals, and fish in the lake and rivers. The earliest records of man are from the Early Stone Age, found near Karonga and the Linthipe River near Lilongwe. The former includes an elephant butchery site complete with choppers, scrapers and knives, and fossilised elephant remains thought to be between 50 000 and 100 000 years old. By this time the fauna would have become more similar to that occurring today. Evidence of man from the Middle, and especially the Later Stone Age is much more widespread, the latter including skeletal material and many artefacts used to make hunting weapons and domestic tools. Besides hunting these people gathered fruits, roots and other plant parts, an essential part of their diet. They occupied rock shelters and caves, and are thought to have been the artists of red geometric paintings found on the rock walls. The paintings comprise circles, stars, ladders, parallel lines and more complicated designs typical of the central African schematic art tradition, and are very different from the Bushman rock art found in the south with its characteristic animals and people. The best Stone Age paintings in Malaŵi are in a series of rock shelters at Chencherere in the Chongoni Forest Reserve: they can be visited in a day trip from Lilongwe[10].

Rock paintings in one of the rock shelters at Chencherere. The red geometric shapes were probably drawn by people of Stone Age culture, and the white figures by Iron Age Maravi. I. VINCENT/SARTOC

From the findings of burial site excavations these people are thought to have been short in stature and robustly built, with both Negroid and Bushmanoid characteristics. They occupied the north-western lakeshore and the plateau area from about 8000 BC to around the end of the fifteenth century AD, and isolated pockets of these people may have survived into the last 200 years. They would probably have had a relatively small impact on their environment, as their numbers were always relatively low and their needs for natural resources were very simple. Gathering of plants would have had a small and very localised impact on the vegetation; fires might have had a more widespread effect. Their hunting activities may have affected certain wild animal populations on a small scale though the effect would have been much less significant than that of the Iron Age people.

Iron Age

The earliest evidence of Iron Age man is from Phopo Hill, near the present-day boundary of Vwaza Marsh Game Reserve in northern Malaŵi. There, remains dating back to around AD 200 have been found, including pottery, iron slag, tuyère fragments and pieces of bone. From around this time until the fourteenth and fifteenth centuries Bantu people are thought to have moved southwards through Africa in successive waves of small groups, some settling in present-day Malaŵi. They brought with them not only knowledge of iron-working, but also livestock and seed for cultivation. The latter would have included finger millet, first cultivated in the highlands of what is now Ethiopia around 3000 BC[11], and still grown in a few plateau areas of Malaŵi today.

The Bantu occupied both southern and northern Malaŵi, plateau and rift valley, around the same time. It is thought that they would have been welcomed by the hunter-gatherers because of the new sources of food and technical skills they brought with them. Their need for land for cultivation and grazing, at least initially, would probably not have seriously conflicted with the needs of the hunter-gatherers as numbers were small, and it is thought that a symbiotic relationship probably existed between the two groups. The gene pool from which the present population of Malaŵi derives is considered to contain a significant element from the hunter-gatherers.

At some time between AD 1200 and AD 1500 the Maravi people migrated from an area in present-day Zaïre into what is now Malaŵi (see map 1.4 on page 16). By the beginning of the sixteenth century the Maravi empire was developing, with centralised rule over the previous inhabitants. At its greatest it encompassed part of eastern Zambia, central and southern Malaŵi and northern Mozambique. It operated under a chieftainship system, with its own beliefs and traditions. The site of creation of man and animals was believed by the Maravi to be in the Dzalanyama Hills south-west of present-day Lilongwe; on a small hill there are footprints in the rockface, believed to have hardened in the sun when man took his first steps. There were many rain shrines with rituals involving fire and animal sacrifice which were necessary to ensure rain for the crops; some are still in use today, such as Bunda Mountain south of Lilongwe[12].

The Maravi gradually became subdivided into three main groups: the Sena and Mang'anja, who inhabited large areas of the lower Shire Valley, and the Chewa who occupied parts of the plateau and rift valley in what is now central Malaŵi. In the north the Tumbuka and associated smaller tribes of mixed

Trap set by local people for hippopotamus, seen by Livingstone on the Shire River. A beam armed with a spear head or spike coated in poison was suspended from a forked pole by a cord which continued down to the path below. It was held there by a catch which was released when the hippo stepped on it, causing the animal to be impaled by the poisoned spear. Livingstone's boat the *Ma Robert* is in the background.   DAVID and CHARLES LIVINGSTONE

origins moved in from present-day Tanzania and north-eastern Zambia, settling around Karonga and Mzimba. Large areas of the country still remained uninhabited by man, such as many of the highlands and areas with no surface water.

The impact of the Iron Age people on the environment would have been greater than that of the Stone Age people; wood was required for iron-smelting (see pages 38 and 39), pastures for livestock, fertile lands for cultivation and cleared areas for settlements. In small pockets the natural vegetation cover would have become greatly modified. It is likely that wild animal populations were beginning to be significantly affected by human activity in certain locations, probably more through loss of habitat than direct hunting. At that time hunting weapons were still fairly primitive and hunting was restricted to a few people who had permission to do so from the local chief. The art was surrounded by mystical beliefs: hunting magic was essential for the success of

the hunt and protection of the hunter. Animals were believed to have mystical powers to harm, and hunted animals could take vengeance on any hunter unprotected by magic with a madness akin to rabies. This power was quite separate from physical strength and defences such as horns and teeth; the duiker, for example, was believed to be a more potent avenger than the elephant. The protective magic involved many rituals, chants and charms and was inherited through the male line of the tribe, thus limiting the number of hunters in any one settlement. In addition the custom of totemism amongst certain clans protected individual species; if the clan were named after an animal, then none of its members could kill that species or eat its flesh.[13] Some of these beliefs are still practised in parts of Southern and East Africa today.

This situation continued into the eighteenth century, with the slow but steady expansion of settlements and cultivation, and production of iron. However, the peaceful era was then interrupted by new waves of invasions and the relatively defenceless society went into decline. In the 1830s the warlike Ngoni, pastoralists fleeing from Chaka and his Zulu warriors in the south, crossed the Zambezi River and moved northwards. One group entered Malaŵi near present-day Dedza, crossing to the south of Lake

Malaŵi before continuing north. A second group moved northwards along the western side of present-day Malaŵi, close to the watershed. In the 1850s and 1860s these groups re-entered the country, the former settling near Dedza and Ntcheu, and the latter in present-day Mzimba and Dowa Districts (see map 1.4 on page 16). They attacked settlements in these areas, killing adult men and capturing women, children and cattle. The Chewa attempted to defend their villages by surrounding them with walls and ditches: remains of fortified villages may still be seen today in Kasungu National Park. However, widespread destruction of many settlements resulted and the small groups who escaped were forced to live in remote and unsuitable places such as the mountains (including the Nyika) and the rift valley escarpment. The Ngoni settled with their large herds of cattle in dense settlements under strong chieftainship in the areas they had taken, using their captors as domestic slaves. Their agricultural system was apparently more intense than that previously practised there and had an adverse impact on the environment. Overgrazing by large numbers of low quality cattle and possibly monocropping resulted in loss of fertility and soil erosion. It therefore became necessary every so often to move to areas as yet unaffected.

The Ngoni made their presence felt in the centre and north of Malaŵi; the south, however, did not escape invasion. The Yao tribe originating from the lands east of Lake Malaŵi moved westwards into present-day Malaŵi, initially because of drought. They settled around the southern shores of Lake Malaŵi, in the Shire Highlands to the south, and along the lakeshore towards Salima where they climbed the escarpment to the edge of the Lilongwe Plain. They also attacked settlements, enslaving the inhabitants.

Trading

The ease with which the Yao captured slaves attracted Swahilis and Arabs engaged in slave-trading operations on the east coast of Africa based at Zanzibar, and from the 1840s onwards a number of Swahili people followed them into the area, introducing aspects of Swahili culture which still exist in Malaŵi today. Portuguese traders also had an interest in obtaining slaves; the slave-trade in west Africa was suppressed in 1840, and with continued demand for slaves in Brazil the half-caste Portuguese traders operating from Portuguese territory on the coast turned their attention to the area of Lake Malaŵi.

Several trade routes from the east coast of Africa crossing present-day Malaŵi to the interior had been in existence for a long time, possibly from the twelfth century AD (see map 1.4 on page 16). They were used to carry headloads of cloth, beads and later guns from the Arab traders at the coast to exchange inland for ivory and copper. It is likely that certain crop plants reached Malaŵi by this route. For example maize, thought to have been introduced to the east coast of Africa by the Portuguese in the seventeenth century after the discovery of America, was probably taken inland by Arab traders in the 1800s[14]. Rice, which had been introduced to Madagascar from south-east Asia in the early centuries of the Christian era, was later established on the African continent by the Arabs[11].

Early crossings of Lake Malaŵi by traders were made by dugout canoe, stopping overnight on islands, though dhows were introduced by the Arabs in the nineteenth century. Well-worn paths climbed the escarpment of the rift valley and crossed the plains to the west. Thus the slave-traders had ready-made transport routes for slaves who were marched in chains and stocks to trade centres on the lake: Karonga, Nkhotakota and Mponda's (near Mangochi). Nkhotakota was a particularly important centre, being an extension of the Omani Arabs' empire at Zanzibar and run by Jumbe, a self-styled Sultan. The slaves were taken in dhows across the lake, from where they were marched to the slave-markets on the coast. In 1870 it was estimated that Nkhotakota and Mponda's each had an annual turnover of 10 000 slaves. They were brutally treated, being beaten, bound, yoked together and made to carry headloads of ivory and other goods to the coast. The majority did not survive; Dr David Livingstone, visiting the area in 1861, was horrified by what he saw, and estimated that only one in ten survived this treatment. He recorded the going price for a slave as one gun, though cloth and beads were sometimes bartered instead[15].

Missionary activity

Livingstone, a Scottish missionary-explorer, had already made several long journeys in southern Africa. In 1858 he was sent by the British Government to open up routes to the interior of Africa for exploration and trade. He sailed up the Zambezi, hoping to discover a route in from the east coast, but

Slaves being marched to the coast, seen here by David Livingstone near the Ruvuma River east of Lake Malaŵi. If slaves became unable to march they were sometimes killed by the slave traders who were enraged at losing the money they had paid for them, or determined that other traders would not benefit from the slaves should they recover after resting.
H. WALLER

found his passage blocked by the rapids at Cabora Bassa in present-day Tete Province of Mozambique. He then turned his attention to the great northern tributary of the Zambezi which he had passed downstream: the Shire River. He sailed up the Shire in his steamer the *Ma Robert* in January 1859 only to discover more rapids, today called Kapichira Falls in Majete Game Reserve, which impeded navigation. However, in subsequent visits he proceeded overland past this impediment, sailing up Lake Malaŵi and exploring parts of the land area of present-day Malaŵi. He followed the trade route from Nkhotakota west through the present-day game reserve, passing across what is now Kasungu National Park where he was much impressed with the quality of the iron he saw being produced but recorded few wild animals. The routes followed by Livingstone through present-day Malaŵi are shown on map 1.4 overleaf.

On his last journey in search of the source of the Nile Livingstone crossed the Lilongwe Plain in 1866,

heading towards the area which is now eastern Zambia. He commented on the large-scale human settlement and the paucity of wild animals: from his and other records it seems that in the central plateau area large mammals were confined to the major river valleys and areas of forest.[16] By that time firearms had been introduced by the traders and there was a good market for ivory, leopard skins and other trophies as well as a heavy demand for meat for domestic consumption. Man was having a significant impact on wild animal populations in certain areas, though in some places animals were still abundant. Faulkner, on an expedition in search of Livingstone the following year, recorded near the confluence of the Shire and Rivi Rivi Rivers south of the present-day Liwonde National Park: *an open plain appeared, and this was literally overstocked with game, all apparently feeding towards the river. There were koodoo, pallahs, hartebeest, gemsbock, and reedbock; wherever the eye turned antelopes of some kind were to be seen. I never saw such quantities of game*[17]. Faulkner was a keen hunter and gives a lucid account of the part he played in reducing the quantity of big game in the country.

Other Europeans visiting the area at that time had more humanitarian concerns, however. Livingstone was so appalled by the social and economic situation created by the slave-trade that, besides the

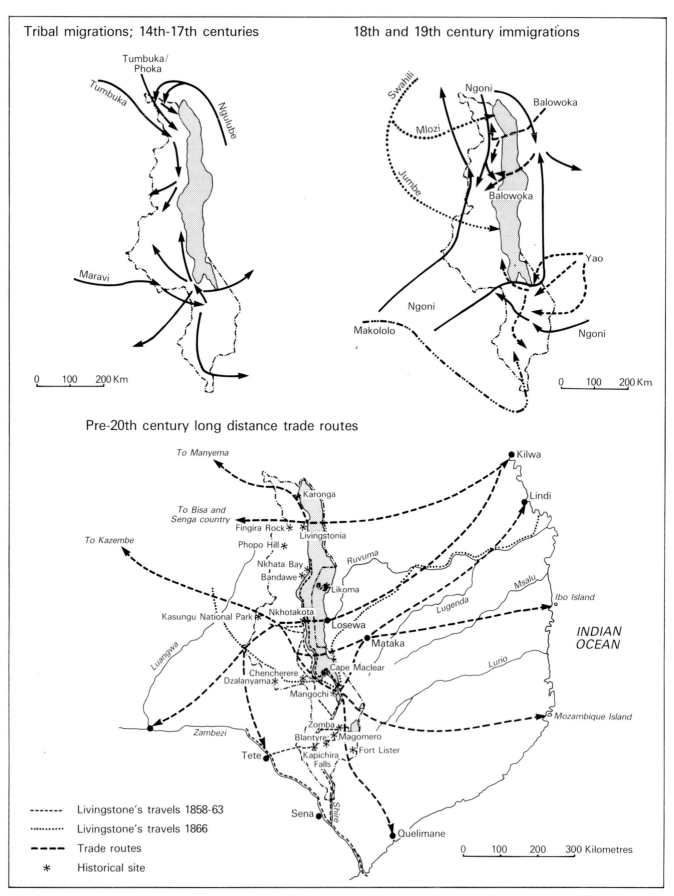

Tribal migrations; 14th-17th centuries

18th and 19th century immigrations

Pre-20th century long distance trade routes

------- Livingstone's travels 1858-63

·············· Livingstone's travels 1866

━ ━ ━ Trade routes

∗ Historical site

Map 1.4 Historical map

St Michael's Church built by the Church of Scotland Mission in Blantyre. Dedicated in 1891, the church still stands today.
THE ROYAL COMMONWEALTH SOCIETY

Mandala House, built in 1882, originally the headquarters of the African Lakes Company in Blantyre and now a national monument.   F.L.M. MOIR

introduction of Christianity, he recommended that alternative commercial activities be initiated to replace slaving. These included agriculture, as he considered the agricultural potential of this new land to be high. He himself died by the Bangweulu Swamps in present-day Zambia in 1873 on his journey in search of the source of the Nile, and consequently did not see the wave of missionary activity which followed his recommendations. In 1875 the Free Church of Scotland established the Livingstonia Mission at Cape Maclear on Lake Malaŵi, which had been named by Livingstone after his friend Sir Thomas Maclear, the Astronomer Royal at the Cape of Good Hope.[18] This site lies within the present boundary of the Lake Malaŵi National Park. The missionaries, however, found malaria to be so great a problem that the mission was moved, first to Bandawe further north on the lake, and later to its present site at Livingstonia, on the escarpment in a much healthier climate. Other missions were establishing bases in Malaŵi at the same time. The Church of Scotland founded a mission in the Shire Highlands, around which the city of Blantyre developed. The Universities Mission to Central Africa established its first settlement at Magomero but this was short-lived; armed force had to be used to prevent slaving activities, and a series of disasters, ending with the death of the leader of the group, Bishop Mackenzie, forced the withdrawal of the mission to Zanzibar. It returned afterwards, however, and established a mission at Likoma Island on Lake Malaŵi where a cathedral was later built. The mission was strategically placed to assist in controlling the slave-trade, and had a boat on the lake to intercept Arab dhows carrying slaves. Apart from this activity, missions were spreading Christianity to the local people and providing some basic schooling.

These missionary activities stimulated a group of businessmen from Glasgow to set up the African Lakes Company in 1878, whose purpose was to promote trade in goods in order to phase out the slave trade and supplement the missions' activities. It was based in Blantyre at Mandala House, and later opened a depot at Karonga with a steamer on the lake. The company still exists today as Mandala Limited. Encouraged by these new developments, planters and traders from various countries arrived to negotiate land rights with local chiefs.

Nyasaland Protectorate

A British Consul was appointed in 1883, accredited to the 'Kings and Chiefs of Central Africa' to look after the British interests in the area. It had gradually become clear that a defence force was necessary to protect the missionaries and traders from hostile tribes and slave-traders, as they would otherwise have been forced to leave. Also, the Portuguese were becoming suspicious of the sudden British activity around Lake Malaŵi. Previously they had occupied only a few parts of their East African territory, on the coast and the Zambezi River, and had charged customs duties on goods being transported on the Zambezi between the newly opened area and the Indian Ocean. Their boundaries to the interior had never been defined, but now that the potential of the land around the Shire River and Lake Malaŵi was starting to be developed they became interested in claiming that area as Portuguese territory. Lengthy negotiations were initiated, interspersed with skirmishes with local tribes. Following a new threat of Portuguese invasion in 1889, the Makololo and Yao areas in the south of present-day Malaŵi were declared a British Protectorate by the acting consul. The Makololo area is significant as these people had been porters who accompanied Livingstone from western Zambia, settling near Chikwawa after the explorer's first visit there.

In 1890 the British and Portuguese Governments finally agreed on the location of the boundary between the two territories, south of Nsanje, where it today marks the international border across the Shire Valley between Malaŵi and Mozambique. At that time Harry Johnston, then British Consul in Mozambique, travelled north and instigated treaties with the local chiefs in the Lower Shire, the Shire Highlands and areas west of Lake Malaŵi. In Karonga he negotiated a truce between the Arabs and the African Lakes Company, where trouble had broken out amongst the different trading groups. In 1891 the Nyasaland Districts Protectorate was declared, administered by the Foreign Office of the British Government. It included the land of the Protectorate declared in emergency in 1889; the western catchment of Lake Malaŵi which Livingstone had stated to be necessary for the control of the slave trade; and part of Lake Malaŵi including Likoma Island on account of the missionary activity there. Its boundaries were those of present-day Malaŵi.

Johnston was appointed as Commissioner and Consul-General of the new Protectorate. Much of his time was occupied by military campaigns and control of the slave trade. Another important task was that of sorting out land tenure: he organised enquiries to ratify all existing land claims, and then concluded treaties with all the chiefs of the Protectorate to secure control over the remaining land. He also created a system of district administration run from *bomas* (administrative centres). These collected taxes and customs duties; directed the police force; administered justice; and in some cases operated a postal service with an internal network of

A stock of ivory at the African Lakes Company's store in the late 1800s. Between 1891 and 1904 80 tons of ivory were exported from the Protectorate, which must have had a large impact on the elephant herds of the region.   H.H. JOHNSTON

runners. Now a national monument, the post office half way between Zomba and Blantyre on the M1 marks the site where runners exchanged mail bags carried between these administrative centres. Zomba was made the capital of the Protectorate.

Thus by the end of the nineteenth century law and order were becoming well established. The Ngoni and Yao were contained in areas they had conquered; the Chewa, Tumbuka and other peoples were safe from slavery and able to return to areas with a more favourable environment; missions were spreading Christianity and opening schools and hospitals; roads were being constructed and new areas being opened up for commercial agriculture.

The indigenous population of the Protectorate at that time was probably smaller than it had been for centuries. Foreigners had been entering the area since the 1500s, bringing with them diseases to which the African had little or no resistance. Some of these diseases caused serious and often fatal epidemics. In addition the Ngoni wars and slave trade had had a tremendous impact on the numbers of people and their social structure.[19] Many wild animal populations were also at a low ebb. Hunting of trophy species such as elephant and leopard for their ivory and skins respectively had been practised for some time, the trophies being sold to traders. Now, however, more firearms were being imported and settlers, traders and explorers such as Faulkner had been taking their toll, aided by the opening of access routes to previously remote areas. Between 1891 and 1904, 80 tons of ivory worth £50 000 were exported from the Protectorate[20]. Hunting pressure on smaller animals such as antelope, pigs and rodents for subsistence would have decreased somewhat, due to the decline in the human population mentioned above, but this effect may have been outweighed, at least in certain areas, by the devastation of the rinderpest pandemic.

Rinderpest, or cattle plague, is a highly contagious virus disease endemic in parts of Asia. It is thought to have been introduced into North Africa by an Italian contractor who shipped cattle in from India for the Italian army during its Eritrean campaign in 1887[21]. The disease spread like wildfire on the African continent where susceptible species had no resistance to it. Vast numbers of cattle, buffalo, many antelope, warthog and bushpig died as the disease spread in all directions. It moved south down the Rukwa Valley from Lake Tanganyika and reached the northern shores of Lake Malaŵi around July 1892. From there its course is unclear. Stevenson-Hamilton stated that it missed the land to the east of the lake but swept down the west side[22]. Other writers reported that it seemed to stop at the north of Lake Malaŵi, and Harry Johnston recorded that the rest of the Protectorate escaped due to the prompt action of his Administration in creating a rigid cordon to prevent southward movement of infected cattle until the pandemic was over[23]. In a separate report, however, he stated that the disease did spread southwards from the northern end of the lake but seemed to become attenuated and eventually died out[24]. He does not record how far south it reached, though Sharpe[25] stated that it never reached the districts to the south of the lake, suggesting by implication that it may have affected central parts of the country as well as the north.

To the west of the Protectorate rinderpest reached the southern end of Lake Mweru on the present-day boundary between Zaïre and Zambia in 1892[20], and spread southwards to the Zambezi Valley. It reached the lower Zambezi south of Malaŵi in 1896, though it apparently missed the Quelimane District of present-day Mozambique[26], and so would not have spread into the Protectorate by that route, partially confirming Sharpe's observation. Although rinderpest reached parts of present-day eastern Zambia the Luangwa Valley was apparently not affected at that time, and the disease does not seem to have spread into the Protectorate across the western watershed. Thus it seems that much of the country escaped, though the north-east and possibly some central parts were affected.

In the north the impact of rinderpest was considerable. The Wankonde people living on the north-western shores of Lake Malaŵi lost 95% of their considerable cattle herds, resulting in severe hardship as milk was an important part of their diet[23,27]. Rinderpest may have been another factor contributing to the human population decline at that time, because of both the impact on domestic stock and the effect on hunting. The impact on wild animal populations in the affected areas would have been considerable. Species most affected were buffalo; antelope such as eland, kudu, bushbuck, reedbuck and duiker; and warthog and wild pig. Antelope such as sable, roan, hartebeest, waterbuck and impala were apparently much less affected, and elephant, zebra, hippo and rhino were not affected at all.[22,27]

The susceptible wild animals would often have been among the most common species, and with their death many ecological balances must have been upset. There would have been many secondary effects: scavengers such as jackals, hyenas and vultures would have feasted for a short while on the carcasses and perhaps had a short-lived population boom. After that they would have gone hungry, as would many of the large predators such as leopard and lion, and their population levels probably declined accordingly. Buffalo and antelope have a very significant effect on vegetation, buffalo consuming and trampling coarse grass, and the various antelope species grazing and browsing a wide range of plant species and plant parts: grass, herbs, shrubs and trees; leaves, twigs, flowers and fruits. In their absence unconsumed plant growth would often have accumulated, perhaps smothering the new growth after a year or two. Productivity of the vegetation may have declined, affecting the surviving herbivores such as zebra, hippo and rhino, whose populations in turn may have declined. Alternatively in some areas they may have increased with the reduced competition for food from the antelope and the buffalo. Unfortunately these events went undocumented.

The importance of preservation of big game was recognised in those early years of the Protectorate, and on the suggestion of Alfred Sharpe, a keen hunter who was later to become Governor of the Protectorate, two game reserves at Lake Chilwa and Elephant Marsh were declared under the Game Regulations in 1897. Villages of local people occurring within these areas remained, however, and by 1902 the Lake Chilwa Reserve was repealed. In 1911 the Elephant Marsh lost its reserve status but a new reserve in Central Angoniland was declared, covering parts of Lilongwe and Dedza Districts.[19,20]

This situation remained for the next 16 years. In the meantime, wild animal populations at least in the north would have been recovering from rinderpest. Many animals would have moved on to the previously cultivated land which had been deserted during the times of the Ngoni wars and slave-trading and had reverted to bush. However, this expansion of range was short-lived. The human population was also expanding fast; with the great majority of people dependent on subsistence agriculture, the demand for land was increasing each year.[19] The diet of the local people was undergoing a change, as their traditional crops of finger millet, pearl millet and sorghum were partly replaced by the more recently introduced maize, cassava and rice. Maize was rapidly becoming the staple crop in many parts of the country, giving better yields but requiring a higher level of soil fertility and greater degree of crop husbandry. Possibly the change to maize and consequent intensification of agriculture resulted from the rapid increase in human population and demand for larger food supplies. In addition to subsistence agriculture, Europeans were opening new estates for coffee, cotton and tobacco; initially their activities were centred on the Shire Highlands but they later expanded into other areas. Between the First and Second World

Wars many areas were opened up for cultivation: especially tea and coffee estates around Thyolo and Mulanje, and small-holder African farming of cotton in the lower Shire Valley and tobacco on the Lilongwe plains.

The development of agriculture would have meant a significant loss of range for many wild animal populations, as well as increased hunting pressure and competition for grazing with the expanding cattle herds. As more and more land was cleared the importance of conservation was not forgotten, and between 1928 and 1941 a further eight game reserves were proclaimed: Thangadzi Stream, Lengwe, Chidiamperi, Kasungu, Nkhotakota, Viphya, Ngara/Nabtundu and Kazuni Lake. However, management at that time was minimal and four of the reserves were later deproclaimed, as was the Central Angoniland Reserve. In 1947 the Nyasaland Fauna Preservation Society (now the National Fauna Preservation Society, NFPS) was established with the aim of doing everything possible to preserve the dwindling wildlife. It has since played a significant role in this field.[13]

The conflict between wildlife and agriculture was not one-sided; in many cases animals raided crops and livestock and caused extensive damage. In 1947 the Department of Game, Fish and Tsetse Control was set up with the initial aim of controlling marauding animals. The department went to work with some enthusiasm: in 1951, for example, 12 500 crop-marauding animals were killed in Central Province (now Region) alone.[19]

Subsistence agriculture with intensively cultivated small fields, near Ngala Mountain in Central Region.   JUDY CARTER

Tobacco crop, with tobacco barns for curing tobacco in the background.   MICHAEL GORE

Rockface on Chipata Mountain in Nkhotakota Reserve. The reserve was first gazetted by the Protectorate Administration, and covers a large area of escarpment wilderness. CAROL CRAWFORD.

Agriculture and the Protectorate Administration had many other problems besides wild animals. Farming was a very labour-intensive activity and the wages paid to its workers had always been low. Many men left the Protectorate to seek better paid work in the mines of South Africa and Zimbabwe (then Rhodesia). Protest about the working conditions on estates had begun in 1915, led by the Reverend John Chilembwe, and continued for the next few decades. The Nyasaland African Congress (NAC) was formed in 1944 as the first indigenous political party in the country, and when the unpopular Federation of Rhodesia and Nyasaland was imposed by the British Government in 1953 the voice of objection became louder. Five years later Dr H. Kamuzu Banda, a medical doctor who had been born in Kasungu but had studied and worked outside the Protectorate for nearly forty years, returned to the country and took over the leadership of the NAC. His campaigning led to clashes with Federation officials. A state of emergency was declared, the party banned and the leaders and some 1000 supporters imprisoned. However, Dr Banda was released in 1960 by the then British Colonial Secretary, Ian Macleod, and invited for meetings in London. The following year elections were held, and the new Malaŵi Congress Party led by Dr Banda came to power.

Republic of Malaŵi

Independence was attained in 1964, and in 1966 the country became a republic within the British Commonwealth with Dr Banda as President. It was called Malaŵi, a name deriving from the Maravi people meaning 'fire flames'. There are various traditional beliefs about its derivation, including one where a group of ancestral immigrants adopted the word when they looked down from the high plateau on to Lake Malaŵi 'which shimmered like flames in the sunshine'.[8]

By the time of Independence many developments had occurred: cities, towns and villages had grown up; a transport network of road, rail and air had been developed for internal and external communication; schools and hospitals had been established in the major settlements; agriculture was still expanding; an administration system was in operation and tourism had started in a small way. This was the development which the newly independent government inherited, but there was still much to do. The government drew up its policies and priorities for action. Despite the many other urgent issues and ever increasing pressure for land for agriculture and forestry, it was resolved that game animals and wildlife in general should be afforded as much protection as possible. The value of the resource was at that time considered to be its potential as a tourist attraction; a possible source of food; and a scientific and educational asset of national importance.[13]

At Independence the country had five game reserves: Lengwe, Majete and Mwabvi (formerly Thangadzi Stream) in the Shire Valley; and Kasungu and Nkhotakota in Central Region. The first national park was declared in 1965: Malaŵi (now Nyika) National Park in the north. In 1970 Kasungu and Lengwe were given national park status, and Liwonde National Park on the upper Shire was proclaimed in 1973, the same year that the Department of National Parks and Wildlife was established. The Vwaza Marsh Game Reserve was declared in 1977 and the Lake Malaŵi National Park in 1980.[19] Since their initial proclamation several parks and reserves have been extended, mainly to ensure conservation of water catchments in areas unsuitable for agriculture.

Zebra on the high Nyika Plateau, Nyika National Park.
FRANK JOHNSTON

The Shire River flowing through Liwonde National Park.
FRANK JOHNSTON

The national parks and game reserves

Malaŵi now has five national parks and four game reserves, from the high Nyika Plateau in the north to Mwabvi Game Reserve in the far south in the lower Shire Valley. All major landscape types are represented, as are almost two thirds of the country's 29 major vegetation types[28]. Nyika National Park, covering all the Nyika Plateau within Malaŵi, is an outstanding and beautiful example of the high mountainous areas. On the Central African Plateau, Kasungu National Park with its *Brachystegia* woodland, broad grassy *dambos* and a variety of large mammal species, is representative of what much of the main plateau area must have been like in the past. The Vwaza Marsh Game Reserve to the north conserves a wider variety of vegetation types, including the marsh itself, and has a tremendously diverse birdlife. To the east of the plateau on the rift valley

escarpment Nkhotakota Game Reserve protects a variety of habitats, from the cool slopes of Chipata Mountain clad in evergreen forest, down the escarpment in a tortuous series of hills, valleys and ridges covered with *Brachystegia* woodland, to the flatter, hot lands of the rift valley floor. Further south Lake Malaŵi National Park conserves part of the waters of Lake Malaŵi, twelve of its islands, and some steep, rocky slopes and hills of Nankumba Peninsula. The *mbuna*, colourful cichlid fish, are particularly numerous around these shores, and colonies of white-breasted cormorants nest on some of the islands.

Lake Malaŵi drains into the Shire River which flows through Liwonde National Park. This relatively small park has a great variety of habitat types and wild animals: scenery and game-viewing are exceptional, with large numbers of crocodile and hippo in the river and herds of sable antelope and elephant on the floodplains and in the woodland behind. As the Shire flows on down the rift valley descending the long rapids it passes Majete Game Reserve, an area with a beautiful river frontage and spectacular wooded hills to the west. Further south is Lengwe National Park, covering an attractive area of thicket and savanna in the east where the population of nyala antelope has made a great comeback; in the west of the park a great wilderness area backs on to the Mozambique border with some very spectacular sandstone outcrops. Finally, in the very south of the country lies Mwabvi Game Reserve, a mosaic of woodland, thicket and *dambo*, home of one of the two black rhinoceros populations in Malaŵi.

In these areas animals are protected by law and the natural vegetation cover is maintained as far as possible, often by controlled burning. In a few cases where animals no longer have access to perennial water sources, artificial water supplies have been introduced. Communities of large mammals in the parks have in many cases recovered from the ravages of hunting and, apart from the absence of one or two species, are probably reverting to a situation similar to that which existed before the Iron Age. Some of the species which disappeared from the parks are now being reintroduced. Legislative protection of the game reserves is not as comprehensive as that of the parks, and in practice they are less intensively managed and developed as most of the limited resources of the Department of National Parks and Wildlife are channelled into the parks at present. The reserves do, however, still have many of their original large mammal species, albeit in reduced

The wilderness of Nyika National Park.   JUDY CARTER

numbers. Poaching for subsistence and/or trophies continues to be a problem in all the protected areas but is especially serious in the reserves.

Many of the national parks have been developed for tourism in an unobtrusive fashion and visitors can see them in relative comfort. The reserves are less well developed, but for those who enjoy some adventure off the beaten track they are ideal. One of the greatest attractions of a tour of Malaŵi's protected areas is the tremendous variety of animal and plant communities, landscapes and scenery. Coupled with this is the wide range of possible activities for the visitor: they include game-viewing by vehicle, from hides and on foot; and bird-watching in a wide variety of habitats and altitudes where about 550 bird species have so far been recorded. There is also a great diversity of smaller animals such as butterflies, reptiles and amphibians. Wilderness walking on the escarpment slopes and high mountains provides an opportunity for healthy outdoor exercise in the midst of challenging scenery, perhaps backpacking and camping out at night under the stars; there are also many opportunities for less strenuous walking in interesting and scenic surroundings. Lake Malaŵi offers a strong contrast to the terrestrial protected areas, with a great potential for water sports in the warm blue waters of the lake and a chance to observe the highly coloured *mbuna* cichlid fish around the rockfaces.

The future of the parks and reserves

The national parks and game reserves are a remarkably rich and diverse part of Malaŵi's national heritage. However, as in many African countries, competition from other land-uses is increasing exponentially and poses a potential threat to the continued survival of the plant and animal communities in these protected areas. Malaŵi's human population is growing rapidly and as the majority of people are dependent on agriculture for their livelihood the demand for land for cultivation is also growing. Increases in the size of the national livestock herd and demand for firewood and poles are causing further pressures on the land. As the problem of reconciling a finite land resource with increasing demands for new production areas continues, conflicts between production interests and current conservation policies will intensify.

The most recent population census in 1977 recorded 5 547 460 people in Malaŵi, giving an average density of 59 people per km² of land area. This is more than four times the average for Africa. The population contains a high proportion of young people and is estimated to be increasing at an annual rate of 2.9%. By the year 2000 it is expected to exceed 10 000 000. There is relatively little urban employment or prospect for large-scale industrial growth in the future and most people will remain dependent on agriculture, either through subsistence farming on customary land or from employment on freehold and leasehold estates. Agriculture is the most important economic activity in the country. In 1983, a year when many southern and eastern African countries were badly affected by drought, besides feeding her own people Malaŵi exported over 265 000 000 Malaŵi kwacha worth of agricultural produce, mainly tobacco, tea, sugar, maize, pulses, cotton, groundnuts and coffee[29]

With the expanding population the demand for

A steep slope cleared for cultivation near Mzuzu in Northern Region.   JANET AND JOHN HOUGH

new land for cultivation is ever-increasing. Much of the land in Malaŵi, however, is unsuitable for cultivation. An evaluation of potential land-use reveals that a large proportion of the country comprises mountains, steep slopes, and areas with infertile or poorly drained soils; only 37% of the total land area of the country has been classified as suitable for agriculture. Much of this is already under production and the remaining available land with good agricultural potential is rapidly being opened up; if present trends continue, all of it will be under cultivation by the year 2005. In some of the more densely populated districts the land crisis has already occurred on a local scale, and people have had no alternative but to clear steep slopes, stream banks and other unsuitable areas for subsistence agriculture. With the removal of permanent vegetation cover topsoil has been lost in some of these fragile areas, resulting in a decrease in fertility and crop yield; some areas have been permanently abandoned after a year or two as they were no longer worth planting. There can be long-lasting indirect effects, for example on the local water regime. A good vegetation cover enables the soil to retain a relatively large proportion of the rainfall, which is then released slowly to springs and streams later on; destruction of the vegetation and loss of the soil may result in flash floods during the rains and premature drying up of streams and wells during the dry season. The eroded soil is usually washed into rivers, and the resulting siltation of rivers and lakes can have an adverse affect on fish populations and therefore fisheries; on the management of dams and hydro-electric plants; and on the quality of water supplies downstream.

One solution to the problem is to cultivate the fertile areas more intensively, for example by irrigating: there is potential for expansion of irrigated agriculture on parts of the lakeshore and the Shire Valley. More intensive cultivation can also be achieved by reducing or eliminating the period when the land lies fallow to recover its fertility, and compensating by applying larger inputs of artificial fertiliser or manure. The former commodity has to be imported, however, involving expenditure of the country's limited foreign exchange. Transport routes to landlocked Malaŵi are affected by the politics of surrounding countries, and transport costs add considerably to the price of the fertiliser. More intensive cultivation necessitates a greater degree of management. Soil conservation measures must be adequate to ensure sustainable production of high yields in the future. Control of pests often becomes a major issue, especially if large areas are planted with a single crop, or if the same crop is grown year after year on the same ground with no rotation.

Cultivation is the main agricultural activity in Malaŵi, though in parts of the country there are large numbers of livestock. Estimates of the size of the national herd vary according to method; one of the larger estimates gave over 1 400 000 head of cattle,

1 600 000 goats and 100 000 sheep on customary land in 1981. Livestock is owned by a small minority of people, and is grazed on *dambos*, in natural woodland and on arable land after harvesting. In some parts of the country heavy grazing pressure is causing localised destruction of the grass cover, sometimes with consequent soil erosion and gullying on slopes. The system of communal grazing involves a series of complex social and environmental issues. Ownership of a large herd of livestock in some parts of the country is considered a status symbol, and is also a traditional source of wealth used to support the family. On customary land no individual is therefore prepared to reduce the size of his flock or herd to alleviate grazing pressure, especially as other owners are extremely unlikely to follow suit. The national herd is currently increasing at a rate of 5% per annum; if this trend continues it will more than double its 1981 size by the year 2000, with a corresponding increase in demand for pasture if the present grazing system continues unchanged. A greater degree of livestock management is likely to become necessary, perhaps through higher levels of offtake and better pasture and grazing management, and an increase in the feeding of crop residues to cattle in stalls.

Livestock, however, provides a relatively small part of the nation's animal protein, about 70% being obtained from fish in the lakes and rivers. In some areas catches have been greatly increased in recent years, but it will not be possible to increase yields indefinitely in the future to keep pace with the expanding human population. Fishing is discussed further in subsequent chapters.

Cattle grazing on a *dambo* during the rains. The national herd is estimated to be increasing at a rate of 5% per annum.
MICHAEL GORE

Large areas of natural forest and woodland are being destroyed each year in Malaŵi for various reasons: clearance for new cultivation; excessive utilisation by livestock; uncontrolled fires; urban expansion; and excessive timber and firewood extraction. This is precipitating a widespread shortage of firewood and timber. In all rural and many urban areas firewood is the main domestic fuel; vast amounts are also consumed in the process of flue-curing tobacco and smaller quantities for processing tea and drying fish. It has been estimated that on average 4.2 cubic metres of firewood are used to prepare each tonne of flue-cured tobacco; in 1986 about 20 000 tonnes of flue-cured tobacco were auctioned in Malaŵi, revealing the scale of the problem. Research is currently being undertaken to reduce firewood consumption by the tobacco industry through use of more efficient techniques.[30] In addition to firewood, poles are needed for construction, and timber for many purposes: there is particular concern that stocks of some of the indigenous high-grade hardwood tree species are becoming seriously depleted. Many plantations of exotic trees have been established but they may not be able to meet future demand for firewood and poles, particularly in the more densely populated areas. With the continued increase in population, demand will rise while areas of natural woodland continue to disappear, and the problem will become more acute.

As the land crisis develops it is inevitable that the national parks and game reserves will come under increasing pressure from other land-uses. They occupy 11% of Malaŵi's land area, much greater than the overall average of just below 4% for all African countries south of the Sahara. Gazetted forest reserves, some used for production forestry, cover about a further 8% of the land area. At first sight this seems a large proportion of conserved land. However, much but not all of it is unsuitable for agriculture. An assessment has been made of the potential contribution of all the national parks, game reserves and forest reserves to the land crisis predicted for 2005 when all available agricultural land in the rest of country will be under cultivation. Assuming that the current rate of increase in the demand for land remains constant, it has been estimated that the opening up of all the protected areas would only relieve the cultivation problem for another four years, when the situation would be back to square one. In the meantime many of the habitats and animal communities of the parks and reserves would have been lost, some of them irreparably. This would seem to be an extortionate price to pay with part of the country's rich heritage for a mere four years' grace in the exponential problem. Nevertheless, the threat is there.

National parks and game reserves are more likely to survive in the future if they can provide tangible benefits to the local people living nearby, as well as to the nation in general. Their management may have to be adapted to allow controlled exploitation of their resources on a sustained basis with minimal environmental impact: cutting of poles, collection of firewood and other forest products, and carefully controlled hunting for example. Malaŵians from all parts of the country could be encouraged and assisted to visit the parks and reserves for education and recreation, enabling them to appreciate and benefit from this part of their heritage. Revenues from foreign tourism could be maximised as far as possible, but without adversely affecting the environment or the aesthetic values of the parks and reserves. It is, however, important that a full dependence on tourism does not develop as it is a fickle industry at the mercy of regional and world recessions, fuel prices, fashions and politics, and as such is not a completely reliable source of revenue.[31] Careful planning would be necessary to avoid conflicts between the different activities in each area. (Sources of information:[19,32,33])

Chapter Two

The high mountains and plateaux

Dark and mysterious, their peaks often banked in cloud, the high mountains of Malaŵi loom steeply above the surrounding plains, some of their slopes covered with a dense jungle of damp evergreen forest. For centuries they have been the source of many mystical beliefs amongst the peoples living in the less hostile lands below, and have occasionally provided a wild refuge during bleak times of persecution by invading tribes.

The mountains and high plateaux occur in isolation along the length of the country, many of them near the lip of the rift valley escarpment and on the western watershed. In their exposed positions they have cool, wet climates and are important water catchments for the rest of the country. They often have spectacular, rugged scenery with fast

flowing mountain streams, moorland, evergreen forests and high rocky peaks, offering excellent wilderness walking in a pleasantly cool climate even at the hottest time of year. Many are gazetted as forest reserves, often involving some plantation forestry as well as conservation of the natural vegetation in unaffected areas. One, Nyika, is a national park.

The most northerly mountains are the Misuku Hills, taking their name from the delicious fruit of a common tree of *Brachystegia* woodland, *Uapaca kirkiana*. They comprise a series of steep-sided hills and ridges, overlooking the deep valley of the Songwe River on the Tanzanian border. South of these lie the Mafinga Mountains on the Zambian border, and to the south-east of them lies Nyika, the most extensive high plateau not only in Malaŵi but in the whole Central African region. On all sides it has steep dramatic scarps. To the east they form the wall

Chambe peak on the Mulanje Massif with the Phalombe Plain in the distance.   JUDY CARTER

Inselbergs rising above pine plantations and *dambos* of the southern Viphya Plateau. JUDY CARTER

Natural vegetation still occurs in the *dambos* and less accessible areas of the plateau, and inselbergs break the monotony of the pines.

In central Malaŵi the Dowa Hills add interest to the landscape, as do several isolated inselbergs and hills south of Lilongwe; they offer many opportunities for day excursions from the capital[10]. To the south-west on the Mozambique border lies the Dzalanyama Range, traditionally believed to be the site of creation, now partly used for cattle ranching and plantation forestry. The remaining natural woodland offers excellent bird-watching and hill walking. Also near the border is Dedza Mountain, its flanks planted with conifers while the plateau on top retains some ever-green forest and sub-montane grassland, with magnificent views across Lake Malaŵi to the east on a clear day. Further south, overlooking the Shire Valley, lies the Kirk Range with some interesting peaks to challenge the rock climber.

Across the broad valley of the Shire River to the east and south-east of the Kirk Range are the mountains of the Shire Highlands. Many peaks rise above the main plateau, creating a spectacular skyline. Mountains such as Chiradzulu, Thyolo and Soche have isolated areas of dense evergreen forest, though

Aloe chabaudii on Dedza Mountain; aloes grow in many rocky areas on the high mountains and plateaux. JUDY CARTER

of the rift valley, continuing downwards to the shores of Lake Malaŵi. The high plateau has an open, rolling landscape with isolated mountains to the north. Nyika National Park is described in greater detail later in this chapter.

On a clear day from the south of the Nyika Plateau it is possible to see across to the north and south Viphya Plateaux, long, narrow formations running parallel with the rift valley. The southern plateau is covered extensively with forest plantations, although since their establishment in the 1950s transport costs have soared and it is now not viable to transport timber and firewood south to the main centres where it is required. Long-term plans exist for a pulp mill on Lake Malaŵi or the Shire River at Liwonde to utilise this enormous resource.

unfortunately the forests of the latter two and some of the rare species they harbour are under threat from illegal wood cutting in this densely populated region. The city of Blantyre is ringed by the peaks of Ndirande, Soche and Michiru. The latter is a steep-sided mountain with a plateau on top; there are breathtaking views from it on a clear day. Under a programme of multiple land-use the lower slopes are planted with eucalypts for firewood and a small area is used as a dairy farm; natural woodland is maintained on the steeper slopes to protect the water catchment; and the plateau area is afforested for timber production. A nature reserve covers one large valley from the summit to the base of the mountain, protecting *Brachystegia* and *Acacia* woodland and a small patch of evergreen forest west of the summit. Michiru is an excellent area for bird-watching and walking, and is very convenient for a half-day visit from Blantyre.[34]

Zomba Plateau

At the northern end of the Shire Highlands lies the Zomba Plateau, a massif rising up almost sheer from the surrounding areas. The plateau is divided into two sections by the Domasi River: Zomba and Malosa. A road from Zomba town, the former capital which still houses the Parliament and university, winds up the slopes of the plateau through forestry plantations and past ravines with lush, evergreen vegetation. On top of the plateau a network of roads and paths takes the visitor through shaded plantations to natural grassland and patches of evergreen forest — on foot, by vehicle or on horseback. The clear streams draining from the plateau tumble down some picturesque waterfalls and wind through sombre green glades where tree ferns stand sentinel. Although small, rainbow trout in the streams and dams provide sport for the angler. After a day's walking, riding or fishing, it is pleasant to relax with a drink and perhaps a meal on the terraces of the Ku Chawe Inn, perched on the very edge of the plateau. The inn provides comfortable accommodation and there also is a campsite nearby; alternatively the plateau is close enough for a day visit from Blantyre. From viewpoints around the edges of the plateau there are spectacular views in all directions: over Zomba town to the hills of Blantyre; towards Lake Chilwa and across the Shire Valley to the Kirk Range. Finally, 40 km away across the Phalombe Plain is the highest and most impressive of all Malaŵi's mountains: Mulanje Massif.

View from Chingwe's Hole on the edge of the Zomba Plateau, with the Shire River in the far distance.   DENIS TWEDDLE

Tree fern and other riverine plants by one of the streams on Zomba Plateau.   JAMES OGLETHORPE

Mount Mulanje[7,35]

Rising almost sheer from the heat of the plain below, above the verdant shimmer of the tea estates at its base, are the hills and peaks of this remarkable mountain. More than 1000 m up from the plain a series of plateaux and basins perch on the outer shoulders of the massif. These are rolling, grassy uplands dissected by deep, forested gullies and ravines, down which fierce torrents rush after rain giving rise to spectacular waterfalls as they plunge off the edge of the plateaux to the plains far below.

From the plateaux huge boulder-fields and deeply fissured rock slabs and walls tower up to the main peaks, a challenge to both climber and walker. The highest peak is Sapitwa, 3002 m above sea-level. Chambe Peak on the north-west side of the massif offers the longest rock climb in Africa, 1700 m of

roped climbing which was first ascended in the 1970s. The scale and magnificence of the massif are such that its atmosphere has to be experienced to be understood: it is difficult to describe the beauty of the golden sunrise on Chambe Peak, the sense of achievement in hiking to the top of a peak with breathtaking views all around, or walking on plateau paths through steep patches of cool, sombre forest and along sunny ridges high above the rest of the world.

Linked by these paths are the isolated timber-built forestry huts on the plateaux; with their blazing log fires they provide a welcome refuge from the night chill and inclement weather. A visit to Mulanje outside the wet season does not guarantee good

Boulder-strewn flank of Sapitwa, the highest peak on Mulanje, rising from a sea of cloud. JUDY CARTER

The massive 'Rabbit Ears' on the route to the summit of Sapitwa. JUDY CARTER

White-necked raven, commonly seen on Mulanje.
MICHAEL GORE

African foxgloves and everlasting flowers on Luchenya Plateau, Mulanje.   DAVID WOODFALL

weather: mist may descend at any time, and cloud on Chiperone Mountain to the south in Mozambique signals the advent of a spell of cold weather when the shelter of the hut will be much appreciated.

Even if the weather does not look good enough for a day's hike there are many other possible activities on the mountain. Various streams on and below the plateaux have been stocked with rainbow trout, and licensed angling can provide a reasonable day's sport with plenty of exercise. Birdwatching can be rewarding. Mulanje covers a wide range of habitats from *Brachystegia* woodland and riverine forest on the lower slopes to the grasslands and montane evergreen forest of the plateaux, with pockets of heathland in less accessible areas, overlooked by the rocky peaks. Many birds of the higher areas are not found on the plains surrounding Mulanje. Interesting species of the grassland include the red-tailed flufftail and swee waxbill. Bar-tailed trogon, olive-breasted mountain bulbul and red-faced crimsonwing occur in the montane forest. The augur buzzard and white-necked raven are often seen in flight; less common

are the blue swallow and scarce and mottled swifts. Mammals are not common, though klipspringer, dassie, vervet and blue monkeys, red rock hare, red duiker, bushpig, bushbuck, porcupine and leopard are amongst those which do occur.

For the casual as well as the more dedicated botanist the mountain provides a fascinating range of rare and interesting plants, many of which are found only on Mulanje. A variety of primitive plants occurs: tree ferns, liverworts, horsetails and other ferns, and the cycad *Encephalartos gratus* which is endemic to the lower streambanks of Mulanje and nearby Milanje Mountain in Mozambique. Orchids abound at various altitudes. They may be seen on a day visit from Blantyre to Likubula Falls at the foot of the mountain; higher up they are common in the wet grassland areas, and epiphytic orchids occur in the woodland. Elephant's tongue occurs in damp, shaded places, its large, pale green leaf flattened against the rock face. On the plateaux many different species of everlasting flowers add colour to the grasslands, including the endemic pink-flowered *Helichrysum whyteanum*. Proteas abound, and aloes provide a splash of red on the rock outcrops. In the higher areas of the massif there are various heaths,

Mulanje cedar.   JUDY CARTER

and a very conspicuous plant, the stag's horn lily. This has a woody stem from which the grass-like leaves spike outwards and white flowers bloom at the end of the dry season. It grows in extremely exposed sites, clinging to fissures of rock and is used extensively for handholds and belay points on many rock-climbing pitches.

One of the most striking plants on the mountain is Mulanje cedar which is at the northern limit of its range here. Only on Mulanje do individual trees grow over 40 m tall; such specimens can be almost two metres wide at the base and up to 200-300 years old. Their grey trunks and drapes of old man's beard and other lichens give them a timeless air. Laurens van der Post described them in his book *Venture to the Interior*, growing *at first, in small clusters driven back into odd, remote nooks of the valley, but then, as we went deeper into the valley, there appeared in the central gash of it a real, dark, brooding, resentful forest of them. It was rather an awe-inspiring sight. They looked, in an odd way, prehistoric; lovely, but long before human time. I would not have been surprised to see a pterodactyl fly out of them. All around the edges*

their branches were festooned and heavily hung with long garlands and veils of lichen and moss.[36]

Susceptible to fire, Mulanje cedars do not occur as extensively now as they once did: frequent fires started on the plateaux and slopes by local hunters have taken their toll of young and old trees. Ironically, an occasional intense fire is necessary for the very early stage of the cedar's development, as it reduces competition by clearing the grass or other undergrowth and the fertile ash provides nutrients for the germinating seedlings.

Around 1900 until 1956 cedar was cut by Government and concessionaires, both for use within Malaŵi and for export. However, since 1901 planting of cedars has also been practised, and in some cases it is now difficult to tell which stands are natural and which are planted. Sawing of cedar is today confined to dead trees. Pine plantations in Chambe and Sombani basins were established from 1949 to 1966 with the aim of creating favourable conditions for the establishment of cedar later. However, cedars were not planted in these locations and the pines matured; they are now spreading on the plateau, and are being exploited for timber. Since there is no vehicular access to the plateaux, felling, sawing and

Lichen community on a tree trunk. JAMES OGLETHORPE

Pit sawing on Chembe Plateáu, Mulanje: trunks are sawn into planks by two men using a long saw, whilst a third drives in wedges to force the saw-cut open. JUDY CARTER

carrying of timber is almost entirely a manual operation on the mountain. Sawing pits are set up near felling sites, and huge two-handled, long-toothed saws are used to cut up the logs, expertly handled by one man standing on a platform and another in the pit below. Long planks of sawn timber are carried balanced on the head or shoulder to the top of the skyline cable hoist at the edge of Chambe plateau, or sometimes carried all the way down to the foot of the mountain.

Mulanje supplies timber to the heavily populated Southern Region of Malaŵi where there is a high demand for wood. The mountain also provides the surrounding areas with a reliable, clean water supply, and is the source of much enjoyment for walkers and climbers. However, other land-uses have been considered for the mountain. Lichenya Plateau has large bauxite deposits up to 15 m thick which, in changing economic climates, could become feasible to exploit. This would necessitate the construction of a road, probably via Chambe basin, which in turn could make further forestry operations a viable proposition. Tourism on a much greater and commercial scale would also become possible. At the base of the mountain the intense pressure for firewood and for more land for subsistence cultivation is forcing local

people to open up new areas of woodland inside the forest reserve, sometimes destroying evergreen forest as well as *Brachystegia* woodland. This is particularly serious on the southern slopes where the survival of several rare species of forest trees and ferns endemic to Mulanje is threatened[37]. Time will show whether Mulanje, the most spectacular of all upland areas in Malaŵi, will remain as it is today.

Map 2.1 *Nyika National Park*

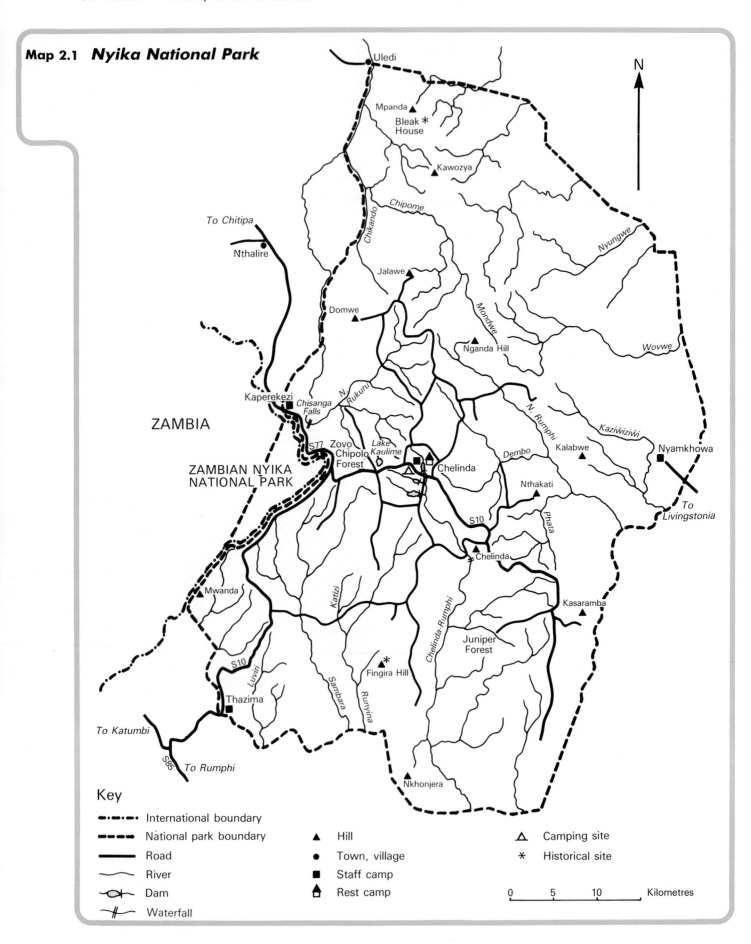

Key

- ·–··–··   International boundary
- – – –   National park boundary
- ▬▬▬   Road
- ⌒⌒⌒   River
- ⬭   Dam
- ⫠   Waterfall
- ▲   Hill
- ●   Town, village
- ■   Staff camp
- ⛺   Rest camp
- △   Camping site
- ✳   Historical site

0   5   10   Kilometres

Nyika National Park [19,31]

Name derivation

From the name of the plateau. The Nyika people migrated to the area from southern Tanzania and presumably gave the plateau its name. The word *nyika* has various meanings including 'from where the water comes' [36], or 'wilderness', and is also a type of thorn bush in Swahili.

Declaration

First gazetted as the Malaŵi National Park in 1965, it covered only the high plateau area. The name was changed in 1969, and in 1978 the park was expanded to include the lower slopes of the plateau for water catchment conservation purposes.

Present size

3134 km²

Location

Northern Malaŵi, adjoining the Zambian border, covering the whole of the Malaŵi part of the Nyika Plateau.

Landscape type

Rolling, high plateau and associated mountains and escarpments.

Vegetation

Short montane grassland, *dambo* and patches of evergreen forest on the high plateau; *Brachystegia* woodland and protea/heath scrub on the escarpment. Of special interest are the wild flowers, including terrestrial and epiphytic orchids; over 120 species of terrestrial orchids are known to occur and the Nyika is the richest orchid area in south-central Africa.

Large mammals

Commonly seen on the high plateau: reedbuck, roan, eland, grey duiker, bushbuck, klipspringer, zebra, warthog, leopard. Seen in parts of the lower areas: elephant, greater kudu, grey duiker, buffalo, baboon. Less commonly seen but occurring in the park: blue monkey, vervet monkey, dassie, Cape clawless otter, side-striped jackal, ratel, civet, genet, mongoose (various species), spotted hyena, lion, serval, caracal, genet, dassie, bushpig, hippo, puku, hartebeest, blue duiker, red duiker, porcupine.

Birds

Birds of the high grasslands, including Denham's bustard, wattled crane, red-winged francolin, white-necked raven and augur buzzard. Birds of high altitude evergreen forest, including cinnamon dove, bar-tailed trogon and starred robin; rarely, white-chested alethe, Sharpe's akalat and olive-flanked robin. Species typical of *Brachystegia* woodland occur on the lower slopes. Over 350 species have been recorded in the park and three birds are endemic to the Nyika: subspecies of red-winged francolin, greater double-collared sunbird and Baglafecht weaver.

Other animals

The Nyika chameleon is endemic to the Nyika and Viphya Plateaux; endemic to Nyika are the Nyika dwarf toad and Nyika squeaker (a forest frog). Grass snakes are rarely seen. Three species and four sub-species of butterfly are endemic to the Nyika Plateau. Rainbow trout have been introduced to the streams and dams of the plateau.

Sites of special interest

Lake Kaulime; Chisanga Falls; Chelinda Falls; Chelinda Dams; Juniper Forest and other evergreen forests including Zovo Chipolo; Stone Age rock shelters, especially Fingira Rock; iron smelting sites; and Bleak House, originally built by missionaries from Livingstonia.

Access

Road: via Rumphi through Thazima Gate, and via Chitipa through Kaperekezi Gate. From Lilongwe, follow the M1 north towards Mzuzu. It is tarred all the way except a portion over the Viphya Plateau which can give problems during the rains. From Mzuzu follow the M1 past the airport towards Karonga. Turn off left just after Bwengu onto the S85 to Rumphi. Drive straight through the village and follow the S85 for 59 km to its junction with the S10. Turn right along the S10 to Thazima Gate, 8 km away. Chelinda Camp is 56 km inside the park from Thazima. It is not advisable to arrive at Thazima later than 4 pm.

In the north, follow the M1 to Mwendendendo, the S85 to Chisenga and the D5 to Nthalire. From there the S77 leads up the escarpment to the park entrance at Kaperekezi. This is about 22 km from Chelinda, and it is not advisable to arrive at the gate later than 5 pm.

All the roads in the north are untarred. Two-wheel-drive vehicles with good ground clearance can negotiate the access roads with careful driving in the dry season; from June to the start of the rains in November-December. At all other times four-wheel-drive is recommended until the access roads are upgraded.

Distances from the main centres to Thazima:

Mzuzu:	129 km
Lilongwe (via Mzuzu):	507 km
Blantyre (via Mzuzu):	854 km

There is a network of single-track roads in the park as shown on Map 2.1. These are passable throughout the year.

Access by light aircraft is possible; there is a grass surfaced landing strip at Chelinda.

Continued

Visitor facilities

Chelinda camp: four self-contained chalets each with two double bedrooms, sitting room, kitchen and bathroom; and six double bedrooms with shared kitchen and dining room. All self-catering with cooks available; hot and cold running water; electricity in the evenings. Campsite in Chelinda Forest with minimal facilities. Small shop stocking certain non-perishable items, and petrol pump. Information room on the park's ecology and management.

Forest cabin with minimal facilities, sleeping four, in Juniper Forest.

Zambian Rest House in Zambian Nyika National Park run by Zambian authorities; access through Malaŵi park with no border formalities; sleeps eight; self-catering.

Advance booking is recommended for accommodation in the Malaŵi park.

Paths to Zovo Chipolo Forest, Chisanga Falls, Juniper Forest and Jalawe Rock.

Visitor activities

Game-viewing and bird-watching on foot or by vehicle. Walking (with or without a hired guide). Overnight wilderness trails (with a hired guide). Photography. Angling by licence on the three dams and streams for rainbow trout (streams throughout the year and dams from 1st September to 30th April); some angling equipment is available for hire, and there is a boat on one of the dams. Visiting Fingira Rock.

Administrative arrangements

Advance reservations for accommodation in the Malaŵi park and overnight wilderness trails should be made at the booking office, Department of National Parks and Wildlife, PO Box 30131, Lilongwe 3 (tel 730 853). Park fees are charged for visitors and their vehicles as well as for accommodation. The service of a game-scout guide can be hired at Chelinda.

Best time to visit

Game-viewing:	October to April
Bird-watching:	November to December
Wild flowers:	December to March and August to September
Walking:	May to November
Angling:	November to January
Scenery:	November to May

Access for two-wheel-drive vehicles: June to November

The park is open throughout the year.

The rains fall mainly from December to April.

During September to November temperatures on the plateau are agreeably warm, a pleasant contrast to the heat in lower areas. In July and August weather on the plateau can be very cold, with occasional frosts at night. Temperatures during the rest of the year are relatively cool.

Nyika National Park

In the north lies the most extensive of all the high mountainous areas: Nyika Plateau. As the density of the human population in the surrounding areas of the Northern Region is much lower than that around Mulanje, and as the Nyika has greater legislative protection as a national park, its wilderness status is more secure than that of Mulanje.

Nyika provides a surprising contrast to Mulanje: the high plateau has a gently undulating topography with comparatively few rock outcrops and a very open vista. It is only on the edges of the plateau that steep, craggy slopes occur, as the escarpment plunges rapidly to the flatter lands below. Ascending the escarpment to the high plateau is like leaving Africa for part of Europe. Once clear of the *Brachystegia* woodland and protea scrub the rolling grasslands have the atmosphere of a Scottish moor: bracken on the freely draining slopes; lichen-covered rocks; bright green mosses and ferns at the heads of valleys, below which grow small, dark patches of forest; and bracing winds which sweep the raven and buzzard across the sky. One is only brought back to tropical reality when a zebra wheels round across the track, snorting indignantly at being disturbed, or a Denham's bustard stalks away on its long legs.

History of Nyika

Man has used Nyika for many years. Rock shelters on various parts of the plateau show evidence of Stone Age occupation, and Fingira Cave in the south was used by hunter-gatherers 3000 years ago. These people left geometric rock paintings, and excavation of the site revealed artefacts, bones, shell and human skeletal material. From analysis of the animal bone it is known that they hunted reptiles, birds, rodents, monkey, large and small carnivores, zebra, pig, duiker, and medium and large antelope. These findings correspond well with the present animal communities, suggesting that environmental conditions have not changed greatly during the past 3000 years.[38]

After 400 years of settlement at Fingira, for some reason the site was abandoned. The high plateau was subsequently used by Iron Age people who hunted

Northern Nyika National Park.   FRANK JOHNSTON

Fingira Rock on the southern side of the Nyika Plateau. A cave in the side of the rock was occupied by Stone Age hunter-gatherers 3000 years ago.   FRANK JOHNSTON

and smelted iron there. For many centuries they did not inhabit the high areas, however, but dwelt in the foothills below, making excursions up the slopes to the plateau to pursue these activities. Only in the nineteenth century were a few settlements established on the escarpments of the plateau and in the southern hills by the Phoka people who were forced to take refuge at this altitude during the Ngoni wars.

Perhaps because the remote and awesome plateau was uninhabited for so long and because it yielded highly prized iron and meat, the Iron Age people who lived in its shadow evolved a complex mythology concerning the Nyika. It was believed, for example, that the only natural lake on the plateau, Lake Kaulime, was the sanctuary of a spirit taking the form of a great snake. The spirit looked upon the animals of the plateau as its own, and permitted only one to be killed by hunters at any one time. So strong was this belief that it may account for the survival of the herds of animals on the plateau today.[13] When men did hunt there, they used various hunting methods including game pits and nets: with the latter, nets made of bark rope were stretched across gaps in the forest, and animals were driven into the nets where they were killed by spearmen who had been hiding in the undergrowth. Even large antelope such as eland and roan were hunted in this fashion.[39] The snake spirit had other powers besides controlling hunting: if a sick person managed to touch the tail of the snake he would be instantly cured, but if someone went to the lake for no good reason he would be caught and carried off to the snake's hole in the bottom of the lake[36]

Iron smelting was also steeped in mythology; traditional ritual and use of local medicines were believed to be just as important for successful smelting as the technical aspects. Smelting was practised on the plateau by the Phoka people until the 1930s and a few old smelters are still alive today, mostly men once apprenticed to their fathers who had been chief smelters. Many signs of smelting are still apparent on the plateau: remains of kilns and slag are widespread, and deep, narrow shafts in the hillside indicate where the iron ore was mined.

Smelting took place in two stages: a large primary furnace (known as a ng'anjo) was filled with charcoal, wood, ore and slag from previous smelts, and fired to produce a sintered sponge of slag containing small pieces of iron. This was then resmelted in a small secondary furnace (kathengo) to produce a solid bloom of iron with some slag in it. Goatskin bellows were used with the kathengo to attain the high temperatures required; in contrast the ng'anjo produced its own draught, an unusual feature of traditional iron-smelting which appears to have been invented in West Africa and was confined almost completely to the African continent. Nyika ng'anjo were built of clay, shaped like a cone with the point cut off and standing up to one and a half metres tall; several tuyères (ceramic air pipes) near the base provided ventilation.

The Phoka people believed the process of smelting to be closely linked to human fertility. The newly completed basic structure of a ng'anjo was considered to be a young woman ready for marriage; once smelting was underway the furnace became 'our wife'. While the ng'anjo was in use, for about a week the small smelting team would remain there in isolation, celibate. Fertile women were not allowed in the team as they were considered detrimental to the smelting process, especially if pregnant. No washing of the body was allowed during that time, and peaceful conduct amongst members of the team was also essential.

The firing of the kathengo involved very little ritual, but a complicated ritual was followed during the preparation and firing of the ng'anjo, combined with prayer and extensive use of medicines. Components of the latter included hippo hide (one of the most important items); heel of zebra hoof; paws of aardvark, hedgehog and tree dassie; skin of ratel; a sacrificial brown rooster; python vertebrae; fish; several species of insects; many different plants; red ochre; mica; graphite and various artefacts. Many of these medicines were also used traditionally by the Phoka for matters related to witchcraft; against epidemics threatening a community; and for venereal diseases which reduced fertility. Other items used were symbols of fertility and plenty, and the remainder symbolised qualities desired for smelting and its end product: strength, toughness, hardness, wiliness and speed. The various medicines were gathered over a large area ranging from Lake Malaŵi to the Nyika Plateau.

Iron smelting involved many different activities: charcoal preparation, mining of ore, transporting materials, building furnaces, gathering medicines, making tuyères, brewing beer and smelting. The full process took three months from July to October, after harvesting and before preparation for planting the next season's crops. At times as many as fifty people were involved, including women and children. The maximum amount of iron resulting from a single, labour-intensive smelting was only enough to make

The Chelinda pine plantations, established before the park was gazetted. They now provide refuge for animals such as leopard.   JUDY CARTER

provide shelter, timber and firewood for the camp at Chelinda, a small amount being sold outside the park. The forest also provides refuge for some wild animals, especially in bad weather.

The high plateau was declared a national park in 1965. In 1978 this was extended to include the lower slopes, involving the resettlement of some local people; the extension ensured the conservation of the large water catchment by protecting the vegetation cover. The rivers rising on the plateau supply water to many settlements and small-scale agricultural projects around its base and along the lakeshore plain from Karonga to Chiweta.

There is a high annual rainfall on the plateau (1200 mm average at Chelinda), and water is plentiful. It drains from the springs and *dambos* into the peaty mountain streams, running darkly and swiftly to the edge of the plateau, tumbling down rapids and waterfalls such as the picturesque Chelinda Falls on the way. On the sides of the escarpment the waterfalls are longer, as the water plunges down steep slopes on its course to Lake Malaŵi.

The Chisanga Falls, where the North Rukuru River leaves the plateau on the west side, are parti-

Chelinda rest camp, overlooking one of the dams stocked with rainbow trout.   FRANK JOHNSTON

about four hoes and some smaller tools. The impact on the vegetation of the plateau would have been considerable: a metric ton of charcoal was needed for each smelting, prepared from about 88 m^3 of wood from the slow-growing shrub *Phillippia benguelensis*. (Information on iron smelting:[40])

Until late in the nineteenth century, only the Phoka people ventured on to the high Nyika. With the declaration of the Protectorate, however, various naturalists visited the plateau, collecting biological specimens from the unusual plant and animal communities there. By 1933 the juniper forests were being protected from fire, and in 1948 the area in the south of the present-day park, now called the Juniper Forest, was made a reserve. The grasslands were protected and hunting prohibited in 1951. The Colonial Development Corporation (now Commonwealth Development Corporation) planted pines and eucalypts at Chelinda in the 1950s, then intended for pulp-wood.[13] However, although growth rates of the trees were amongst the best recorded in the country, the remoteness of the area made transport costs prohibitively expensive and the plantation was not extended. The trees are now mature and

The North Rukuru River plunging down the Chisanga Falls on the west side of the Nyika Plateau. DAVID ELIAS

remain on the high grasslands throughout the year. Zebra, roan and eland are more gregarious, especially the latter which may be seen in herds of 100 or more. They are very mobile, and during the dry season when the nutrient value of the forage declines and temperatures on the high plateau are low these species move to lower areas of *Brachystegia* woodland. It may be that the shelter of the Chelinda plantations enables some, especially zebra, to stay longer on higher ground, but after May few are to be seen there. They return later in the year when temperatures are higher and forage has improved, first with the green flush stimulated by the grassland fires, and then with sustained growth after the start of the next rains.

Smaller antelope occurring on the high plateau are bushbuck, klipspringer, and three species of duiker: grey, blue and red. All are well adapted to survive in the conditions prevailing there. For example, they are selective feeders and choose the most nutritious plant species and parts of the plants, such as new leaf rather than stem. These small antelope are able to feed selectively because they require small amounts of food compared to, say, a zebra or an elephant. While the latter have to feed by bulk to obtain enough food, consuming large mouthfuls of forage in which they cannot select individual leaves, flowers or stems, small antelope can take a bite here and a nibble there of the most nutritious food available to obtain a high quality diet. Differences in feeding behaviour amongst the

cularly spectacular. The Manchewe Falls near Livingstonia, fed by water from the park, are the longest falls in the country: twin cascades plunge 300 m to the valley below[41].

On the plateau itself there is very little standing water. Three dams, constructed near Chelinda in the early 1960s during forestry operations, add interest to the scenery and provide good trout fishing. Roan antelope may often be seen grazing the waterweeds growing underwater in the lower dams. Lake Kaulime, west of Chelinda, is the only naturally occurring lake on the plateau, home of the snake spirit protecting the plateau's animals.

Animals of the Nyika

The most common species of large herbivore are reedbuck, zebra, roan, eland and warthog. The reedbuck, by far the most numerous species at present, are dispersed over the plateau in small groups: they

Young male reedbuck. Reedbuck are the most common large mammal on the high Nyika Plateau. DAVID ELIAS

Young roan antelope on Nyika. Roan frequent the high plateau grasslands during the rains; with the onset of the cold dry season they move to the *Brachystegia* woodland on the lower slopes.   FRANK JOHNSTON

A herd of eland on the rolling Nyika grassland. Eland is the largest antelope in Malaŵi.   JUDY CARTER

Adult male bushbuck. On Nyika bushbuck frequent the more densely vegetated *dambos* and streams, and the edges of the plantations.   FRANK JOHNSTON

various herbivores are discussed further on page 59 onwards. The small antelope on Nyika (excluding reedbuck) are predominantly browsers: they eat broad-leaved plants such as herbs and shrubs rather than grass, which is eaten by grazers. It is likely that, at least in some of their habitats, browse is more readily available than grass during the dry season, and possibly retains a higher nutritive value. Thus they are able to survive the year on the high plateau, whereas many larger animals move away.

In addition, the small antelope ensure they have enough to eat by holding territories which they defend, sometimes with a mate, against intruders of the same species. Boundaries of a territory are often marked: the grey duiker for example has scent glands in front of the eyes which it rubs against bushes and grasses to mark its patch. Other animals may mark territory by scraping or urinating. The territory is an area large enough to supply all the animal's needs: mainly food, water and shelter. This limits the number of animals of a given species in any one area, ensuring that each individual, providing he/she holds a territory, has adequate resources to live and breed.

The small antelope avoid competition for resources between different species by occupying different habitats. Bushbuck are usually found along the more densely vegetated *dambos* and streams; the grey duiker are on higher grassland areas. Klip-springer occupy rock outcrops, feeding on herbs and shrubs growing amongst the boulders. They are extremely agile and scale rocky areas with ease, walking on their hooftips, the hooves having the consistency of hard rubber. Blue and red duiker live

Adult male grey duiker. The line in front of the eye is a scent gland used for marking territory.   JUDY CARTER

in the dense patches of evergreen forest which occur in drainage lines below the *dambos*.

Another interesting animal occurring in the forest patches is the blue monkey, which spends most of its time in the high canopy; the forests often echo with its soulful call. On the floor of the forest the largely nocturnal bushpig roots for food in the undergrowth, and the chequered elephant shrew feeds on insects such as ants and beetles.

One of the main predators of animals such as the bushpig and small antelope is the leopard; they are common on the plateau and are often seen around the Chelinda pine plantations, especially at dusk. Less common is the serval cat, which preys on reptiles, rodents and birds as well as small antelope, and the side-striped jackal which feeds on reptiles, rodents, insects and wild fruits, besides scavenging on kills of other animals.

Between the main plateau and Kawozya Mountain to the north, nearly 1000 m below them, lies the valley of the Chipome Stream. Elephant and buffalo occur in the *Brachystegia* woodland of the valley and on the *dambos* flanking the Chipome and its tributaries. Little is known about these small, isolated populations which live in the shadows of the high mountains. They have occupied a valley which, before it gained national park status, supported a small human settlement with subsistence cultivation. Sitting on Jalawe Rock on the northern end of the high plateau one can now look down into the valley below and watch these animals peacefully feeding along the line of the stream or resting in the shade,

A family of klipspringers near Jalawe Rock. These small, surefooted antelope are especially adapted to live on rocky hills.   JANET and JOHN HOUGH

Visitors sitting on Jalawe Rock at the northern end of the main plateau watching elephant in the *dambos* of the Chipome Valley far below.   DAVID ELIAS

Denham's bustard. Nyika has the largest breeding population of this species in the country.   MICHAEL GORE

quite unaware of being observed. More widely spread in the lower areas of *Brachystegia* woodland are the shy, graceful kudu antelope.

The birds of the park are of great interest. On the high grasslands the internationally endangered wattled crane is commonly seen in pairs near *dambos*. Nyika has the largest breeding population of this species in the country, as well as Denham's bustard. The red-winged francolin, often viewed crouching immobile or scurrying away in the grassland, is a subspecies found only on Nyika Plateau. The most commonly sighted birds of prey include the striking augur buzzard, and the bateleur and black-breasted snake-eagles. Many smaller raptors also occur, and after a hatch of termites in the lower areas during the rains, kestrels, kites and lanner falcons provide an exciting spectacle, swooping and turning to catch and eat the insects on the wing. (Information on termites is given on page 75.)

For the dedicated bird-watcher, however, the isolated patches of evergreen forest harbour the most interesting birds. These forests contain more species than any other in Malaŵi, some of them reaching the most southerly limit of their range here. Many of the birds frequent the high canopy and can be difficult to see, but bird-watching can be aided by the use of a portable cassette player and directional microphone. By recording the call of a bird and then playing its voice back, the bird becomes understandably curious and will often come closer for a better look at the supposed intruder. Species which may be seen include the bar-tailed trogon, cinnamon dove and starred robin; among the rarer ones are the white-chested alethe and olive-flanked robin. Brown-necked parrots often move into the forest patches to feed on the fruits of the huge aningeria trees, and rameron pigeons and green loeries feed intensively on the fruit of the Cape olive when they mature every two years. Many of the birds which breed in the forests are very territorial, and a breeding individual may occupy the same small area for many years[42]. Other species do not breed there but use the plateau as a feeding and resting ground during migrations. Most activity occurs in November and December at the beginning of the rains, and this is the most rewarding time for bird-watching.[43,44]

Vegetation of Nyika

The evergreen forests are fascinating places. There is a sharp contrast as one leaves the exposed, short grassland of the ridges and enters the tall, sombre half-light of the cathedral-like forest which clothes the valleys of the plateau. The wind suddenly drops and new noises become apparent: the trickling of a stream, or the call of a bird invisible in the high canopy. Some of the trees reach a great height and have massive, fluted trunks with great buttresses at the base to help support their weight on the steep slopes with their thin soil cover. Everywhere there is an upward struggle as the plants compete for light, and creepers use the existing trees for support to reach the canopy above. In the humid atmosphere ferns and lichens grow on the trunks and branches of the larger trees, and epiphytic orchids abound, producing delicate sprays of dangling flowers during the rains. Tree ferns grow along the streams. Two forests on the south of the plateau are dominated by juniper, some specimens of which reach a great height. The species is on the southern limit of its natural range here, occurring more commonly on the slopes of the high mountains in Tanzania and Kenya where it produces valuable timber.

The main threat to the survival of the evergreen forest is fire. Although some controversy exists as to the former vegetation cover, it is generally considered that the forests were once much more widespread on the plateau. An increasing frequency of fires started by man, felling for iron smelting, and also possibly a shift in climate to drier conditions caused a reduction in the forest cover. When fire penetrates the dense outer growth of a forest patch and reaches the canopy, many susceptible plants are killed and the whole structure of the forest is destroyed. The environmental conditions change so much that other

The inside of an evergreen forest on the slopes of Nkhonjera Mountain on the southern side of the plateau. There is a sudden change as one enters the shelter of the forest from the exposed grassland outside.   DAVID ELIAS

Early burning on the Nyika Plateau. Areas of grassland are burnt rotationally by the park management early in the dry season to remove the accumulated dead grass and reduce the risk of fierce uncontrolled fires damaging the evergreen forests.   DAVID ELIAS

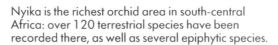

Nyika is the richest orchid area in south-central Africa: over 120 terrestrial species have been recorded there, as well as several epiphytic species.

Bulbophyllum acutisepalum, an epiphytic orchid of the *Brachystegia* woodland.   DAVID ELIAS

Disa erubescens carsonii, an orchid of the *dambos*.
DAVID ELIAS

Herschelia baurii, a grassland species.   DAVID ELIAS

Aerangis montana, an epiphytic orchid.   DAVID ELIAS

Eulophia odontoglossa, common in montane and upland grassland, though scarce in woodland.
FRANK JOHNSTON

Holothrix longiflora which occurs locally in woodland near Fingira Rock.   FRANK JOHNSTON

Protea angolensis var. *trichanthera* found on the ascent to the Nyika Plateau.   JUDY CARTER

Everlasting flowers which carpet the grasslands during the dry season.   JUDY CARTER

colonising plant species often invade, and the forest does not regenerate.

Fuel for fire on the grasslands builds up during the rains, when the grass grows faster than the herbivores can consume it. In the dry season this growth dies and becomes dry. In successive rains, more grass will grow and much of this, too, will accumulate. Over a number of years a considerable amount of dead grass builds up. Apart from eventually stifling the growth of new grass, this is a considerable fire hazard: if set alight, especially at the end of the dry season when the plant material is tinder-box dry, the grassland burns extensively and fire is likely to spread to the adjacent forest. The park management therefore burns blocks of grassland each year, early in the dry season, to avoid hot fires which could damage the forests. In successive years the blocks are burnt rotationally, so that no area is left to accumulate dead grass for more than three or four years. This not only protects the forests but ensures that new grass can grow, unhindered by old, dead material. Grazers such as zebra and roan depend on this grass for much of the year.

Uncontrolled fires started by poachers are a severe problem in the park, both on the high plateau and in the *Brachystegia* woodland below where dry plant material also accumulates. The fires may be started to drive animals into snares or to smoke out bees' nests for honey, or simply to facilitate walking in the woodland. In dry conditions, fires can spread unchecked over large areas, sometimes destroying evergreen forest patches in their path.

The grassland communities contain many other plants besides grass. After the fires the charred landscape suddenly becomes a mass of colour as flowers appear seemingly from nowhere, stimulated by the burn. There are few times of the year when there is not a spectacular floral display on the high plateau. After the rains start the delicate terrestrial orchids flower in the grasslands and *dambos*, including many different species of *Disa*, *Satyrium* and *Habenaria*. The plateau is the richest orchid area in south-central Africa: over 120 species of terrestrial orchid have been recorded there, at least six of which are thought to occur nowhere else in the world[19]. Towards the end of the rains, as other flowers are fading, proteas deck the slopes above the *Brachystegia* woodland in pearly pinks and whites. Later, as the weather cools and grassland dries to a rich golden hue, aloes add a splash of scarlet and everlasting flowers produce brilliant yellow mats of colour which decorate the landscape for many months to come.

Nyika wilderness

Walking on the high grassland across the carpets of flowers or through the high pines of Chelinda Forest is one of the most pleasurable experiences of a visit to Nyika. Laurens van der Post described a 1949 expedition on foot to the mystical plateau in his book *Venture to the Interior,*[36] and apart from the development of Chelinda, the landscapes and fauna which he saw remain much the same today. There are waterfalls, evergreen forests and Stone Age rock shelters to visit, birds and mammals to watch, and flowers to find. Views are breathtaking, especially on the edges of the plateau where the escarpment drops away and one can see north and eastward to the lakeshore plains and across the shimmering Lake Malaŵi to the distant hills of Tanzania; or south to the Vwaza Marsh and Viphya Plateau. The margins of the plateau are truly wild areas, where the terrain is too steep for vehicles and man seldom ventures. It is here that walking becomes a real wilderness experience, following narrow game paths created by countless wild hooves: along ridges, by streams and across steep slopes. The area is so extensive that one can spend four or five days in this wilderness, walking by day and camping at night under the brilliant African stars beside the rushing streams, or in the shelter of the evergreen forest.

To the north of the main plateau Kawozya Mountain rises majestically up from the Chipome Valley, leading on along an isolated ridge to the twin peaks of Mpanda Mountain overlooking Karonga and Lake Malaŵi. This is a fascinating walk, crossing the elephant-inhabited *dambos* of the valley and climbing the *Brachystegia*-covered lower slopes of Kawozya to the high heaths and the grassland. On the exposed shoulder of Kawozya the trail passes a magnificent isolated yellow-wood tree, *Podocarpus falcatus*. The only one of its kind for miles around, it is the origin of many local beliefs. Known as *mbonekera* (literally 'the tree which is seen from afar') an infusion made from the bark is believed to make the imbiber much admired, especially by members of the opposite sex[45]. It is fortunate that *mbonekera* grows in such an isolated refuge!

Past the peak of Kawozya, a long ridge of waving oat-like grass leads to Mpanda Mountain. At the far end there are groves of *Acacia abyssinica*, a striking flat-topped thorn tree, and the valleys to either side are filled with the dense, dark canopy of evergreen forest. At the end of the ridge, overlooking Lake Malaŵi and in the shadow of Mpanda, stands the

Mbonekera, 'the tree which is seen from afar', on the ridge of Kawozya Mountain.   JUDY CARTER

Other wilderness trails are shorter. One incorporates angling: walking is combined with the pleasure of playing an elusive rainbow trout in the dark, fast waters of the North Rumphi Stream, camping overnight on the banks and roasting the day's catch for supper over an open fire in the velvety Nyika night. Another trail leads one way off the plateau along the remote and isolated Kalabwe Ridge between the North Rumphi and Kaziwiziwi Valleys, towards the mission at Livingstonia outside the park. From here, walkers can continue down the steep, wooded escarpment to the lakeshore plain and the blue water of the lake, perhaps catching the *Ilala* steamer back to civilisation in the south.

Wilderness walkers climbing the twin peaks of Mpanda Mountain, with the peak of Kawozya in the distance.
JUDY CARTER

ruin of Bleak House. This isolated dwelling was built by missionaries from Livingstonia around 1900 when they hoped to spread Christianity towards Karonga; it was later used by the owner of a cotton ginnery as a hunting lodge before it fell into disrepair. Finally, on the summit of Mpanda, there is a kaleidoscopic view as far as the eye can see, of mountain, valley, forest, water and sky.

Chapter Three

Central African Plateau

The main plateau areas, lying between about 800 and 1400 m above sea-level, cover approximately three quarters of Malaŵi's land surface. They are mostly part of the old Central African Plateau which extends across Central and Southern Africa, now much fragmented by rifting and downcutting of rivers. In Malaŵi these areas have a warmer climate than the high mountains and plateaux which rise above them, but are much cooler than the low-lying lands of the rift valley below. The soils are variable: in places they are very fertile and support intensive agriculture, but large tracts of plateau have infertile, leached, sandy soils. The natural vegetation is normally *Brachystegia* woodland with *Acacia* and *Combretum* in more fertile areas; *dambos* often occur along drainage lines with marsh in flooded areas.

There are three main areas of plateau, the most extensive being in the west and covering the Lilongwe, Kasungu and Mzimba areas. Much of it has gently undulating topography, interrupted occasionally by isolated inselbergs which rise above the surrounding land. Meandering rivers with many ox-bows traverse the area, flanked by broad, grassy *dambos*. The general direction of drainage is to the north-east, and before the development of the rift valley it is likely that these rivers continued eastward, forming the headwaters of the Rovuma, Luwegu and Ruaha Rivers which flow through northern Mozambique and southern Tanzania to the Indian Ocean. Rifting would have resulted in their eventual capture, diverting their waters southwards to the Shire and Zambezi[5]. The plateau is bounded by the edge of the rift valley in the south-east and the Viphya Plateau in the north-east, though in the west it continues across the border, extending into Zambian territory until it is cut by the Luangwa Valley. To the north it is interrupted by the high

The Central African Plateau near Zomba, at the end of the dry season. JAMES OGLETHORPE

Part of the new Capital City of Lilongwe. REX PARRY

Nyika Plateau, but continues beyond it to the Misuku Hills and the Tanzanian border.

The Lilongwe Plain has very fertile sandy clay soils and is intensively cultivated for maize and other crops; it is also densely populated and supports the new capital, Lilongwe. In the heart of the city between the old town and the new capital centre lies the Lilongwe Nature Sanctuary. It protects an area of *Combretum/Piliostigma* woodland, with clumps of bamboo on lower ground and evergreen trees along the Lingadzi River. In this small area 200 species of birds have been recorded, including rarities such as the red-winged warbler. Pied mannikins are sometimes seen in the bamboo thickets, and African broadbills may be heard displaying at dusk[44].

Heuglin's robin with young in the Lilongwe Nature Sanctuary.
MICHAEL GORE

Crocodile occur in the river, and large mammals such as bushbuck, grey duiker, bushpig, porcupine, leopard and spotted hyena frequent the woodland. Nature trails lead through the area, and in the quiet heart of the sanctuary it is difficult to remember that one is in the centre of Malaŵi's capital city. The main objective of the sanctuary is conservation education: the Department of National Parks and Wildlife has many informative exhibits on display in the Education Centre as well as a few captive orphaned animals. It is well worth a visit, and is very accessible from the rest of the city.

West and north of the Lilongwe area the soils are poorer and large areas are cultivated for tobacco. Much of the natural woodland in the Kasungu area has been cleared for firewood which is used in the processing of flue-cured tobacco, and acute shortages of fuel are now occurring. Kasungu National Park which lies along the Zambian border, however, harbours a wide variety of large mammals in extensive *Brachystegia* woodlands. Further north along the border, just south of the Nyika Plateau, lies the Vwaza Marsh Game Reserve, an area with diverse wetland and woodland habitats and a hot, dry climate contrasting strongly with the high Nyika.

The second plateau area is the relatively small Chiripa Plateau which stands isolated at the southern end of Lake Malaŵi, rising between the two

Paradise flycatcher nesting in the Lilongwe Nature Sanctuary. The small neat nest is made of bark, roots and grass, bound with spider web. MICHAEL GORE

arms of the lake and extending southwards between the Bwanje and Shire Valleys. The northern part of this plateau contains the Phirilongwe Forest Reserve, a rugged wilderness much dissected by drainage lines and harbouring an elusive population of elephant which still occasionally moves eastward to the vicinity of Nkhudzi Hill in the Lake Malaŵi National Park.

The third plateau area lies to the east of the Shire Valley and includes the Shire Highlands, the Phalombe Plain, the low-lying area of Lakes Chilwa and Chiuta, and the hilly area of the Namwera region. It is a heterogeneous area due to the effects of rifting and later downwarping, which have resulted in a gradual drop in altitude from the Shire Highlands towards the lower lying Phalombe Plain and Lake Chilwa. The Shire Highlands have many interesting shaped hills rising from the plateau to create breathtaking skylines. The area has a high density of human settlement including the towns of Blantyre, Limbe and Zomba, and has some of the most intensively cultivated land in the country, the major crops being maize, tobacco and tea. Much of the natural vegetation has been cleared and soil erosion is a serious problem in some places.

In contrast the Phalombe Plain is a vast, flat area with a few isolated hills. It is one of only two areas

Fishermen and dugout canoes at Lake Chiuta; the channel leads to open water in the distance. DENIS TWEDDLE

in Malaŵi known to have supported large herds of Nyasa wildebeest; this species unfortunately disappeared from the area around 1925 due to human pressure[13,19]. Now much of the Phalombe Plain is heavily cultivated, its soils consisting of a deep layer of sediment, with a series of terraces indicating previously higher levels of Lake Chilwa. At one stage this lake was continuous with Lake Chiuta and covered much of the plain; it is thought to have drained northward into the Rovuma basin in Mozambique and hence to the Indian Ocean. It is now separated from Lake Chiuta by a wind-blown sand-bar and has no surface outlet. Shallow and partly covered by swamp, the lake is fed principally by rivers from Zomba Plateau and Mulanje Mountain. It undergoes large fluctuations in level which are related to rainfall. In drier years the amount of water in the lake is drastically reduced, and salinity and alkalinity become so high that most of the fish are forced to retreat to the purer waters of the inflowing rivers. Lake Chilwa supports a very productive though rather unreliable fishery. Under favourable conditions it has the highest productivity of all the fisheries in the country, and in 1979 when the lake level was relatively high it yielded 25 846 metric tonnes of fish, 43% of the national catch that year. At the other extreme, however, in 1968 and 1973 the lake dried out completely and yields were extremely low, causing severe social hardship. Lake Chiuta also supports a fishery, but it is much less productive than

the one found at Lake Chilwa.

To the north and north-west of Lakes Chilwa and Chiuta, the expansive plains are interrupted by a series of isolated inselbergs. Further north the larger massifs of Mangochi Mountain and the Namwera Hills rise up steeply from the surrounding areas, the latter flanked on the west by the lakeshore plain and traversed in the east by the Mozambique border. Tobacco is grown extensively around Namwera, and large tracts of woodland have been felled to provide firewood for tobacco curing. Shortages of firewood are becoming acute in the area and if present trends continue, supplies from natural woodland are likely to be completely exhausted in a few years' time. The slopes of Mangochi Mountain are protected as a forest reserve, however, and support some evergreen forest besides montane grassland and deciduous woodland. Elephant from Liwonde National Park in the Shire Valley migrate to the slopes of the mountain during the rains, living in the woodland and drinking from temporary water sources. Remains of a fort may still be seen on the mountain, a relic from the early days of the Protectorate. (Geographical and agricultural information:[5,6]; Lake Chilwa:[3,46])

Kasungu National Park[19,31,47]

Name derivation

From the administrative district in which the park lies. The name originated from Kasungu Hill, and oral tradition holds that it is derived from the Chichewa word *kusunga* (meaning 'to keep safe'). In this area people were protected by the first Chief Mwase from raids by warrior tribes and wild animals.[48]

Declaration

In 1922 the Fort Alston Forest Reserve was gazetted, covering much of the existing park area. This was part of a programme to control sleeping sickness transmitted by tsetse fly. In 1930 the area was declared a game reserve, and in 1970 it gained national park status, with a slight reduction in area. A buffer zone was gazetted in 1977.

Present size

2316 km²

Location

Central Malaŵi on the Central African Plateau, along the western border with Zambia.

Landscape types

Flat to undulating topography dissected by broad drainage lines; a few isolated inselbergs particularly in the west.

Vegetation

Mainly *Brachystegia/Julbernardia* woodland in the plateau areas, grassy *dambos* supporting orchids and other wild flowers, and open woodland of *Pericopsis*, *Combretum*, *Albizia*, *Acacia*, *Piliostigma* and *Terminalia* along the valleys of the major drainage lines.

Large mammals

Most commonly seen: elephant, zebra, warthog, reedbuck, roan, sable antelope, hartebeest and buffalo. Also occurring: vervet monkey, baboon, wild dog, ratel, zorilla, various mongoose species, spotted hyena, cheetah, lion, leopard, genet, aardvark, dassie, black rhino, bushpig, hippo, bushbuck, kudu, eland, grey duiker, waterbuck, puku, impala, klipspringer, oribi, grysbok, porcupine.

Birds

Birds of *Brachystegia* woodland and *dambos*; water birds on Lifupa Dam. Over 300 species have been recorded in the park.

Other animals

A few species of fish occur in the dam and streams.

Sites of special interest

Rock shelters, rock paintings, remains of fortified villages, iron smelting kilns, hills in the west and north, Black Rock, Lifupa Dam.

Access

The park is reached by vehicle from the M1 Lilongwe — Mzuzu road. Near the turnoff to Kasungu town on the opposite side of the road the D187 leads off west to the park; it is well signed. This road is mostly untarred, but is passable for saloon cars with good ground clearance virtually all year round except after very heavy rain. The park entrance gate is reached after 38 km, and Lifupa Lodge lies about 14 km inside the park. There is a network of game-viewing roads, most of which are closed during the rains (approximately December to April); during the dry season they are passable for saloon cars. The roads are shown on Map 3.1

Continued

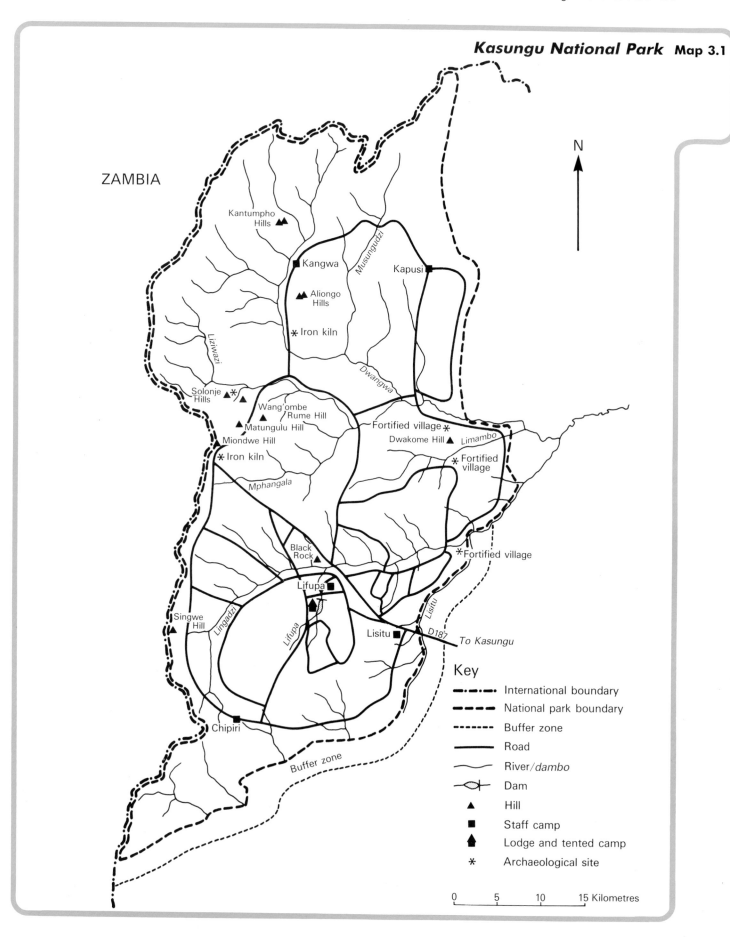

Kasungu National Park Map 3.1

N

ZAMBIA

Kantumpho Hills

Kangwa

Kapusi

Aliongo Hills

Musungudzi

* Iron kiln

Liziwazi

Dwangwa

Solonje Hills *

Wang'ombe Rume Hill

Matungulu Hill

Fortified village *

Dwakome Hill Limambo

Miondwe Hill

* Iron kiln

* Fortified village

Mphangala

* Fortified village

Black Rock

Lisitu

Lifupa

Singwe Hill

Lingadzi

Lifupa

Lisitu D187 To Kasungu

Chipiri

Buffer zone

Key

▬·▬·▬·	International boundary
▬ ▬ ▬	National park boundary
- - - -	Buffer zone
▬▬▬	Road
∿	River/*dambo*
⊱✛	Dam
▲	Hill
■	Staff camp
⬟	Lodge and tented camp
*	Archaeological site

0   5   10   15 Kilometres

Distances from the main centres to the entrance gate are:

Lilongwe: 165 km
Mzuzu: 289 km
Zomba: 446 km
Blantyre: 512 km

There is a grass-surfaced airfield at Lifupa for light aircraft.

Visitor facilities

Lifupa Lodge offers accommodation in comfortable rondavels, and has full restaurant and bar facilities, swimming pool, petrol pump and shop. There is also a tented camp nearby, with facilities for self-catering visitors. There is a hostel for student groups. A museum provides information on the national park.

A marked trail leads through some of the western hills and incorporates rock shelters and paintings.

The services of a game-scout guide may be hired to escort visitors by car or on foot in the park.

Visitor activities

Game-viewing and bird-watching by vehicle, on foot and from the lodge; walking; looking at plants; visiting archaeological sites; photography.

Administrative arrangements

Reservations for Lifupa Lodge at the time of writing are made with Halls Car Hire in Blantyre (Box 368, tel. 620 498/633 907). The gates of the park close at 6 pm and open at 6 am. Park fees are charged for visitors and their vehicles.

The services of a game-scout guide may be arranged at the park headquarters at Lifupa.

Best time to visit

Game-viewing: August to January
Bird-watching: November to December
Walking: June to September
Historical sites: June to September
Looking at plants: August to September; November to February
Photography: August to February

Note that most of the game-viewing roads are closed during the rains (approximately December to April). Temperatures from May to August inclusive are normally pleasantly warm in the park. During September to November they can be uncomfortably hot. The rest of the year is intermediate.

A herd of elephant on a *dambo* in Kasungu National Park. The wet black marks on their sides are from a recent bath at a waterhole. MICHAEL GORE

Kasungu National Park

Kasungu National Park has the largest elephant population in the country, thought to number about 800 animals at present[47]. Late in the afternoon after the heat of the day, small family groups of elephant can often be seen browsing tranquilly on coppiced *Brachystegia* growth, their ears flapping gently to cool themselves as they move slowly through the woodland. From time to time a mother may make a low rumbling noise to her calf, warning it not to wander too far, and occasionally the dominant cow of the group may raise her trunk above her head to scent for possible danger. Gleaming tide marks on their backs indicate that they have bathed earlier in the day at one of the various water holes in the park, where they often wallow in the mud to smother parasites clinging to folds of skin and spray water on to their backs with their trunks to cool themselves.

Steep-sided inselbergs rise above the *Brachystegia* woodland in the west of Kasungu National Park. JUDY CARTER

The park also supports many other large mammal species including buffalo, zebra, black rhino, many species of antelope, and predators such as lion, leopard and cheetah. Game-viewing at certain times of the year is very good, especially along some of the valleys and *dambos* which dissect the undulating plateau areas of *Brachystegia* woodland. During the rains and after the fires the *dambos* have a multitude of orchids and other wild flowers. On the Zambian border to the west a series of hills rises above the rest of the park, a fascinating wilderness area to explore on foot. There are also many late Stone Age and Iron Age archaeological sites to see. With its comfortable and attractive lodge, Kasungu currently receives more visitors than any other park in the country.

History of Kasungu National Park

The park area has a rich history. Records of Middle Stone Age settlement exist from sites just across the

border in Zambia in use as long ago as around 40 000 BC, and it is likely that these hunter-gatherers also used the present park area from time to time. Late Stone Age people inhabited rock shelters in the park, particularly around the Miondwe Hills, and their small, sharp, quartz flake tools may still be seen in the vicinity of the rock shelters today. There are also various rock paintings consisting of faint red and purple geometric shapes, thought to have been drawn by these people or the Early Iron Age people who moved into the region around AD 100: these paintings may have been significant in initiation rituals or rain-making ceremonies. (The white paintings of geometric figures are much more recent and were connected with the Nyau cult, a Chewa secret society: they may have been concerned with Nyau initiation rites.) A foot trail today leads the visitor through open woodland into the wilderness of these inselberg hills, to the rock shelters and paintings.

When the Early Iron Age people moved into the area they started cultivating and smelting iron; they also hunted. At this time wild animals were probably reasonably abundant, though population densities would never have been very high because of the intrinsically low carrying capacity of the area. From about AD 1100 onwards successive new groups of people moved into the area from the west, developing villages in the valleys where the soils were more fertile than on the plateau. They grew crops on a system of shifting cultivation, and probably kept a few livestock, tsetse fly permitting. Hunting was still an important source of meat and skins, and as the Arab and Portuguese traders extended their trade

A candelabra tree growing in the rocky western area of the park. CHRISTOPHER CARTER

Iron-smelting kiln or *ng'anjo*. A few kilns still stand in the park, relics of the smelting industry which continued in the region until about 1930. CHRISTOPHER CARTER

Blacksmiths at work forging hoes from locally smelted iron, seen by Livingstone to the south of the present-day park in 1866. Each blacksmith would make several hoes a day, and the sound of the hammer was heard from dawn to dusk. The hammer was a large stone bound with strips of bark for handles; tongs were made from bark; the anvil was a large stone sunk into the ground; and the bellows were made from goatskin.   DAVID LIVINGSTONE

network into the area, in the nineteenth century, elephant were hunted heavily for ivory with the new firearms which the traders introduced. By about 1850 the Mwase family was in control of the Kasungu Plain, having probably originally come as agents for the traders and ousted the traditional leaders they found there. They ruled over the local people and protected them from attacks by other armed slaving groups and also from wild animals; at this time the Kasungu Plain was very prosperous. The Mwase traded as far as Quelimane and Zanzibar on the coast of the Indian Ocean, and inland to Tete.

This was the situation when David Livingstone crossed the park area in 1863. He commented specifically on the iron smelting activity in the Kasungu area, noting that every third or fourth village had a kiln, or *ng'anjo*. He obtained a sample of iron which was later analysed in Europe and found to be of exceptionally high quality. A few iron smelting kilns may still be seen standing in the park today, tall structures built of clay from termite mounds. The Kasungu *ng'anjo* are taller than those built by the Phoka on Nyika (page 38), being up to 2.3 m tall. They are shaped like a cylindrical chimney, wider at

the base than at the top. A constriction about a third of the way up on the inside creates two chambers, the lower one being where the smelting occurred. The Chichewa-speaking Chulu people of the Kasungu region differed slightly from the Phoka in their smelting traditions, though they also had well developed ritual, prayer and taboos, and used many medicines.[40]

The intensive smelting activity would have affected the species composition of the woodland, about 15 tons of wood from mature specimens of the timber tree *Pterocarpus angolensis* being used to produce one and a half metric tons of charcoal for each smelting[40]. Clearance of valley areas for shifting cultivation and the effects of grazing livestock would also have had a significant impact on the habitat and hence on wild animal populations of the present-day park area. Hunting for subsistence would have further reduced the numbers of the smaller species. Livingstone saw only a few hartebeest and zebra, and no sign of elephant. For some years the Mwase's hunters had been obtaining ivory from the Luangwa Valley to the west, suggesting that elephant had been more or less eliminated from the present-day park area.

The period of relative peace and prosperity of the human population which Livingstone witnessed was soon to be ended. In the next few years the Ngoni started raiding the Kasungu area from their newly established base at Mzimba. The Chulu people attempted to defend themselves by retreating into fortified villages: each village consisted of a closely clustered group of huts surrounded by a ditch and an earth wall, probably with a wooden stockade on top. The defence was not always successful, however; the Ngoni decimated villages in the northern part of the park around 1870. Mwase was the only chief in the area to resist the invaders successfully when they attacked his stockade at Linga near Kasungu Hill in 1873. Remains of fortified villages may still be seen in the park today: usually a circular or oval ditch up to 100 m in diameter, with a low bank on the inside. In some cases the bases of huts can be traced.

The unrest caused by the Ngoni was finally quelled with the establishment of the Protectorate, whose boundary ran along the western limit of the present-day park area. Chief Mwase attempted to resist the British but was defeated by a British military expedition which shelled his fortified village from the slopes of Kasungu Hill. The Fort Alston military post was established just outside the present boundary of the park in 1897.

Following the destruction of many villages by the

Ngoni, wild animals moved back into the abandoned and overgrown fields of the former settlements. With them they brought the tsetse fly: it entered the park area from Luangwa in 1910, and in 1922 an epidemic of sleeping sickness broke out in west Kasungu. The area was evacuated by the Protectorate Administration, the people resettling both to the east, and to the west across the border. The evacuated area was declared the Fort Alston Forest Reserve; in 1930 it was also declared a game reserve. Animal populations started to build up again in the reserve, elephant moving in from the Luangwa Valley. With the removal of the people from the tsetse-infested land sleeping sickness disappeared, although tsetse are still present in the park. In 1955 Chief Mwase requested that some of his people be allowed to return, and a few villages reoccupied the south-eastern part of the reserve. This land was excised and the rest of the area raised to national park status in 1970, the year in which the lodge was opened. (Historical information:[47])

Vegetation of Kasungu

Most signs of human settlement have now disappeared and plant succession has occurred in the previously cleared areas. The plateau which comprises most of the park was probably least affected by human activity: it consists mostly of undulating terrain covered in tall *Brachystegia* woodland and in general has fairly infertile soils. Some local variations occur, however: in the flatter, southerly end of the park the soils are pale, sandy and very infertile due to the underlying quartz, and support scattered, medium sized trees. By contrast, in parts of the undulating eastern central area outcrops of base-rich rock have given rise to heavy, red, fertile clays. *Brachystegia* trees here are interspersed with species from the valley woodland: *Combretum*, *Pericopsis* and *Terminalia*; the trees grow densely and are much stunted and coppiced because of elephant pressure.

Grass growth beneath the trees of the plateau woodland is generally short and sparse. Somewhat surprisingly, however, it has a relatively high nutrient content. Most of the soils are freely draining and little water is retained in the topsoil, so there is not enough water for the plants to produce large amounts of fibre which would make the grass less digestible and nutritious. The small amount of grass which does grow therefore has a relatively high nutrient content and supports various species of antelope.

The woodlands are dissected by a network of grassy *dambos* which drain towards the major rivers of the park; many of the game-viewing roads in the park follow the lines of *dambos*. Most of them are relatively infertile as they have sandy soils and are waterlogged for much of the year; they are known as sour *dambos*, and their grass has a very low nutritive value except possibly for the green flush of young grass which grows on the damp soil in the ashes following grass fires in the dry season. There are, however, saline seepages along their margins and at the bases of termite mounds in the *dambos*: these seepages provide salt licks for elephant and other animals. The sour *dambos* have wonderful displays of orchids, lilies, gladioli and other flowers at the start of the rains.

In contrast, a relatively small number of *dambos* in the park have fertile, clay soils and are known as sweet *dambos*. They occur in the basic rock outcrop area of the eastern-central plateau and in the larger river valleys on the east side of the park, supporting a high quality grass growth. In the valleys the original sandy plateau soil has been removed by the down-

A herd of buffalo on one of the many *dambos* of the park during the rains.   MICHAEL GORE

cutting action of the rivers, and subsequent weathering of the underlying rock has produced a reddish-brown clay loam on the valley slopes with an accumulation of clay in the valley floor creating sweet *dambos*. In a few places obstructions such as a hard sill of rock across the valley has halted the down-cutting process, and an accumulation of clay has built up behind producing a wide floodplain of high quality grass: there is one such area on the lower Lingadzi River near the park boundary. The fertile soils of the valley slopes support open woodland with tree species such as *Pericopsis, Albizia, Terminalia, Combretum* and some *Acacia*. The grass on the slopes is very tall, and although initially nutritious it develops so much fibre that it eventually becomes unpalatable by the end of the rains.

The park management burns the central *dambo* and valley areas of the park in the middle of the dry season to prevent hot, damaging fires in the valleys later in the dry season. This also improves game-viewing as visibility is better and many animals are attracted out of the *Brachystegia* woodland on to the green flush of grass which grows after the fires. Most of the *dambos* have pools of standing water during the dry season so water availability is not a problem.

Animals of Kasungu

Kasungu National Park has a variety of habitats and food sources for the herbivores of the park. As on Nyika, each species is specialised to exploit a certain part of the vegetation and hence avoid excessive competition with the others. In Kasungu, however, there is a greater diversity of large herbivores and the situation is more complex. Large animals such as elephant, buffalo, zebra, eland and hippo graze non-selectively in the tall grass valley areas, consuming large amounts of grass often of relatively low quality. They comprise about 80% of the biomass of large mammals in the park. Apart from the hippo these species do not hold territories but move in herds over a large home-range.

Buffalo are normally found in large herds, grazing on medium to tall grasses; they move from the valley slopes to the clay floodplain areas at the beginning of the dry season when the grass in the former becomes unpalatable. Towards the end of the dry season the large herds split up, perhaps because of scarcity of food; they cannot use the new grass growth stimulated by the fires unless it grows tall enough for them. Smaller groups of buffalo become scattered throughout the valleys and sometimes wander into the plateau areas, using the sour *dambos*.

Zebra occur in small herds, comprising a number of mares and young animals accompanied by a stallion: at maturity young males are driven away from the family group and form bachelor herds. Unlike the antelope and buffalo, zebra have upper incisors and are able to bite off both closely cropped and tough grasses which the former cannot utilise; they can therefore consume a very wide range of grass heights and qualities. They have inefficient digestive systems compared to the ruminants, and consequently eat large quantities of food which is often of low quality. They use the tall grasses of the valleys during the rains, moving to the eastern plateau areas when the valley grasses become unpalatable in the dry season, until the fires start when they move on to the burnt areas, presumably for the mineral in the ash. Once the grass grows they again concentrate in the valleys. The home-ranges of different herds overlap freely.

Hippo are also able to graze the grass very short, using their wide, horny lips to grip the grass close to the ground and tearing it off by swinging their heads. They graze at night, spending the day lying on sandbanks or submerged in water to regulate their body temperature. During the dry season the only water body large enough for them is Lifupa Dam, and they can often be seen from the lodge. When the rains come they disperse to pools on the Lingadzi River and to dams outside the park. Male hippo are very territorial and defend their stretches of water fiercely, theatening each other with wide open mouths revealing their formidable canines which have developed for fighting and defence rather than feeding. It is likely that the dam is too small for more than the fifteen or so animals which presently occur in the park, as young hippo are regularly killed by adults.

The other two species which graze non-selectively, elephant and eland, also consume browse material at certain times of the year especially in the dry season when the remaining grasses are extremely unpalatable. Elephant stay on the valleys later than most other animals apart from buffalo as they are able to use very low quality grass, but eventually even they move off the valleys at the end of the rains into the adjacent coppiced *Brachystegia* woodland, where they obtain the bulk of their forage by browsing. They have had a profound effect on these areas, causing dense, coppiced growth of the trees. They remain here for quite a time, not returning to the *dambos* immediately after the fires as the green flush does not produce a large enough quantity of grass for them. Once the rains have started, however, and the valleys again have adequate amounts of palatable grass, they return there. Eland, the largest antelope, overcome the problem of dry season forage in a different way. As on Nyika they are extremely mobile, the herds having very extensive home-ranges, and they move out of the area possibly to the north of the park or even across the border into Zambia. At this time they consume mainly leaves and shoots of herbs and bushes.

The smaller antelope are more selective in their feeding habits; their smaller stomachs require less bulk food but the smaller body size means that they have a higher metabolic rate and therefore require higher quality food. They are adapted to select for the most nutritious plant species and sometimes the best parts of the plant. Selective grazers such as the sable, roan and hartebeest mainly use the plateau woodlands, grazing the sparse but nutritious grasses there. As the carrying capacity of the plateau is generally low they occur in relatively small numbers, ranging widely over the area. They are most commonly seen when they move on to the *dambos* after the fires in the dry season to graze on the green flush, at which time they calve, returning to the woodland with the rains. Although they have similar diets they do each have some specialisation to reduce direct competition. Sable prefer short to medium height grass and graze fairly selectively; they occur mainly in the north of the park as the coppicing of woodland by elephant in the central area has suppressed grass growth. Roan are slightly larger in body size than sable, and are therefore probably less selective and capable of using taller grass. They have a wider range in the park and are seen more often in the valleys than sable, though they generally prefer the plateau woodlands. The hartebeest is smaller than the other two and is probably more selective; its long pointed face allows it to pick out the more nutritious green leaf from the thin wiry grasses of the sour *dambos* and surrounding woodlands. It is found most commonly in flat areas prone to waterlogging, particularly in the north-east of the park, but may also be seen in the sour *dambos* of the central area.

In contrast to these woodland species the waterbuck selects for soft, sweet grasses with a high moisture content. It also has a high water requirement, so it occurs only in the vicinity of open water. With its rather pointed muzzle it can select the more nutritious leaves from the coarse grasses of the valleys, but it prefers a leafy green sward: the optimal habitat for it is the clay floodplain area on the lower Lingadzi River. Unfortunately this area is on the park boundary and disturbance from outside, especially poaching, has scattered the waterbuck into surrounding areas of less suitable habitat. It remains to be seen whether the species will survive in the park.

Another antelope of the wetter areas is the puku; it prefers swampier areas than the waterbuck, and is smaller in body. Previously common on the large *dambos* of the region, particularly along the Bua and Rusa Rivers, the puku was heavily hunted by local

A male puku. In 1984 all but one of the puku which had recently appeared in Kasungu were females, so a number of young males was captured in the Luangwa Valley and released in the park to ensure the survival of the species there. CAROLINE CRAWFORD

Kasungu oribi.   JANET and JOHN HOUGH

people and disappeared completely from the Kasungu area in the 1930s. In 1978, however, a single female appeared at Lifupa Dam, to be followed in subsequent years by other females and one male. A similar phenomenon occurred in Vwaza Marsh Game Reserve, and two females also appeared on the high Nyika Plateau. The origin of these animals is a mystery: they may have been small, isolated groups of survivors from the original Malaŵi populations which wandered up the water courses into the protected areas, or they may have dispersed along *dambos* in the Luangwa catchment in Zambia and crossed the watershed into Malaŵi. The fact that all but one of the new arrivals were female may be related to the strong territorial behaviour of the male puku, which like the male waterbuck holds a small territory during the mating season and defends it rigorously against other males. Females are not territorial and are much more mobile, grazing through the area in groups: a receptive female is covered by the male in whose territory she happens to be at the time. To ensure the viability of the Kasungu puku a number of young males was captured in the Luangwa Valley in Zambia and translocated to Kasungu National Park in 1984. Once that population builds up, young males from it can be moved to Vwaza Marsh Game Reserve to ensure the survival of its population.

Slightly less selective in its feeding habits than the puku and waterbuck is the reedbuck. This is surprising as it is smaller than the other two; its nutritional strategy is not yet fully understood. It survives on the sour *dambos* and woodland margins throughout the year, living in small groups which remain within the small home-range; a number also occur on the clay floodplain areas of the lower Lingadzi River. The little oribi, very selective in its diet and more restricted in its home-range, grazes in

the most fertile *dambo* and floodplain areas living in pairs or small groups. It is not very numerous in the park as the amount of suitable habitat is limited.

Warthog and bushpig also graze selectively; the bushpig in addition consumes browse and animal material. Warthog select short nutritious grasses which they cut off with their incisors, and can often be seen going down on their knees to graze. They occasionally root in the soil with their snouts, consuming bulbs and tubers, and may also take leaves and fruits at certain times. They concentrate on the *dambos* immediately after the dry season fires, consuming ash presumably for the minerals it contains. They feed on the nutritious green flush which then develops, remaining in the valleys during the rains. When the valley grasses become unpalatable they move into the *Brachystegia* woodland to feed on the more nutritious grasses there. They live in family groups or sounders, the two parents normally being accompanied by their young. They are diurnal, often sleeping at night in enlarged aardvark burrows where they also produce their young. Bushpig on the other hand are largely nocturnal, living mainly in the woodland in small sounders, each with a dominant boar. They move extensively over a large home-range in response to food availability, and their diet includes roots, bulbs, grasses, seeds and fruits, as well as a smaller amount of insects, birds' eggs, reptiles and carrion. They root more and graze less than the warthog, often excavating extensive areas and probably playing an important role in preparing seedbeds for various woodland plant species.

Another selective mixed feeder is the impala. It mainly grazes on short grasses, using the patches of short nutritious grass surrounding the larger termite mounds in some of the valleys (see page 75 for information on termites) and the mown sward of the Lifupa airfield; during the dry season it feeds increasingly on nutritious parts of herbs and shrubs such as fruits, shoots and young leaves. The impala population was probably greatly reduced by the human settlement in the valleys; it is now recovering although it is not very large.

A few herbivores in the park hardly ever graze, instead consuming browse material from herbs, shrubs and trees. They include kudu, bushbuck, grey duiker, grysbok and black rhino; all but the black rhino are selective feeders. In general the browsers occur in the fertile valley woodlands. They do not make much use of the *Brachystegia* areas: only elephant browse the coppiced *Brachystegia*, when the valley grasses are too coarse and dry for them or when the valleys have been burnt, at which times there is no other bulk forage available for them. Otherwise the plateau trees are little used because they are unpalatable: many produce chemicals which make them poisonous or bad-tasting. This phenomenon may be related to soil fertility: in fertile areas trees can easily replace foliage removed by browsers, but in these woodlands the soil is not fertile enough to permit much extra growth so the plants may have developed this mechanism to prevent browsing. Certainly many of the *Brachystegia* woodland species contain a variety of chemicals, and are much used by local people for a wide range of traditional medicines. *Brachystegia bussei* seems to be particularly immune from elephant attack, and this graceful tree can be seen in tall groves on the crests of ridges, standing high above the surrounding coppiced woodland.

The browsers in the park therefore have a restricted range, and they comprise a relatively small proportion of the herbivores. Black rhino probably number about twenty; they are rarely seen, living solitarily in the denser areas of valley woodland and browsing relatively unselectively on shoots, leaves and young branches of shrubs and small trees. They always defecate in particular places, scattering the dung in these middens with their hind legs. Males defend a territory of sorts, marking the boundaries with middens, urination spots and rubbing places. The only other place where black rhino are known to occur in Malaŵi is Mwabvi Game Reserve; their international conservation status is discussed on page 154.

Kudu feed more selectively than the rhino. They are able to forage up to a height of over two metres, giving them access to plant material which is out of reach of the smaller browsers. They live in small herds and are numerous in the park, though they are well camouflaged and are often difficult to see in the woodland. The smaller bushbuck live singly or in pairs in small home-ranges, and may dig up roots and tubers as well as browsing on leaves, tender shoots and fruits.

Grey duiker also live alone or with a mate, defending a territory against intruders and supplementing their browse diet with animal material such as insects and carrion. The smallest antelope of the park, Sharpe's grysbok, has a greater water requirement than the duiker, and probably only holds territories in areas adjacent to permanent water. It lives singly except during the mating season, and besides browse material it may consume young grass and roots.

Preying on this complex community of browsers, grazers and mixed feeders is a variety of carnivore species, also specialised in their feeding habits to avoid excessive competition. The largest carnivores are lion, leopard, cheetah, spotted hyena and wild dog. Cheetah and wild dog have very large home-ranges which probably extend into Zambia: sometimes they are not seen in the park for long intervals, and then suddenly they are sighted frequently again. Both species catch their prey by running them down in a fast chase. Wild dogs hunt co-operatively in packs which normally number about ten animals; during the chase a few individuals stay close to the prey animal, pressing it hard while the others follow at a more leisurely pace, taking over from the leading dogs when they tire. As the prey animal becomes exhausted it slows down and the dogs bite and snap at it till it falls. It is then devoured rapidly, and normally nothing is left over for a second meal. Hyena have been known to steal carcasses from wild dog in the Serengeti, though it is not known if this happens in Kasungu. Wild dog normally hunt animals such as warthog, reedbuck and impala, but are capable of taking prey as large as a kudu. Like many other dog species they have a complex social organisation. The pack often has a communal den where a number of litters produced by different females are

Male kudu in Kasungu National Park at the end of the dry season. The *Brachystegia* woodland behind has been coppiced by browsing elephant. JANET and JOHN HOUGH

Cheetah frequent the more open areas of the park, relying on their tremendous speed to catch their prey. They usually hunt alone.   MICHAEL GORE

reared together; each litter comprises on average nine to ten pups. Other members of the pack bring food to the den, regurgitating it for the pups to feed on. While rearing young the pack is fairly sedentary: young animals are not strong enough to follow the pack on its long wanderings until at least seven months old.

The cheetah, although also a chase predator, has very different hunting techniques and other habits to the wild dog. It hunts singly or less often in small groups, relying on its tremendous speed: it is the swiftest running animal in the world and over short distances can sprint at speeds of over 110 km per hour. After approaching the prey as closely as possible

it puts it to flight and runs it down, overthrowing it by side-swiping it with a front paw and seizing it by the throat until it dies of strangulation. Cheetah hunting alone prey on smaller animals than wild dog, taking young antelope or small animals such as oribi, impala, grysbok, warthog, hares, and birds such as guineafowl. Adults of larger antelope species may be taken if they hunt in groups. Cheetah take only one meal from each kill and eat rapidly. Their kills are occasionally scavenged by lion, leopard and hyena before they have finished, and very rarely by large numbers of vultures: being relatively small cheetah are not able to stand up to the other large carnivores.

The female cheetah rears her litter alone, concealing the cubs when young in dense vegetation. On average she produces three to four cubs. While they are less than six weeks old she feeds them on regurgitated meat, an unusual habit for a cat. Later on she teaches them to hunt, sometimes capturing animals live for them to practise on. By the time the cubs are about 15-17 months old they are more or less able to hunt for themselves, and leave the mother to disperse on their own.

The chase predators, cheetah and wild dog, hunt during daylight and prefer relatively flat, open habitats where visibility is good and they have a better chance of running down animals. They rely on being able to approach fairly close to their prey before the chase, and consequently cannot afford to hunt in the same area for very long or the prey animals become too wary. Hence they are nomadic except when rearing young, moving over a very extensive home-range. Even taking this into account their population densities are comparatively low in Kasungu National Park as the habitat is not ideal for them. Lion and leopard, by contrast, hunt by stalking or ambushing their prey, getting so close before the prey animal becomes aware of their presence that they need make only a short rush and pounce to catch it. They therefore prefer habitats with adequate cover for concealment such as tall grass, thicket or broken terrain, and mostly hunt at night. Their densities in the park are high considering the relatively low carrying capacity for prey species. They do not compete directly with cheetah and wild dog because they hunt in the more densely vegetated areas.

Lion have the most highly developed social organisation of all the large cats. Apart from a few nomadic males they usually live in prides consisting of one dominant adult male and sometimes others which are subdominant; several lionesses which are often related to one another; and various cubs. The group is fairly stable though the dominant male may periodically be challenged and displaced by another. A new male may kill all the existing cubs in the pride which would have been fathered by his predecessor. This reduces future competition for his own cubs, which can now be conceived sooner. Cubs are reared jointly by the lionesses of the pride; a lioness will even suckle cubs which are not her own and should a mother die her cubs will be brought up by the rest of the pride. Cubs are dependent on the pride for at least the first two and a half years of life, after which time the young males are chased out by the dominant male.

Co-operation within a pride extends to hunting. Lions will often spread out to encircle a prey animal, and some may drive it towards others positioned in dense cover waiting to ambush it. Lionesses usually do most of the hunting; they are more efficient

Adult male lion in Kasungu National Park. Lion use dense cover to stalk and ambush their prey, members of a pride hunting co-operatively together. MICHAEL GORE

hunters than the males as they can run faster, and can stalk better with their smaller body size without the hindrance of a mane. The prey is knocked down by one or more lions. Small animals are then usually killed by a bite on the back of the neck; larger animals are often held by the throat and suffocated or strangled. The carcass may then be moved to another location or consumed on the spot. The dominant male which has been following the hunt usually feeds first, the lionesses waiting till he has finished. They in turn feed before the cubs. If all the carcass is not consumed at once lions will remain in the area until ready for another meal; one or two may stay to guard the kill while the rest sleep in the shade, their abdomens grossly distended. At such a time prey animals may graze close to the pride, aware that they are safe as the lions are not hunting.

Lions' diets are varied: they have been known to take antelope of all sizes; young elephant, hippo and rhino; and other animals including buffalo, warthog, bushpig, porcupine, baboon, hares, birds and crocodile. Besides hunting they may scavenge the kills of other predators and consume any animals which have died from disease. In Kasungu National Park they have specialised in killing young elephant, perhaps because elephant are among the more commonly occurring species of large herbivore; it is not known how they fend off attacks from adult elephant attempting to defend their calves. The lion population of the park is thought to number between 20 and 40 animals, usually occurring in small groups of not more than three animals. Like the cheetah and wild dog they may also move across the border into Zambia from time to time as lion have large home-ranges.

The leopard in contrast tends to consume smaller species than the lion as it is lighter in body and normally lives solitarily unless a female is accompanied by cubs. This therefore reduces competition between the two species. Another difference is the size of home-range: that of the leopard is much smaller, covering only a few square kilometres. The home-ranges of a male and a female leopard may overlap though it seems that males will exclude each other from their own areas. The female produces up to three cubs which she keeps hidden in dense vegetation. The young stay with her for a period of between one and two years, by which time they are able to fend for themselves and disperse.

Leopard are extremely adaptable, being widespread throughout Africa in many different habitats including desert, mountain, forest, savanna and cultivated land, even surviving in urban parks and other open spaces in the centres of many African cities including Lilongwe. Although in recent years leopard skins were fetching high prices on the world market the leopard population in Southern and East Africa was never seriously endangered. (The Convention for International Trade in Endangered Species, CITES, has since placed very stringent regulations on trade in leopard skins worldwide as a further protection.) Reasons for the leopard's successful survival in many parts of the continent include their secretive, nocturnal habits and extremely adaptable and variable diet. They kill small and medium sized antelope, normally up to reedbuck size though in the Serengeti they have been recorded to take larger antelope probably weighing up to 150 kg, two to three times the weight of the leopard itself. At the other end of the scale they have been observed eating baboons, monkeys, warthog, bushpig, porcupine, aardvark, dassie, rodents, small cats, jackals, birds, tortoises, snakes, frogs and catfish. In areas of human settlement they will take small-stock, poultry and domestic cats and dogs, as well as some of the wild animals which constitute pests in these areas.

Hunting by stealth, the leopard's excellent camouflage and intimate knowledge of the terrain in its home-range enables it to ambush its prey which it seizes by the neck to break the spine. Small kills are consumed immediately, but larger carcasses which cannot be eaten in one meal are dragged into the branches of a tree and stored for later, out of the reach of scavenging lion, hyena and jackal. Large carcasses may last a leopard as long as five days. Leopard are common in Kasungu National Park though they are not often seen because of their secretive habits.

Spotted hyena are opportunists, killing for themselves if they have to but otherwise scavenging on

Spotted hyena are opportunists, often scavenging on the prey of other large carnivores, though they do also hunt for themselves. MICHAEL GORE

the prey of other large carnivores, attracted by the sound and scent of kills. At a lion kill they may try to sneak in before the lions have finished eating but are usually kept hovering on the sidelines till the latter are satiated: stealing kills from cheetah and wild dog is easier. They have very powerful jaws and teeth enabling them to crunch up bone which other predators may leave; the digestive system is efficient, their droppings consisting mainly of mineral matter from bones. Hyena are especially important in cleaning up dead animal material which may often be carrying disease, so reducing the risk of infection to other animals.

Hyena have a much looser social organisation than lion or wild dog. They live in small groups or packs, a number of which are associated in a clan. Each clan has its own territory with a centrally located communal den where the females raise their cubs; unlike the lioness, however, a female hyena suckles only her own cubs, which usually number two. The cubs do not normally eat meat until six months old, unlike the large cat species. They are dependent on their mother for about 18 months.

Another nocturnal scavenger which often appears at kills is the side-striped jackal, hanging around in the background waiting for the left-overs of the larger animals. It also hunts for itself, catching small mammals, birds, reptiles and insects and foraging for birds' eggs and vegetable matter.

The sight of a pride of lions sleeping off a heavy meal or lazily playing with its cubs may provoke the thought that the life of a predator is an easy one. This is far from the truth: the predators often work hard for their kills, and perhaps on average for all species only 50% of hunts are successful. Prey species are well adapted to avoid capture: most are able to run fast and have excellent senses of sight, hearing and smell, the large eyes being positioned on the side of the head to give them a wide field of vision. (This contrasts with carnivores whose eyes are normally forward-looking to enable them to judge distances better.) When being hunted they have various techniques to confuse their pursuers: some may zigzag and swerve, and herds of antelope may scatter so that the predators do not know which individual to follow, while other animals such as zebra may stay in a tight bunch so that the predator cannot pick out a single animal. Wherever possible predators select the slowest, easiest looking animal: often young, old or sick. This must exert a strong genetic selection pressure in the prey populations; it also has the function of limiting the occurrence of disease and therefore

keeping the animal community healthy. Despite selection of the easiest animals, capturing and killing the prey can be a dangerous business with the risk of injury from hooves, horns and teeth of a panicking victim and sometimes a protective mother. Killing strategies are therefore adapted to minimise injuries. If a predator is injured it may not be able to hunt for itself or keep up with the rest of its group, and will probably not survive long. (Information on vegetation, mammals and ecology of Kasungu National Park:[47]; social organisation of antelope:[49]; wild dog:[50]; other predators:[51,52]; additional information on mammals:[53].)

Management aspects

Kasungu National Park supports a wide diversity of large mammal populations living and interacting in a complex community. For many animals the park area is adequate for all their needs, but for a few with more extensive home-ranges such as eland, elephant, cheetah and wild dog it is too small and they move periodically outside its boundaries. To the west the Zambian territory adjacent to the park is very sparsely settled though it is traversed by the main Chipata-Lundazi road. Between ten and 20 km from the Malaŵi border lies the Lukusuzi National Park, a large area of plateau woodland stretching to the edge of the Luangwa Valley. Some of the more extensive home-ranges cover parts of both parks, and there has been some discussion between the two countries on the possibility of managing both areas as one conservation unit with the creation of a corridor between them.[54]

To the south-east of Kasungu National Park there is a buffer zone between the park boundary and the land beyond it: the latter is extensively cultivated for tobacco and subsistence crops such as maize and ground nuts. Despite the buffer zone food crops are sometimes raided by animals such as elephant, buffalo, bushpig, baboons and monkeys. A solar-powered electric fence was installed along part of the south-eastern boundary in 1982 which has proved extremely efficient in preventing elephant and buffalo from moving into the cultivated area. This is a great advance on previous control methods for elephant which involved attempting to scare them back to the park, and ultimately shooting between 20 and 30 each year. The problem of crop raiding was being aggravated by poaching which had increased almost four-fold in recent years in response to a rapid rise in the black market value of ivory. Poaching pressures

Lifupa Lodge, Kasungu National Park. There is often good game-viewing and bird-watching from the terrace outside the bar, overlooking the dam.   CHRISTOPHER CARTER

from the west and north were forcing the elephant to concentrate in the south-east corner of the park where they were over-utilising and damaging the woodland as well as causing an increase in crop raiding. In 1981 at the height of the problem at least 55 elephant were poached, and between 1977 and 1982 the elephant population was estimated to have declined drastically to about 800 animals. The anti-poaching campaign was greatly intensified in 1982 with excellent results: along with the introduction of the electric fence that year elephant mortality in the park has been greatly reduced, and the population is now thought to be increasing at over 5% per annum.[47]

Thus elephant will continue to graze in the valley woodlands and use the natural salt licks of the *dambos* for years to come. They may be watched from a vehicle on the game-viewing roads, and are some-times seen across the dam from Lifupa Lodge, drinking and perhaps bathing at the water's edge. Even if there are no elephant there are usually hippo to watch from the comfort of the lodge, basking on

Saddlebill stork, often seen feeding near the edge of the water at Lifupa Dam.   JANET and JOHN HOUGH

the far shore or partly submerged in the water during the day, emerging at sundowner time for a night's grazing. There are also many interesting birds around the dam: herons, ibises, plovers, saddlebill stork, wattled crane during the rains, and occasionally osprey and other birds of prey overhead. After a long game-viewing drive or tramp in the western hills it is very pleasant to relax with a drink and a pair of binoculars on the lodge terrace, or perhaps to stroll around the grounds for a better view of the birds in the nearby reeds.

Vwaza Marsh Game Reserve [19,31,55,56]

Name derivation

From the Vwaza Marsh in the north of the reserve. The word *vwaza* may have an onomatopaeic derivation from the sound of walking through mud.

Declaration

The Lake Kazuni area was proclaimed a game reserve in 1941, and deproclaimed in 1950. In 1956 the Vwaza Marsh Game Controlled Area was proclaimed and the area was declared a game reserve in 1977 [13,19].

Present size

986 km^2

Location

North-west Malaŵi on the Zambian border, to the south-west of the Nyika Plateau.

Landscape types

Mostly flat, alluvial land with a large marsh in the north and lake in the south-east; extensive hills in the east and south, and isolated hills in the north-west.

Vegetation

Lake and marsh vegetation; floodplain grassland and *dambo*; riverine forest; thicket; mopane, *Brachystegia* and *Combretum* woodland.

Large mammals

Most commonly seen: elephant, warthog, kudu, roan, hartebeest, bushbuck, grey duiker, impala and buffalo. Also occurring: vervet monkey, baboon, wild dog, ratel, hippo, civet, various species of mongoose, spotted hyena, lion, leopard, aardvark, dassie, zebra, bushpig, eland, reedbuck, waterbuck, puku, sable antelope, grysbok, klipspringer, porcupine.

Birds

Birdlife is extremely diverse due to the large variety of habitats including open water, and over 250 species of birds have been recorded in the reserve. They include Swainson's francolin (not known to occur anywhere in Malaŵi) and the rare white-winged starling. Birds of prey are often particularly abundant in the valley of the South Rukuru River.

Other animals

The reserve contains many fish species found in Malaŵi only in the South Rukuru catchment [57].

Sites of special interest

Lake Kazuni, Zaro Pool, Vwaza Marsh, eastern hills, Iron Age site on Phopo Hill (just outside the reserve).

Access

Road access is normally via the entrance at Lake Kazuni. Approaching from Mzuzu and Rumphi, follow the S85 west from Rumphi towards Nyika. 10 km from Rumphi turn left on to the S49 which passes by the entrance to the reserve after 19 km. The track to the reserve entrance barrier is signposted: it leads straight on as the main road turns sharp left away from a hill to cross the bridge over the South Rukuru River. This entrance can also be approached from the south on the S49: the reserve entrance is 48 km from Euthini.

Approaching from the north it is possible to enter the reserve at Kawiya in a vehicle with good ground clearance in the dry season, preferably four-wheel-drive. Coming from the Nyika Plateau this provides an alternative route to Rumphi, travelling through the reserve to Lake Kazuni. After leaving Nyika National Park by the Thazima Gate follow the S10 for 8 km to its junction with the S85. Turn sharp right downhill and follow this road for 6 km when the D13 branches off to the left and leads to the reserve entrance after 5 km.

At the time of writing the S85 and S49 were untarred and could give problems during the rains, sometimes even for four-wheel-drive vehicles. Plans do exist to upgrade them to all-weather standard.

Distances from the main centres to Lake Kazuni:

Mzuzu:	91 km
Lilongwe (via Mzuzu):	469 km
Blantyre (via Mzuzu):	816 km

Inside the reserve a spine road connects Kawiya and Kazuni, and there are various other game-viewing roads as shown on map 3.2. The road network is not always maintained and it is advisable to request up-to-date

Continued

Vwaza Marsh Game Reserve **Map 3.2**

ZAMBIA

Turner Camp

Vwaza Marsh

Hewe

D13

To S85 and
Nyika National Park

N

Kawoyeka

■ Kawiya Camp

Vumu

Thundiro

○ Kamarang'ombe

Khweta

Kawuwu

Kasitu

▲ Kam'gondo Hill

○

▲ Mahohe Hill

To Katumbi

Thungundu

Phakasero

D11

Khaya Camp △

Bururuji

▲ Mbuna
Hill

Chanawe

Kasinje

Kavezi

▲▲▲
▲▲
Kapata Hills

Mphangara

To Rumphi

Njaie

○

S49

Phetekeza
Hill ▲

Luwewe

Jozga

○

▲▲
▲

Phopo
Hill ▲

Chankwazi

Kazuni
Camp ■

Mupando

Chalepweteka

Uyuzi
Hill ▲

●Filimon
Kumwenda

South Rukuru

△ Zaro Pool

⌂ Lake Kazuni

To Euthini

Key

- ‒·‒·‒· International boundary
- ‒ ‒ ‒ Game reserve boundary
- ——— Road
- ——— River
- ≡≡≡ Marsh
- ○ Permanent water hole
- ▲ Hill
- ● Town, village
- ■ Staff camp
- ⌂ Picnic site
- △ Camping site
- ▲ Tented camp

0   5   10 Kilometres

information on road conditions before entering the reserve. All roads are untarred.

There is no airstrip in the reserve: the nearest is at Katumbi, 7 km from the entrance at Kawiya.

Visitor facilities

There is a tented camp overlooking Lake Kazuni with five tents under thatched shelters sleeping two or three people. Water is drawn by hand from a nearby well; the camp has washing shelters and pit latrines. Cooking is done over open fires; a dining shelter/kitchen is being constructed. There is no electricity supply in the camp. Bedding and cooking and eating utensils are provided, but visitors must take their own food. Camping is possible at Lake Kazuni using some of the facilities of the tented camp, and also in attractive camping sites at Zaro Pool, Vwaza Marsh and the Luwewe River where there are minimal or no facilities. Note that there is sleeping sickness in the area, and although visitors are unlikely to contract it they are advised to avoid bites from tsetse flies during the day by wearing trousers and long sleeved shirts, and keeping car windows closed.

Visitor activities

Game-viewing, bird-watching, walking, picnicking.

Administrative arrangements

Reservations for the tented camp should be made in advance to the Department of National Parks and Wildlife booking office in Lilongwe (Box 30131, tel. 730 853) or the Senior Parks and Wildlife Officer, Thazima, P. Bag 6, Rumphi, tel. Rumphi 50.

It is possible to hire the services of a game-scout guide if requested well in advance from the Senior Parks and Wildlife Officer at Thazima. Visitors walking in the reserve must be accompanied by a guide.

At the time of writing no entrance fees are charged for people visiting the Lake Kazuni area for the day only. Reserve fees are charged for visitors going further into the reserve and for staying overnight.

Best time to visit

Game-viewing: March to November
Bird-watching: all year round
Walking: June to August

Note that the roads of the reserve are closed to vehicles during the rains (approximately December to April). Temperatures in the reserve are pleasantly warm in May to August inclusive; during September to November they can be uncomfortably hot. The rest of the year is intermediate.

Lake Kazuni in the south-east corner of the Vwaza Marsh Game Reserve, during the rains. ERICA MCSHANE-CALUZI

Vwaza Marsh Game Reserve

Below the slopes of Phopo Hill Lake Kazuni spreads across the floodplain, stretching back up the valley of the South Rukuru River. Fringed with grassland and groves of shady trees on higher ground, the lake nestles in a depression at the entrance to the reserve. Openbill storks wade feeding in the open water while a solitary Goliath heron fishes near the extensive reedbeds. White-faced tree ducks wade in the shallows or sleep and preen on the shores. Loud grunts and snorts from the reeds indicate the whereabouts of a territorial male hippo, and impala graze on the floodplain above the water's edge. Towards the end of the rains elephant and buffalo frequent the lake area, emerging from the woodland behind to drink. The rest of the reserve lies to the north-west of Lake Kazuni, and includes the extensive Vwaza Marsh and a large, flat, alluvial woodland area, besides the valleys of the two perennial rivers and hilly land in the east. Vwaza is an attractive area with a wide range of habitat types and high diversity of animals, despite the fact that it has a long history of human occupation and only recently gained protection as a game reserve.

History of Vwaza Marsh Game Reserve

On Phopo Hill by the reserve boundary there is the oldest Iron Age site known in Malaŵi, dating back to the third century AD. During excavation iron slag and fragments of pottery were found there, along with shell disc beads, remains of fish and game animals and signs of dwellings constructed of wood and burnt mud.[8] It is likely that the reserve area was inhabited much earlier than this, however, by Stone Age hunter-gatherers[19]. It continued to be used later on in the Iron Age, and recent signs of iron smelting from the late nineteenth and early twentieth centuries have been discovered to the south-west of the reserve[56]. The Iron Age people would have cultivated land in the vicinity, though they probably did not keep livestock because of tsetse fly which still occur in the reserve today.

From about 1700 onwards various groups of people moved into the region from the west, north and east, probably as a result of disturbances in their homelands. It seems that they integrated with the people already living there, and the Nkhamanga Chieftainship developed east of the reserve which ruled over the smaller clan leaders of the area. At that time

elephant were plentiful in the region. Between about 1770 and 1780 the Balowoka group arrived in the area; according to local tradition they came as traders from beyond Lake Malaŵi, drawn to the area by rumours of the abundant and unexploited source of ivory. They were probably Yao, trading for the Arabs from Kilwa on the coast of the Indian Ocean. They offered goods such as beads and cloth in exchange for ivory and leopard skins and the leader of the group, Mlowoka, married into one of the prominent families of the Nkhamanga Plain to the east of the reserve. He therefore came to control a large part of the ivory trade in the region, being located in a strategic position in rich ivory country on a main trade route between the Bisa people in the west and Lake Malaŵi and the coast in the east. His lieutenants established similar economic bases for themselves, almost certainly including the present-day reserve area.

With Mlowoka's death around 1805-1810 his son inherited his father's wealth and his grandfather's political power in the area, giving rise to the Chikulamayembe rule which had a monopoly over both the ivory from eastern Zambia and the Nkhamanga area, and the distribution of goods from

White-faced tree duck, often seen at Lake Kazuni.
MICHAEL GORE

the coast. No figures exist on the numbers of elephant which were killed around this time but they must have been enormous, hunting occurring over a wide area including that of the present-day reserve and greatly reducing the herds. The Nkhamanga and surrounding areas became renowned throughout East

Africa for their ivory, and other men were attracted to the area including Swahili slave and ivory traders. They smashed the Chikulamayembe monopoly, dealing directly with local leaders for ivory and slaves: the latter were often criminals and orphans. This disruption was followed by the arrival of the Ngoni in the middle of the nineteenth century, who met with little resistance and conquered the local people, ruling there until the creation of the Protectorate. (Historical information:[8].)

At this time parts of the reserve area were probably lightly populated by local people whose major activities would have been cultivation and hunting. In 1941 Lake Kazuni and the land within a five mile radius of it were declared a game reserve[19], which was subsequently deproclaimed in 1950 because of inadequate management resources. In 1956, however, the Vwaza Marsh Game Controlled Area was proclaimed, largely due to the efforts of Chief Katumbi to have the wildlife protected.[13] Although hunting was restricted settlement was not affected until plans were made to gazette the area as a game reserve; this finally happened in 1977 and the people were resettled. The areas they had cultivated, mostly on relatively fertile, freely draining soils near streams and rivers, are now regenerating, many of them covered with a dense, short growth of young *Brachystegia* and *Combretum* trees.

Ecology of Vwaza Marsh Game Reserve

The South Rukuru River is the larger of the two perennial rivers in the reserve. It rises in the southern Viphya Plateau and flows northward near the Zambian border to its confluence with the Luwewe River at Zaro Pool on the southern boundary of the reserve. From there it flows north-east to Lake Kazuni, its broad floodplain lined in places with borassus palms and grazed by buffalo, reedbuck and puku (see page 60–61 for further information on puku). During the dry season other large mammals concentrate near the river valley. The level of Lake Kazuni fluctuates seasonally with the level of water in the river. Longer term variations also occur, and in 1970 it dried up completely and the hippo moved away. Its level is thought to be determined by the relative silting and scouring actions of the South Rukuru River, affected by variations in annual rainfall.[55]

The South Rukuru's tributary the Luwewe drains from the Vwaza Marsh in the north of the reserve, an extensive wetland of reedbeds, grasses and sedges, its margins dotted with termite mounds supporting

Sunrise over the Vwaza Marsh, with the Nyika Plateau in the distance.   STEPHEN TEMPLE

Phoenix palms and other trees. The marsh itself is fed by the Hewe River which rises on the south-western slopes of the Nyika Plateau, including Mwanda Mountain. As the Hewe enters the marsh it flows through an area of papyrus swamp before its waters spread out to cover the rest of the wetland. Like Lake Kazuni the marsh harbours a great variety of waterbirds and a population of hippo. Towards the end of the dry season the southern part of the marsh provides grazing for many large mammals: a nutritious green flush develops in this area of high water-table after the late dry season fires, and is particularly important as much of the rest of the reserve is burnt and dry by then. Animals, especially buffalo, concentrate there for the high quality grazing of the marsh and its floodplains; unfortunately heavy poaching also occurs in the area at this time.

The inflow of water from the Hewe and South Rukuru Rivers is very significant for the reserve as it provides perennial water and permits a greater diversity of habitats including the wetlands. Rainfall over the reserve itself is relatively low as it lies in the rainshadow of the Nyika Plateau to the north, and the Viphya Plateau and south Rumphi Hills to the east[5]. The network of permanent swamp and rivers provides perennial water over much of the reserve, enabling the survival throughout the year of many water-dependent animals. The reserve also protects populations of the South Rukuru fish fauna which includes species not occurring anywhere else in Malaŵi. Outside the reserve the fish are subjected to fairly heavy fishing pressures, so the reserve probably plays an important role in maintaining fish stocks[57]. Surprisingly, crocodile are rare in the reserve.

The Luwewe river drains south from the Vwaza Marsh, a slow-flowing stream in the dry season whose deep channel is shaded by a narrow strip of riverine forest along much of its course. In places a belt of floodplain runs parallel with the river, and many of its tributaries are flanked by grassy *dambos* which provide important grazing for species such as elephant. Although the tributaries stop flowing in the dry season a few of them have permanent waterholes which continue to provide water at this time of year: of particular importance is the Chamawe Stream to the west. Its channel crosses an extensive tract of mopane woodland on a lowlying, alluvial clay plain area. The reserve is one of the most northerly locations in Africa for mopane, an interesting tree which often occurs in almost pure stands on poorly drained clays. Each leaf has two leaflets which give the appearance of a butterfly: hence the name 'mopane' which is a southern Bantu name for butterfly[5]. During the heat of the day the leaflets move close together, presumably to reduce water loss; the tree therefore gives little shade. In the reserve the mopane woodland is fairly open, growing on slightly raised areas of ancient termitaria and interspersed with grassy glades on the lower ground. The area is frequented by grazers such as roan, hartebeest, impala, sable antelope, zebra and warthog after the fires in the dry season when they feed on the green flush of the grassy glades.

During the rains the mopane area becomes very wet and most of the large mammals move into the better drained *Brachystegia* woodland which occurs elsewhere in the lowlying alluvial areas of the reserve, and on to localised areas of higher ground near the Luwewe where the river has created levees. At the end of the rains elephant move into the *Brachystegia* woodland, particularly the fertile areas near streams and rivers which were formerly cultivated by the human occupants of the reserve. At this time the tall grasses of the *dambos* have become unpalatable as in Kasungu National Park (page 60), and the elephant browse on the dense growth of regenerating *Brachystegia* and *Combretum* trees. Although elephant density in Vwaza is too low to create areas of woodland coppice by heavy browsing of mature woodland, the elephant are taking advantage of the man-created coppice. Combined with the action of annual fires in the more open sites of old cultivation where large amounts of dead grass fuel accumulate and destroy young trees, elephant seem to be holding the woodland of these sites in a coppice equilibrium[56].

To the east of the alluvial area the land rises above the plain in a series of pediments and hills, an extension of the foothills of the Nyika Plateau. Rocky, infertile slopes are covered in *Brachystegia* woodland; the more fertile valley areas between the hills have open *Combretum/Pterocarpus* woodland and tall grass, with a few clumps of dense thicket. Saline seepages occur in places, much used by some of the animals: elephant, buffalo and other species frequent the valleys towards the end of the rains and beginning of the dry season until the temporary water sources dry up and they descend to the adjoining plains. The hills are interesting to explore on foot, well-worn elephant paths leading up wooded valleys towards the rocky summits. Troops of baboons are common throughout the year and klipspringer live among the rocks; an occasional shy kudu may be seen on the slopes. From the summits views are spectacular: the hills overlook the South Rukuru Valley, Vwaza Marsh and the rest of the reserve towards Zambia, and the most northerly peaks face towards the Nyika Plateau. The Kapata Hills are a particularly attractive area, and from the narrow ridge of Phopo Hill there is a good view across Lake Kazuni.

Despite the area's protected status the populations of some of its large mammal species remain well below carrying capacity. These are the species of the valleys: elephant, buffalo, zebra and impala, which may still be suffering from the effects of competition with the previous human occupants in those areas. Illegal hunting is probably also responsible, and continues to be a serious problem in the reserve.

The slow-flowing Luwewe River, lined with riverine trees on the left-hand bank.   ERICA MCSHANE-CALUZI

Chikatu Hill in the east of the reserve, covered in *Brachystegia* woodland.   ERICA MCSHANE-CALUZI

Elephant move across the border between the reserve and Zambia, particularly during the rains, and poaching pressures on both sides of the border may influence this movement. Poaching is practised for commercial trophies such as ivory as well as for subsistence, and accounts for the wariness of many of the large herbivores. Large carnivores such as lion and hyena do occur in the reserve, but in relatively small numbers because of the low herbivore density, and also probably because of the use of wire snares by poachers, to which lion are very vulnerable[54]. (Information on animal distribution:[56].)

Smaller animals of the reserve

A small and primitive animal which nevertheless has a very profound influence on the ecology of the reserve is the termite. Signs of it are plentiful: there are large numbers of termite mounds in the woodland and along the fringes of the Vwaza Marsh and valleys. In places the raised areas of old termitaria now support isolated clumps of trees, such as palms around the edge of the marsh. The soil from the termitaria is often much more fertile than that of the surrounding areas.

Despite the fact that the termite is a primitive insect it has a very highly developed social system, with a king and queen whose main function is reproduction; soldiers which defend the colony; and workers which gather food, build the nest and look after the young. All are wingless except for young kings and queens. As most species of termites have soft, thin skins which do not retain moisture very effectively, they usually live in nests where temperature and humidity are carefully controlled. When foraging away from the nest they either travel along tunnels beneath the soil surface or build sealed tubes on the ground with ceilings of masticated mud to maintain humidity. Nests of different species vary greatly in form: the most commonly known is the termite mound standing above ground, made from earth mixed with glandular secretions which dries and hardens to a cement-like consistency. Harvester termites, however, usually build their nests underground. Unlike most other groups of termites, the workers of the harvesters have eyes and a hardened skin and are able to forage in the open, except in very hot weather. Dry wood termites live in dead branches and tree trunks, hollowing out chambers connected by tunnels inside the wood.

Termites feed on dead plant material, breaking up dead trunks, branches, leaves, stems and other

One of the many termitaria in Vwaza Marsh Game Reserve. Over the years the activity of the termites has raised the level of the mound above that of the ground around it; in time this small area may be colonised by a different vegetation to the surrounding area.   JANET and JOHN HOUGH

plant parts and ultimately converting them into living tissue; they are one of the most important links in the recyling of nutrients in the ecosystem. They have various strategies to deal with the normally rather indigestible cellulose of their diet. In some species the plant material is digested several times over, a worker passing on its partially digested food to another, either by regurgitation or by presenting its tail end for the excrement to be swallowed. In this manner all the nourishment is eventually extracted, and the remaining indigestible paste is sometimes used as building material for the nest. Many wood-eating species have colonies of protozoan flagellates in the gut which are able to convert cellulose to sugars; the termites then absorb the sugars, as well as obtaining protein from the digestion of some of the flagellates. Newly hatched termites obtain protozoans by sucking the rear end of adults.

Other species cultivate fungus gardens, where a particular species of fungus is grown on a compost of plant material which has been broken up and moulded into spongy heaps or combs. In some species young termites and the royal pair are fed on a particular stage of the fungus; ultimately the comb is broken down into digestible material by the fungus and is consumed by the workers.

Dispersal to a new colony occurs after heavy rain, when very large numbers of winged young kings and queens are released from the original nest. They fly a short distance before the female lands and sheds her wings. A male is attracted to her by a pheromone and lands behind her, shedding his wings. The pair moves off, the female leading, and she selects a suitable site for a new nest where they construct a chamber and start a new colony. Eggs laid by the queen hatch to produce young workers, and the colony gradually builds up over a number of years. (Information on termites:[58].)

There is great activity around termitaria during a termite hatch, and the majority of young kings and queens do not survive the nuptial flight to produce a new colony as they are preyed upon by many animals. Birds, frogs, lizards, other insects, spiders, and many mammals including man take advantage of the sudden feast which a termite hatch provides. A few more specialised animals feed on termites throughout the year, such as the nocturnal antbear or aardvark (literally 'earth pig'). Its large burrow entrances may be seen in many of the woodland areas of the reserve away from the rocky slopes, though the aardvark itself is very rarely seen. About the size of a pig, it has an arched back, powerful tail and elongated head ending in a long snout with a blunt, pig-like muzzle. Its toes are armed with huge straight claws which it uses for digging out ants and termites from underground nests and termite mounds: these insects constitute its total diet. It catches them with its long tongue which is wetted with viscous saliva; during the rains it consumes mostly termites, ants becoming more important during the dry season when termites are inactive. The aardvark has poor eyesight but its excellent senses of smell and hearing assist it on its nightly foraging: termites under leaf litter or on the move in large columns make small noises which the aardvark is thought to be able to detect.

Aardvark also dig to make burrows for themselves; they may have several entrances to an extensive underground network of tunnels and chambers where they take refuge during the day, or at night if threatened by a predator. They have many enemies which have been known to include lion, leopard, cheetah, wild dog, spotted hyena, python and man: if necessary they defend themselves with their powerful claws. Local people in Southern Africa mostly regard the aardvark with much fear and superstition and it is consequently rarely hunted there. In parts of West Africa, however, the meat is consumed and other parts of the animal used as charms and medicine: teeth are worn round the wrist to prevent illness and bring good luck, and aardvark hair is powdered to form a potent poison when added to local beer. Elsewhere, claws put in a basket used for collecting winged termites after a hatch are believed to increase the harvest. In Malaŵi the only known use of the aardvark was in iron smelting, when an aardvark paw was one of the many medicines used to prepare the large kiln for smelting[40] (see page 38).

The female aardvark bears her young in the burrow: she normally produces one offspring at a time which is thought to remain in the burrow for two weeks, after which it starts to accompany its mother on nocturnal foraging trips. At the age of six months it digs its own burrow and gradually becomes independent. The adult female is thought to remain in one locality while the males wander extensively. Abandoned burrows play a very important role in the ecology of the reserve as they are used as refuges by many other animals including warthog, small carnivores and reptiles. (Information on aardvark:[53,59].)

Another mammal of the reserve which may make use of aardvark burrows at times is the porcupine. Also nocturnal, it stays in burrows or crevices under boulders during the day, emerging at night to feed on roots, bulbs, bark, berries and fruit. The porcupine is rarely seen but its black and white striped quills are often found whilst walking in the reserve. This is the crested porcupine, the largest African rodent, named for its ability to raise its quills when provoked which gives it a crested appearance. It can vibrate the quills to give a characteristic warning rattle and when necessary it charges backwards at its enemy, the hindquarters being well armed with backward-pointing quills. Although it cannot shoot quills they are easily uprooted and often remain sticking into the flesh of its enemy where they inflict sometimes fatal wounds.[53]

The civet is also nocturnal, hiding up in thickets, tall grass or aardvark burrows during the day and feeding at night. It is a very handsome animal, with black spots on the body, a crest of black hairs along the spine and two black collars on the neck. It feeds

Porcupine foraging. A nocturnal animal, the porcupine is active at night, spending the daytime hidden in a burrow or rock crevice. MICHAEL GORE

on carrion and a variety of prey including rodents, birds, reptiles, amphibians and insects, as well as berries and fruits. Territories are marked with an oily musk secretion from glands below the tail: in parts of Africa civet are farmed for this secretion which is used to manufacture perfume.[53] Civet are usually solitary, and they may wander extensively during their nocturnal forays. Droppings are often deposited in the same place each night, and large amounts may accumulate in these middens. A curious feature is the presence of a roll of coarse grass, apparently one in each deposition. Although possibly consumed for

Crowned eagle soaring above the reserve. MICHAEL GORE

roughage, local people have another belief about its function. As the civet travels widely each night and yet likes to defecate in the same midden, they believe that it eats the grass early in the evening to act as a plug until it returns to its chosen spot at the end of the night's wanderings. Civet middens, complete with grass plugs, are sometimes found in the reserve though the civet itself is rarely seen.

Another mainly nocturnal omnivore of the reserve is the ratel or honey badger. This is a stocky animal the size of a European badger with striking markings, the upper parts of its body a whitish grey which contrast strongly with the black underparts. The ratel also rests for most of the day in a burrow, dug either by itself or an aardvark. It feeds at night on small animals such as rodents, shrews, snakes and large insects. It occasionally catches small antelope and may eat carrion; it also consumes roots, bulbs, fruits and honey. Honey is a delicacy to the ratel which it devours along with the pupae of wild bees when it raids bees' nests. Although it sometimes finds nests on its own it is often led to them by the greater honeyguide, a small bird which guides ratels and people to bees' nests with many agitated and repeated calls: its scientific name is appropriately *Indicator indicator*. Once at the nest the ratel breaks it open with its claws, protected from stings by its tough hide and thick subcutaneous fat. Bird and ratel then share the feast.[53,60] The greater honeyguide is not uncommon in the reserve and will sometimes try to summon walkers to a bees' nest.

Even if game-viewing in the reserve is not as good as in some of the national parks of Malaŵi, bird-watching can be outstanding. Walking along the Luwewe River it is possible to see a large variety of woodland and riverine birds, and near the confluence of the Luwewe and Kayezi Rivers there are also many wetland species especially early in the rains. The South Rukuru Valley is an excellent area for many river and grassland birds, and Lake Kazuni and the Vwaza Marsh have a great variety of waterbirds. In the hills to the east, species of the dry, rocky hill habitats occur. Birds of prey can often be seen circling and soaring overhead in the reserve or perched in trees in the woodland, and the diversity of raptors is unusually high due to the wide variety of habitats and abundance of smaller animals. Like the large mammal community (see page 59 onwards) the birds of prey are specialised in their feeding habits to avoid excessive competition between species: diet varies with habitat, hunting technique and body size and conformation.

Black-shouldered kite watching for prey from a perch.
MICHAEL GORE

The largest raptor is the martial eagle which feeds on dassies, monkeys, ground squirrels, game birds, hares and rodents, soaring high over open ground or perching on a vantage point to search for its prey. The slightly smaller crowned eagle preys on dassies, monkeys and small antelope such as grysbok, perching in tall trees in the woodland watching the open glades below for prey. While many raptors may include snakes as a small part of their diet the snake-eagles specialise in catching them, managing to avoid the venomous bite of poisonous species; the black-breasted snake-eagle is even able to consume a snake whilst on the wing. Piracy is practised by the bataleur eagle which often robs other birds such as the ground hornbill of its prey. It also feeds on carrion and sometimes hunts for itself, soaring overhead with a very characteristic tail-less flight while it searches for prey. The smaller long-crested eagle watches from

Lake Kazuni at sunset. The floodplain by the side of the lake provides excellent bird-watching.   JUDY CARTER

dead trees for mice and rats, as well as frogs, snakes, lizards and small birds. The yellow-billed kite is a similar size but has a more varied diet including shrews, snails, insects and carrion; it is very manoeuvrable in flight, often twisting from side to side as it changes direction, grabbing its food deftly from the ground. The smaller peregrine falcon specialises in catching birds such as pigeons and doves by diving down on them at speed from above. Smaller still, the black-shouldered kite feeds mainly on rodents, often watching for them from a perch. The small European hobby feeds mainly on insects, including termites which it catches and eats on the wing. A summer migrant, it may be seen in large numbers in the reserve during the rains[56]. Some raptors hunt in the wetland and areas of open water in the reserve. The fish eagle's main prey is fish from open water, though it will also take rats and young waterbirds. The African marsh harrier flies over marshland, pouncing on frogs, water rats and bird chicks from a low level. (Information on raptor feeding habits:[60].)

The specialised feeders on carrion, the vultures, find their food mostly by soaring high over a large range looking for carcasses of animals which have died naturally or been killed by large predators such as lion. In some species individual birds watch one another in flight, and when they see one bird descending to a carcass all those in sight follow it. Although the density of large mammals and consequently carcasses is not high in the reserve, vultures do appear at carcasses in areas of open vegetation which they can spot from the sky. Up to four different species of carrion-eating vulture may be present at a carcass at any one time; each is specialised in its feeding habits to reduce competition and make optimal use of the available food. The largest is the lappet-faced vulture, a very aggressive bird which normally dominates the much more numerous white-backed vultures, driving them back while it is feeding. The lappet-faced vulture has a very large, strong bill and feeds by tearing off skin and tough meat. It often opens up the carcass which then gives the white-backed vulture access to the meat and soft organs: this species has a long neck adapted for reaching inside the carcass to feed. The hooded vulture is a much smaller bird with a slim bill, and it pecks at scraps around the carcass besides eating a variety of other foods. The white-headed vulture lies between the hooded and white-backed vultures in size, but behaves very differently from the other species. It is much less common than the white-backed vulture and is very timid, rarely feeding beside the other species at a large kill but seeking the carcasses of smaller animals such as hares. It probably also kills a significant proportion of its own food, and is the only species to have a fixed territory.[51,61] Like the spotted hyena, vultures play a very important role in removing the remains of dead animals which are a potential source of disease infection for other animals.

With its outstanding birdlife the Vwaza Marsh Game Reserve provides some of the best birdwatching in the country. This low-lying area is an interesting contrast to the high Nyika Plateau, and it is well worth while making a diversion through the reserve on the return journey south from the Nyika. If the internal tracks are impassable it is usually still possible to get to Lake Kazuni: quite apart from its bird-watching potential this is an excellent picnic spot. The area can be explored at leisure by spending a night at the tented camp, perhaps walking along the floodplain of the South Rukuru River from the lake towards Uyuzi Hill for some interesting bird-watching, or climbing Phopo Hill.

Chapter Four

The rift valley escarpments

Steep and rugged, the escarpments descend from the edge of the main plateaux some 500 m or more to the hot lakeshore plains and Shire Valley. On the western side of the rift valley the escarpment runs almost the entire length of Malaŵi; in the east the only part to fall within Malaŵi is in the south, due to the location of the eastern international boundaries.

The western escarpment is particularly spectacular in the north where the land drops rapidly from the high Nyika and Viphya Plateaux to the lake, a height of 1500 m in places. Viewed from a boat well offshore the full magnitude of the escarpment can be appreciated, as the mountains rise up steeply from the lakeshore towards the high peaks and clouds. Isolated villages hug the lower slopes, their cultivation a pale

The northern rift valley escarpment rising from the shores of Lake Malaŵi. The lower slopes have been cleared by local villagers for cultivation.   JAMES OGLETHORPE

patchwork against the darker woodland, and settlements such as the Livingstonia Mission perch on isolated and restricted plateaux. In 1894 the missionaries chose this site high above the lake for its healthy climate, after experiencing severe losses through malaria at the previous two sites on the lakeshore. Here they developed a farm, school, hospital and the first hydro-electric plant in Malaŵi, besides constructing a large church and spreading Christianity in the area.

Near to Livingstonia are the 300 m high Manchewe Falls, the longest waterfalls in Malaŵi, which drop sheer from the top of the Livingstonia Plateau down into the deep, rocky, fern-lined gorge far below. Behind them is a cave, inhabited last century by Phoka people during times of persecution by the Ngoni: a wet and God-forsaken refuge, reached by a precipitous path down the side of the gorge.

Part of the Manchewe Falls near Livingstonia, the longest waterfall in Malaŵi.   JAMES OGLETHORPE

Gorode, the road with 22 hairpin bends built by the Livingstonia Mission in 1905 which climbs the rift valley escarpment to link Livingstonia with the lakeshore.   JUDY CARTER

Livingstonia is linked to the main Chiweta-Karonga lakeshore road by the renowned *Gorode*, a stone-based road snaking down the escarpment round 22 hairpin bends. Constructed by the mission and local people in 1905, this remarkable feat of engineering is still in good condition today: a test for the nerve of any driver with its sharp bends and precipitous drops on the unfenced downhill side. A few kilometres to the south, an equally spectacular but tarred road now descends the escarpment to Chiweta, linking the northern lakeshore with Mzuzu.

Further south in the country the terrain of the escarpment becomes more tortuous and broken: minor geological faults, slips and downwarps have occurred parallel to the line of the rift valley in places, and deeply cut drainage lines have further dissected the landscape. Waterfalls and rocky gorges occur along the courses of the major rivers such as the Lilongwe and Bua, as they plunge through the escarpment wilderness to the lake and the Shire River. Isolated villages are served by tortuous tracks and roads such as the steep winding Golomoti road east of Dedza.

The soils of the escarpments are very variable. In places, for example along minor fault lines, exposed base-rich rocks have given rise to fertile soils in localised areas. Elsewhere, soils are thin, stony and infertile, with frequent rock outcrops. Many of the escarpment slopes are covered by deciduous *Brachystegia* woodland, the species composition varying with drainage, soil type and slope, and sometimes including *B. boehmii* with its distinctive dark compound leaves, the 'Prince of Wales feathers'. Late in the dry season, when temperatures are high and deciduous trees are coming into leaf, whole hillsides appear aflame with the shimmering, delicate transluscent reds and oranges of the young pigmented *Brachystegia* leaves. These soon turn green and darken as they develop fully.

In places the *Brachystegia* gives way to *Terminalia* and *Combretum* woodland, and along the major watercourses riverine vegetation occurs, with patches of *dambo* at the heads of drainage lines. In the high rainfall area near Nkhata Bay there are evergreen forests, more similar to the coastal forests of East Africa than to the other vegetation types of Malaŵi. They are partially protected by the Kalwe Forest Reserve, and provide habitat for such interesting birds as Gunning's akalat, green coucal, red-capped robin and blue-mantled crested flycatcher[44].

The escarpment areas in general have low agricultural potential because of the steep, broken terrain, difficulty of access and infertile soils in many areas. However, some of the more fertile land is cultivated. On the lower slopes of the escarpment near Nkhata Bay is the only rubber estate in the country. Its regimented rows of trees, each with a spiral cut in the bark and a small cup to catch the raw rubber, are a sharp contrast to the wild tangle of nearby Kalwe Forest. Also in this high rainfall area

Brachystegia woodland coming into leaf in September, the young leaves pigmented red and orange.   JUDY CARTER

are tea estates, and much coffee is produced on the northern escarpments under a smallholder scheme. To the south, agriculture is mostly confined to subsistence crops on the escarpments, often with a system of rotational, or shifting cultivation. On the steep slopes the risk of soil erosion is high, and the clearing of natural vegetation for new cultivation has, in some places, resulted in serious soil loss.

Gullies have often formed along well-used pathways leading down the slopes. Other parts of the escarpment, however, are protected as forest reserves, and there is one game reserve, Nkhotakota, on the western escarpment in the Central Region. The carrying capacity of the escarpments for wild animals is largely determined by the presence or absence of base-rich soils associated with faults and other geological features. In fertile areas it is quite high, and may even exceed that of the plateau areas though the absence of *dambos* on the escarpments makes this uncertain[54].

Nkhotakota Game Reserve[19,31,54]

Name derivation

From the administrative centre of the district the reserve lies in: the town of Nkhotakota. It is reputed that the original village of Kota Kota lay east of the present town, on a site now flooded by the lake. According to an oral belief, the name derives from the Chichewa word *kukhota*, which means 'to meander'. The track which led to the old village apparently meandered.

Declaration

The northern area was gazetted as a forest reserve around 1935; the game reserve was first gazetted in 1954 including an area south of the previous forest reserve; the present boundaries were gazetted in 1970.

Present size

1802 km²

Location

Central Malaŵi, on the western escarpment of the rift valley.

Landscape type

Steep, hilly terrain with ridges and isolated peaks, dissected by watercourses.

Vegetation

Evergreen forest on the slopes of Chipata Mountain; *Brachystegia* woodland in much of the rest of the reserve, with tall grass in wet areas and *Terminalia* woodland in drier parts of the more fertile western areas; raffia palms on the watercourses in the south-east.

Large mammals

Most commonly seen: elephant, warthog, grey duiker, bushbuck, sable antelope, eland, buffalo, baboon. Less commonly seen but occurring in the reserve: Cape clawless otter, civet, various species of mongoose, side-striped jackal, wild dog, spotted hyena, lion, leopard, zebra, hippo, bushpig, kudu, reedbuck, waterbuck, roan, hartebeest, klipspringer, grysbok, porcupine, blue monkey, vervet monkey.

Birds

Birds of *Brachystegia* woodland and riverine woodland, including the palmnut vulture, fishing owl and giant kingfisher. Birds in the evergreen forest have a relatively low diversity but include the moustached green tinkerbird, yellow-streaked bulbul, grey-olive bulbul and wattle-eyed flycatcher[37]. Over 130 bird species have been recorded in the reserve.

Other animals

Fish in the Bua River include catfish and the migratory *mpasa* (lake salmon), *sanjika* and various species of yellowfish which move upstream from Lake Malaŵi to spawn at times of high river levels. The *mpasa* is an important sporting fish. There are many crocodile.

Sites of special interest

Chipata Mountain, Bua River.

Access

The M10 road runs east-west through the reserve as shown on Map 4.1. From the west the reserve is reached by following the M10 through Ntchisi from the M1 turnoff, 25 km north of Lilongwe. The M10 is untarred and can give problems during the rains, but after it has been graded in June it is passable to saloon cars until the onset of the following rains. The untarred S54 road from Kasungu joins the M10 at the western boundary of the reserve, and is an alternative access route from further north on the M1. Three kilometres before its junction with the M10 a track leads off it to the left to Chipata Camp and Chipata Mountain. This is untarred, and can give problems during the rains.

From the east the M10 is reached by turning off the tarred S53 lakeshore road at Nkhotakota. The Department of National Parks and Wildlife office lies a few kilometres along this road, before the entrance to the reserve. A turnoff to the left, 10 km from Nkhotakota, leads to Wodzi Camp.

There is a further entrance to the reserve off the S53, to Bua Camp. Twelve kilometres north of Nkhotakota village an untarred track leads off westward, crossing agricultural land before reaching the reserve boundary after 8 km: this leads to Bua Camp.

Distances from the main centres to the western entrance of the reserve:

Lilongwe (via Ntchisi):	115 km
Blantyre (via Ntchisi):	462 km
Zomba (via Ntchisi):	396 km
Mzuzu (via Kasungu):	325 km

Visitor facilities

There are three attractive camping sites in the reserve: Bua by the Bua River in the east of the reserve; Wodzi, under raffia palms by the Wodzi River; and Chipata, on the slopes of Chipata Mountain overlooking the western part of the reserve towards Lake Malaŵi. Facilities in all the camps are minimal, and visitors must take all their own equipment.

Firewood and water are available; it is advisable to boil drinking water.

The service of a game-scout guide is available if arranged well in advance: this is necessary for visitors

Continued

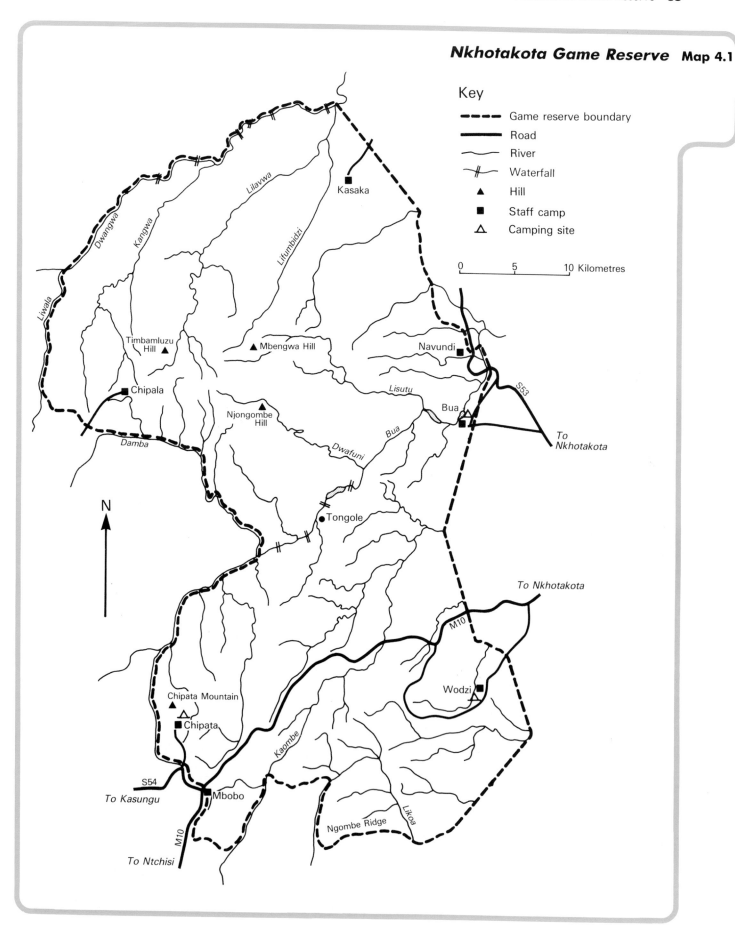

Nkhotakota Game Reserve **Map 4.1**

Key

- – – – Game reserve boundary
- ——— Road
- —— River
- —//— Waterfall
- ▲ Hill
- ■ Staff camp
- △ Camping site

0   5   10 Kilometres

Liwala

Dwangwa

Kangwa

Lilavwa

Lifumbidzi

Kasaka ■

Timbamluzu Hill ▲

▲ Mbengwa Hill

Navundi ■

Chipala ■

Lisutu

Bua ▲

S53

To Nkhotakota

Njongombe Hill ▲

Damba

Bua

Dwafuni

N

↑

—//— Tongole ●

To Nkhotakota

M10

Chipata Mountain ▲

△
Chipata ■

Wodzi ■
△

Kaombe

S54

To Kasungu

Mbobo ■

M10

Likoa

Ngombe Ridge

To Ntchisi

planning to walk in the reserve.

There is a marked trail from Chipata Camp leading to the summit of the mountain.

At present angling is permitted on the Bua River from Bua Camp from the 1st of June to the start of the rains. Single, barbless hooks only are allowed and all fish must be returned live to the river.

Visitor activities

Game-viewing, bird-watching, walking, angling.

Administrative arrangements

Reservations for camping, angling and a guide should be made through the Department of National Parks and Wildlife headquarters, Box 30131, Lilongwe 3 (tel 730 853). Reserve fees are charged for visitors and their vehicles, except when in transit on the M10. Permits for angling must be purchased in advance from DNPW headquarters.

Best time to visit

Game-viewing (though never excellent):	August to October
Bird-watching:	November to December
Angling:	June to July
Walking:	June to September
Scenery:	throughout the year.

Access for saloon vehicles can be problematic during the rains (approximately December to April).

Temperatures during May to August are pleasantly warm; during September to November they can be uncomfortably hot, especially in the lower areas. The rest of the year is intermediate.

Nkhotakota Game Reserve from the slopes of Chipata Mountain, with the Bua River in the distance.   JANET and JOHN HOUGH

Nkhotakota Game Reserve

The game reserve covers a huge area of escarpment wilderness, stretching from the peaks of Chipata Mountain, Timbamluzu Hill and Mbengwa Hill on the uplifted lip of the Central African Plateau, down a series of tortuous, jumbled slopes and ridges to the edge of the flatter, hot lands of the rift valley floor. A large fault running north-south through the reserve, just below the edge of the plateau, has resulted in a step-like formation in the escarpment. A steep scarp on the fault line leads down from the plateau to an area which tilts slightly upwards towards the east until it reaches a line of low hills, the eastern side of which forms another, smaller scarp dropping down to more level land. This large-scale, geological pattern has been dissected by many drainage lines, which in places have cut through the major scarp, causing deep valleys reaching back far into the plateau. Below this, many high, steep-sided ridges have developed as streams have cut deeper and deeper along their courses to the confluences with the major north-easterly flowing rivers: the Bua, Dwangwa and Kaombe.

History of Nkhotakota Game Reserve

Despite the ruggedness of the terrain there is a long history of human settlement in the area of the present-day reserve. In the south an old rock shelter with faint red drawings bears testimony to Stone Age occupation. More recently there was fairly widespread Iron Age settlement. These people cultivated crops, made pottery and probably smelted iron. The majority of them lived around the area of the fault scarp below the edge of the plateau where the soils are significantly more fertile than those of the surrounding region. Remains of pottery are common in the evergreen forest on the slopes of Chipata Mountain, the highest point in the reserve. It is possible that the mountain may have been a rain shrine, or a place of refuge during the Ngoni wars.[54]

In the nineteenth century the reserve area was traversed by the much used trade route running between Nkhotakota village on the lakeshore and Mwase Kasungu on the plateau. Thousands of slaves and tons of ivory passed down the escarpment, to be dispatched to the coast by Jumbe, the self-styled sultan of Nkhotakota. Livingstone himself crossed the reserve area when he travelled inland from the lake to Kasungu.

With the declaration of a forest reserve in part of the area in 1935, and the game reserve boundaries in 1954 and 1970, local people living in the present reserve area were resettled. Although there are still some signs of old settlements and cultivation, they are rapidly becoming hidden as vegetation succession proceeds and the area is reverting to a huge, fascinating but challenging wilderness. Vehicle access has never been developed on a large scale due to the ruggedness of the terrain. There are only a few short tracks, and one unfenced and comparatively little used national road (the M10) which crosses the reserve from Mbobo and Chipata Mountain in the west towards Nkhotakota village in the east. A new national road has been proposed to link Kasungu and Nkhotakota: this would cross the reserve north of Chipata Mountain, opening up a vast new area to vehicular access. At present, however, this and many other areas are accessible only on foot.

Ecology and wilderness of Nkhotakota Game Reserve

Walking along the ridge tops on well-worn elephant paths through open canopy *Brachystegia* woodland,

The Bua River flowing through the reserve. FRANK JOHNSTON

with occasional panoramas of valley landscapes below, a glimpse of zebra stripes blending with the dappled foliage, or even a view of the distant, deep blue waters of Lake Malaŵi, provides a real taste of wilderness. Exploring the courses of the major rivers is more difficult going, sometimes through head-high stands of coarse grass and dense riverine woodland, keeping a wary eye open for elephant and buffalo. In places where the river is wide, easier walking is possible by following the edge of the river-bed at times of low water. The rivers flow through gorges which they have channelled deep into the escarpment, and drop over sills of resistant rock down spectacular waterfalls. A walk up the Bua River from the east leads past wide, deep, dark pools harbouring lake salmon, along grass carpeted banks of silt which become flooded at high water, to rocky areas where the river foams its way through a jumble of boulders, constantly pounding away at the bedrock underneath. Each bend in the river reveals a new landscape, and perhaps a wary group of waterbuck drinking from the

shallows, or a large crocodile basking on a far sand-bank, while waders and other birds forage busily at the water's edge. The woodland to either side frequently echoes with the sound of baboons as males contest for dominance, and young animals playfully mock-fight in the understorey.

The greatest concentrations of large mammals occur in the more fertile areas of the scarp fault, in the valleys of the Bua, Dwafuni and Kaombe Rivers. However, the reserve in general contains relatively few large animals, partly because of the inherently low carrying capacity of much of the habitat but also because of illegal hunting which continues despite anti-poaching measures. Poaching makes animals very wary, so although the reserve is criss-crossed by game trails and much spoor may be evident they are difficult to see, especially when the grass is high. Occasionally elephant may be seen from a vehicle on the M10 or observed from vantage points high on the rocky peak of Chipata Mountain, feeding in the *Brachystegia* woodland on the ridges below. There are many signs of elephant in the evergreen forest which covers the slopes of the mountain; walking is easy there as they keep the understorey open.

The forest of Chipata Mountain is an isolated

The peak of Chipata Mountain from the *Brachystegia* woodland below.   JANET and JOHN HOUGH

A strangler fig enveloping its host. Thin aerial roots hang down from its branches.   JAMES OGLETHORPE

evergreen forest of Ntchisi Forest Reserve 35 km away. (Information on Chipata Mountain[37].)

A marked trail leads up through the forest to emerge in a fringe of candelabra trees at the rocky summit. From here there are views in all directions: eastward over the reserve to Lake Malaŵi; north to the Bua River; west across the Central African Plateau towards Kasungu; and south to the Dowa Hills and Ntchisi Mountain. Other hills in the west of the reserve provide equally scenic views from their summits, particularly Mbengwa and Njongombe, north of the Bua, in a very wild, isolated and beautiful part of the reserve.

Mpasa

Apart from its general value in the conservation of soil, water, wildlife and wilderness, Nkhotakota Game Reserve plays a vital role in the conservation of the commercially important lake salmon. Known locally as *mpasa*, these endemic fish, along with the closely related *sanjika* and various species of yellow fish, migrate annually from Lake Malaŵi up some of the major tributary rivers to breed. Every year when the river levels rise during the rains, adult *mpasa* swim up rivers such as the Songwe, North Rukuru, Luweya, Bua and Linthipe seeking clean gravel beds in which to spawn, returning to the lake a few months later.

The *mpasa* is thought to have evolved from riverine ancestors and although it spends most of its life

community of lowland and sub-montane evergreen species such as the brown-berry fluted milkwood, the bastard white stinkwood and the forest Natal mahogany. Tall and majestic buttressed trees reach up to the dense closed canopy overhead, strangler figs entwined around trunks and competing with other plants for light. Epiphytic ferns grow on the limbs of larger trees. Many shrubs and small trees of the understorey have been severely damaged by elephant; some have adapted to this pressure and now grow horizontally. The elephant are particularly fond of the spiny shaggy-fruited dovyalis.

Birdlife in the forest is rather impoverished, probably because of its isolation from other evergreen forests and the impact of elephant. However, lowland riverine forest birds such as the grey-olive bulbul and wattle-eyed flycatcher occur, as well as species such as the moustached green tinkerbird and yellow-streaked bulbul which may have originated from the

Mpasa or lake salmon. Angling is permitted on a catch-and-return basis in the reserve.   DENIS TWEDDLE

During the rains the *mpasa* migrate up the Bua River from Lake Malaŵi into Nkhotakota Game Reserve, where they spawn in gravel-beds in shallow water.   JUDY CARTER

in the lake it has not developed a breeding strategy there, thus necessitating the migration. Its breeding habits are very similar to those of the Atlantic salmon of the northern hemisphere, which spends most of its life in the sea but returns to its river of origin to breed. The two species also have similar feeding habits, and look very much alike in body shape and colouring (hence the name 'lake salmon' for the *mpasa*). The Atlantic salmon belongs to the salmonid family, however, and the *mpasa* is a cyprinid: in the course of evolution these two groups are considered to have diverged about 100 million years ago, so they are not closely related taxonomically. It is thought that when Lake Malaŵi developed it created new conditions for the riverine fish in the area; the forebears of the *mpasa* occupied a niche comparable to that of the Atlantic salmon, with consequent development of a species very similar to it: an interesting example of convergent evolution[62].

When the *mpasa* migrate up the river, the male establishes a small territory containing a clean gravel bed in shallow water, and patrols it until he is joined by a female. The two fish lie side by side over the gravel in the centre of the territory, and as the eggs and milt are shed the adults stir up the gravel with their large anal fins. Some eggs are fertilised and trapped in the gravel as the adults churn it up; others

are carried away by the current to be consumed by juvenile *sanjika* and small minnows which wait in anticipation downstream from the spawning *mpasa*. The fertilised eggs hatch in the gravel and the young fry frequent shallows and backwaters. Further mortality occurs in the ensuing months, and an extremely small percentage of the fry survives to find its way to the waters of Lake Malaŵi at the beginning of the following rains. The young fish which do reach the lake remain near the river mouth until their second year; they then move offshore until the age of four or five years when they are ready to spawn. By this stage they are large, silvery, salmon-like fish, and may eventually attain weights of nearly 4 kg.

In recent years heavy fishing pressure and in some cases siltation has resulted in a decline of *mpasa* stocks in many rivers, but the Bua still has a large run of *mpasa*. This population is harvested by local fishermen using gill nets at the mouth of the Bua as the adult fish wait for adequate water to migrate up the river, and more are caught in the lower reaches at the start of the migration. Once the survivors have run this gauntlet and entered the reserve they are protected, however, and can spawn in relative peace. Equally important, the spawning beds are protected from siltation and sudden changes in water level which may result from certain agricultural practices and deforestation. Clean gravel and a flow of well-oxygenated water are essential for the development of the fry. (*Mpasa* information:[57,63,64].)

Chapter Five

Lake Malaŵi and the lakeshore plains

At the foot of the escarpments in the hot climate of the rift valley trough lie the fertile lakeshore plains and Lake Malaŵi. Nearly 600 km long, the lake covers two thirds of the length of the country, the plains lying shimmering with heat by its side. Scenery is spectacular, the escarpments overlooking the many moods and colours of the huge, narrow lake. Trees along the shoreline provide perches for the majestic fish eagle, whose soulful voice is a common sound along the lakeshore. The waters of the lake, which provide abundant food for the fish eagle and many other birds, harbour some of the most diverse freshwater fish communities in the world. Two species of otter feed on the fish, living around the rocky shorelines, and man also harvests the lake: along much of the lakeshore small fishing settlements are in evidence. Lake and plain are essential components of the habitats of many animals, and the floor of the rift valley is a highly productive area. In this chapter the lakeshore plains are described first, followed by the lake with its unique fish fauna and the national park which protects part of it.

Lake Malaŵi.　FRANK JOHNSTON

The lakeshore plains

The lakeshore plains vary in width along the length of the country. At the narrowest they are almost non-existent, the escarpments rising steeply from the lake with scarcely any shoreline; at the other extreme they may be as wide as 25 km. Narrow plains in the steep sections of the rift valley were formed by geological faulting which created the step-like plains between escarpment and lake. Elsewhere, monoclinal folding of the rift margin produced more gradual slopes and wider plains, for example in the Salima area. Subsequently, parts of the plains accumulated rock and screes which fell from the escarpments above, along with material carried down by rivers and deposited on the sides of their estuaries. Today in the wider sections there are typically lagoons and

Remote village on the northern lakeshore. There is no lakeshore plain here, and fishing is an important activity for the local people. Tin roofs are a sign of prosperity.   JAMES OGLETHORPE

swamps near the lake, adjoined by flat, open plains, behind which the land rises in a series of low terraces towards the foothills of the escarpments. The terraces represent old shorelines of the lake, dating back thousands of years to periods when the lake level was higher than it is today. Isolated hills frequently rise out of the surrounding plains, especially in the south. [5,6]

The people of the lakeshore plains cultivate the rich alluvial soil and graze livestock on the broad, grassy *dambos* and less fertile areas. In the extreme north the broad, fertile Karonga Plain is cultivated for cotton and rice besides subsistence crops, and there are many cattle. South of Chitimba the escarpments of the Nyika and North Viphya Plateaux continue downwards into the lake with scarcely a break at the lakeshore, and there are very few flat areas in this section south to Nkhata Bay. There is a rice scheme at Limpasa north of Chintheche, but south of this the escarpment closes in again, narrowing the lakeshore plain to a thin strip for a further 70 km. North of Dwangwa it widens again into a broad section which stretches all the way to the south-west arm of the lake. Sugar is grown on a large estate at Dwangwa, and elsewhere there are cotton and rice schemes as well as subsistence cultivation of maize, groundnuts and other crops. The lakeshore plain around the south-east arm of the lake is narrower, and is used mainly for subsistence agriculture and grazing of livestock. Not all of the plain is farmed, however. In the wetter, less fertile and less densely populated areas the natural vegetation remains: grassy *dambos*, *Acacia* and *Combretum* woodland, and swamp and sand-dune vegetation in places by the lake.

There are many striking trees on the lakeshore plain, including baobab, fever tree, wild mango and winterthorn. Baobabs, with their swollen trunks and stubby, twisted, grasping branches are fabled to have been planted upside down, the branches resembling the roots of a windblown tree. The baobab has many uses. Sections of the bark have been cut off the trunks of many trees on the lakeshore plain to be beaten out to make bark cloth, mats, string and rope. A red dye can be made from the roots, and the leaves may be used in cooking. The hard-shelled fruit has a pith around the seeds which contains tartaric acid and a very high vitamin C content: a welcome refreshment during a walk through the woodland of the hot lakeshore plain. The seeds are also edible, and may be roasted and used as a substitute for groundnuts in cooking. A solution made from soaking seeds and pith is used to treat

A large baobab, a common tree of the lakeshore plains. Bats pollinate the flowers of the baobab at night, and in some places local people believe that the flowers are inhabited by spirits.   JUDY CARTER

fevers, and shoots of the germinating seed are eaten as asparagus. Cattle eat the leaves and flowers, and monkeys and baboons break open the fruits to consume the pith. Elephant may eat the bark and soft fibre of the trunk during the dry season if other components of their diet are inadequate. Bats feed on the nectar of the flowers which open at night, incidentally pollinating them. Not suprisingly the tree is surrounded by a wealth of superstition. In parts of Africa it is believed that the flowers are inhabited by spirits, and anyone who dares pick a blossom will be eaten by a lion. Another tradition says a draught of water prepared by soaking and stirring the seeds gives protection against crocodile; imbibing an infusion of bark is believed to make a man strong and mighty.

Another tree around which superstition developed was the fever tree: this time a belief of the early white pioneers in Southern Africa. These striking yellow-barked *Acacias* grow in areas of high watertable by swamps where mosquitoes breed. Before the role of the mosquito in the transmission of malaria was understood, the pioneers believed the tree to be responsible for causing the disease which they often contracted after camping near to fever trees in lowlying areas. The unusual, flaky yellow bark may have enhanced the belief.

Other, more useful trees of the lakeshore plain include the winterthorn and wild mango; the trunks of both these species are carved out to make dug-out canoes, and the latter is also used for making traditional drums by the people of the villages. The wild mango has a dense, spreading, dark green foliage, providing shade in many villages during the hot season. The winterthorn, on the other hand, remains leafless and appears dead at this time, coming into leaf only in the cool dry season when the rest of the bush is turning dry and brown: hence the name of the species. It grows in areas with an underground water supply and can be used as an indicator for the presence of water. The nutritious fruits of both winterthorn and wild mango are eaten by many wild animals; the pods of winterthorn can apparently also be ground up and used as fish poison, and a draught prepared by boiling its bark is used to treat diarrhoea. (Information on trees:[65,66,67])

The people of the lakeshore plains also make use of a number of introduced tree species. Shady mango trees are grown along much of the lakeshore, laden with fruit at the beginning of the rains, and kapok trees have been planted in rows in some of the villages, the fluffy bolls of kapok being used to stuff pillows and cushions. These exotics have been introduced by man at various times in the region's history: some of the lakeshore villages have been on important trade routes between the Indian Ocean and the interior of the continent since around the twelfth century AD. The Arab influence introduced by traders in the nineteenth century still prevails today along much of the lakeshore: in many of the towns and villages Muslims walk in the streets wearing white robes and prayer-caps calling Swahili greetings to one another, and the evocative sound of prayer from the mosque echoes over the surrounding countryside. A few dhows continue to cross the lake between remote Makanjila on the south-eastern shore and Leopard Bay near Salima, carrying passengers, fish, crops, bicycles, miscellaneous luggage, goats and chickens. Reminders of the Protectorate can still be seen in the larger towns. Old colonial administration buildings with large verandahs are

A sign of the Arab influence, dhows are still in use on Lake Malaŵi, crossing regularly between Makanjila and Leopard Bay. JUDY CARTER

still in use, and the Queen Victoria Memorial Clock Tower stands at the southern end of the lake on the Shire River at Mangochi. This carries a plaque commemorating the worst known disaster on the lake when the badly designed m.v. *Viphya* sank in a violent storm off Chitimba in 1946[41]. Disasters on this scale are very rare, however, and the lake continues to be an extremely important transport route in Malaŵi today.

Passenger steamers ply up and down the lake, and a trip on the *Ilala*, with her bar and restaurant services, transports the visitor into another world and time: to Likoma Island with its mission station and cathedral; and to small isolated villages at the foot of the northern escarpment where the *Ilala* is the main link with the outside world. On this journey the scale and magnificence of the lake and rift valley can be truly appreciated, and the many moods of the lake experienced at first hand.

Lake Malaŵi[3,4,5]

The lake exerts a profound influence not only on scenery and transport in the region, but also on climate, hydrology, commerce and tourism. It runs southwards from the Tanzanian border in the north of the country almost to Mangochi, its maximum width being 80 km. In the south it divides into two arms round the Nankumba Peninsula, part of which falls within the Lake Malaŵi National Park. The lake is relatively shallow in these arms at less than 100 m but to the north water depth rapidly increases, reaching the deepest point north of Nkhata Bay. Here the steep-sided escarpments continue downwards from the lake surface at approximately 474 m above sea-level to the great depth of 704 m[6]. This is a remarkable 230 m or so below the surface of the Indian Ocean, some 600 km to the east on the Mozambique coast.

Lake Malaŵi has not always been this deep. It is thought to have originated between one and two million years ago as a small lake at the northern end of its present basin, over 200 m above its present level. As further faulting occurred the rift trough deepened and the lake extended south, capturing rivers from the west and flooding the former head of the Shire River. At this time the lake level was still higher than at present, and therefore much wider in the south. However, more faulting brought the lake to its present level, depth and narrow width, with the Shire River its only outlet. Lake Malaŵi has a relatively small catchment, between three and four times its own area. Besides the land of northern and central Malaŵi as far south as Ntcheu and the southern end of the lake, the catchment includes the narrow eastern escarpment above the lakeshore; the basin of the Ruhuhu River in Tanzania which is its largest tributary; and the south-western part of the Livingstone Mountains and other hills in Tanzania to the north and north-west of the lake.

All the rivers draining into the lake are relatively short by African standards, and there are no large groundwater reserves within the catchment. Input is therefore largely dependent on rainfall, which varies greatly within the catchment area due to the wide range of altitudes. Many of the smaller rivers stop flowing in the dry season, and the lake level fluctuates seasonally within a range of about a half to two metres. Levels are normally highest in May and lowest in December.

Apart from this seasonal variation the lake level also displays longer term fluctuations. During the past 120 years the average annual lake level fell by about four and a half metres between 1865 and 1915, and rose by over six metres from 1915 to 1980. The latter caused flooding in many areas of the lakeshore: many properties had to be abandoned; roads and harbours were adversely affected; agricultural land was lost; trees along the lakeshore died and swamps developed or expanded; beaches were drowned; and erosion was caused by wave action above the new high water mark.[68] Since 1980 the lake level has started to drop again, leaving dead trees and a ragged 'high tide' mark along the shoreline. It is impossible to predict what levels the next few years will see: the situation remains a mystery. Levels could rise again, or alternatively the pattern could reverse and levels could drop significantly, leaving beaches and landing points stranded.

The reason for this fluctuation has been the subject of much debate and various theories have been proposed concerning climatic variations and changes in land-use. The operation of the barrage at Liwonde has only a very small effect, estimated in 1979 to have increased the lake level by 15 cm. There is

The Queen Victoria Memorial Clock Tower at Mangochi. A plaque on the tower commemorates the worst known disaster on Lake Malaŵi, the sinking of the m.v. *Viphya* in a storm in 1946. Behind is the Shire River, flowing out of the lake on its course down the rift valley.   DENIS TWEDDLE

The *Ilala*'s lifeboat is lowered in the shallower waters to collect passengers from remote settlements along the lakeshore. JAMES OGLETHOPRE

When the level of Lake Malaŵi continued to rise in the late 1970s many buildings near the lakeshore were flooded like this one near Karonga, and had to be abandoned.
DENIS TWEDDLE

some correlation between annual lake levels and mean annual rainfall over the catchment, though this alone does not provide a full explanation. Another theory involves changes in the position or intensity of the inter-tropical convergence zone (ITCZ), as this affects the precipitation pattern during the rains. In this theory, rain falling directly on to the lake is considered to be the most significant variable affecting lake level. Most rain falls on the lake from convective thunderstorms at night. It is thought that when the ITCZ lies to the north of the catchment the air mass over Malaŵi originating from further south is relatively stable and there is a correspondingly low incidence of thunderstorms, most rain falling as orographic precipitation over high ground away from the lake. Consequently, the seasonal rise in lake level is less than average. If the ITCZ lies further south, however, rainfall occurs mainly as convective thunderstorms which develop in the unstable air masses from further north. At this time differential cooling of the land and lake surfaces at night results in movement of air from land to lake, and the development of intense convection over the lake. Under such circumstances lake rainfall will be above average, leading to larger than average rises in lake level. Unfortunately there are no rainfall data for the lake surface, though there is some correlation between changes in rainfall trends at certain lakeshore

stations and variability of seasonal rise in lake level during the past forty years.[69]

Other theories explaining the fluctuations of lake level are based on the large-scale clearing of forest and woodland for agriculture which has occurred in many parts of the catchment this century. One concerns convective thunderstorms again: it is thought that land cleared for crops will cool faster at night than it did when it had its original vegetation cover. This should result in an increase in the nocturnal temperature difference between land and lake with a corresponding increase in the movement of air towards the lake. Convection over the lake would be intensified, augmenting the development of thunderstorms when other conditions were suitable, and hence increasing rainfall over the lake.[69] Again, there are unfortunately no climatic data available on rainfall over the lake or wind strength and direction to verify this idea. There is another theory based on changing land-use. Natural forest enables the retention of a relatively large proportion of rainfall in the soil; much of this water is then gradually released to the atmosphere by direct evaporation and indirectly by plants during the process of photosynthesis. Relatively little water therefore reaches the rivers. Destruction of the permanent vegetation cover usually reduces the retention of water in the soil and results in more rapid runoff to the rivers, and hence a greater input to the lake. This process may play a significant role in affecting lake level, though it is extremely difficult to demonstrate[68]. It does not, however, account for all aspects of the recent trends in lake level[69]. There may well be a number of complex factors affecting the pattern of lake level changes during the past century.

The sparkling blue waters of the lake appear very safe and inviting in calm weather. Looks can be deceptive, however, as storms can suddenly spring up, seemingly from nowhere. During the cool dry season (April to August) strong south-easterly winds known as *mwera* can blow unimpeded up the lake at speeds reaching 60-70 km/hr, creating waves sometimes three to four metres high in unsheltered parts and causing strong currents around islands and rocky outcrops. Winds during the rest of the year can also be dangerous.

Deep in the rift valley trough below the bed of Lake Malaŵi, deposits of oil and natural gas have recently been discovered. Their location at a great depth under the lake makes exploitation difficult, but it is possible that they may be tapped one day. This would obviously be of economic benefit to the

Storm over the Maleri Islands in the Lake Malaŵi National Park. JUDY CARTER

country, but would inevitably be accompanied by a risk of environmental pollution from oil spillage which, if it happened on a large scale, could have an extremely adverse effect on some of the plant and animal communities of the lake.

Lake Malaŵi is a highly productive system, supporting a wide range of organisms in complex food chains and webs in various habitats. About 30% of the shoreline comprises steep, rocky shores, the remaining 70% being sandy beaches or areas of water-weed and swamp. The floor of the lake in deeper areas consists of sand or mud. Other habitat types include open inshore waters and the upper 100 m or so of the offshore waters. Most organisms occur relatively near the surface where light and oxygen are plentiful, but fish have been caught from depths of over 200 m, at the lower limit of oxygen in the water. Below this level there is little vertical mixing of water, as the water underneath is colder and therefore more dense than the sun-warmed, less dense layer above it. This phenomenon occurs in many lakes, the division between the two layers being known as the thermocline. The lower layer is deficient in oxygen, but because of the absence of aerobic organisms it may contain concentrations of unused minerals and organic debris which have fallen to the bottom. The upper layer is illuminated by the sun and kept well oxygenated by wave movement and turbulent currents, but plant growth may become limited by a deficiency of nutrients, especially during periods of high plankton production.

The problem is not serious in the south of the lake where water depth is less than 100 m and mixing of oxygen and nutrients throughout the water occurs annually as a result of the *mwera*. Further north, however, productivity is severely restricted by the existence of the thermocline, and the fishery in the north of the lake is much less productive than in the south. An exception to this is near rock outcrops such as Likoma Island where upwelling of nutrient-rich cold water occurs, carried by currents diverted upwards by the rockface.

The fish of Lake Malaŵi[3,4,70,71]

The aquatic fauna of Lake Malaŵi, its tributaries and the upper Shire River has been isolated from aquatic organisms of other water catchments in the region for a great length of time. Once the rift valley and lake were developed and river capture completed, the only remaining link with another hydrological basin was through the Shire River flowing southward to the Zambezi. Falls and rapids on the Shire, however, prevented the migration of aquatic fauna upstream from the Zambezi system, with the exception of the mottled eel (see page 137). This isolation enabled the evolution of many new fish species which are endemic to Lake Malaŵi and occur naturally nowhere else in the world. Along with Lake Tanganyika, Lake Malaŵi contains more species of fish than any other freshwater lake in the world. It is still not known how many occur as new species and subspecies continue to be discovered each year and their taxonomy is very complicated, but the total number in Lake Malaŵi has been estimated to be over 500[72]. Ten families are represented, the great majority of species belonging to the cichlid family. Ninety-eight per cent of the known cichlid species are endemic to the lake. Ten of the cichlid genera comprise the *mbuna*: small, brightly coloured fish normally living around rocks, of which there may be as many as 350 species.

The explosive evolution of the Lake Malaŵi *mbuna* is more outstanding than even the classic example of Darwin's finches on the Galapagos Islands. The process of speciation is thought to have been accelerated by periodic fluctuations in lake level, which would have alternately separated and rejoined rocky habitats. During a period of separation, relatively small populations of a given *mbuna* species would have been isolated from each other long enough for them to undergo evolutionary change, and each population could potentially have given rise to a new species. When the fluctuating lake level next rejoined their habitats the populations would have mixed, the community then containing two or more distinct species derived from the initial one. Periodic fluctuations of lake level would have enabled this phenomenon to be repeated many times, the process of speciation progressing geometrically to produce large numbers of new species in a comparatively short length of time.[72] Another contributory factor in the explosive speciation is the exceptionally good parental care displayed by *mbuna* (see pages 101–102) which results in the production of relatively small numbers of offspring, and reduced dispersal. This makes them more prone to inbreeding and hence speciation.

Nearly every *mbuna* species has a limited distribution in Lake Malaŵi. In some cases a given species may be endemic to a very small area, for example occurring only along a few hundred metres of one particular rocky shoreline. This phenomenon is a result of the *mbuna's* close association with rocks and low level of dispersal, along with the highly fragmented nature of the rocky coastline and the history of fluctuating lake levels. *Mbuna* communities around many offshore islands have a particularly high percentage of endemic species. The limited distribution of many species in the Lake Malaŵi National Park is discussed on pages 108–109.

Large numbers of species coexist in each of the various fish communities in the lake. Many different specialisations and adaptations have evolved enabling the development of a tremendous variety of niches and thus reducing competition between species. Many of the adaptations of these fish are analagous with those of the large mammal communities described in chapter 3. As outlined above, cichlid evolution has been most explosive around the rocky shores. On the upper surfaces of the submerged rocks a carpet of filamentous green algae grows, providing a habitat for other algae, bacteria and protozoa, and various invertebrates such as crustaceans, water mites and the larvae and nymphs of insects. Crabs live in the cracks and crevices. Around these rocks many different species of *mbuna* and other cichlids occur, all highly specialised in their feeding behaviour. Most feed on the algae covering the rocks and have evolved different types of teeth, mouths, body shapes and behaviour to ensure that each species exploits a slightly different part. *Pseudotropheus tropheops* and *Labeotropheus fuelleborni* have close-set, stout teeth which they use to scrape even the most firmly attached algae from the rock surface. *Pseudotropheus zebra*, on the other hand, combs the algae with its long, wider spaced back teeth, taking only the looser algae. Some species suck up loose algae, having a mobile mouth with tooth pads.

Many species have similar diets but avoid competition by exploiting different parts of the habitat. They may live at different depths in the water, using different zones of rock. Some frequent areas of small rocks, whereas others prefer larger rock faces. Smaller mouthed species are able to feed in crevices where larger fish cannot reach. Some species feed intensively on one small rock face; others feed less intensively with more mobility over a larger area. Some have such a limited distribution that they are confined to only one tiny island outcrop. In such a case the equivalent niche on other isolated rock outcrops is fulfilled by other species.

Not all the cichlids are herbivores: some are carnivorous. A few *Labidochromis* species with large

Mbuna. Along with Lake Tanganyika, Lake Malaŵi contains more species of fish than any other freshwater lake in the world. The majority of them are cichlids, almost all of which are endemic to the lake. They include the colourful *mbuna* which live around the rocky shores of the lake.

Female *Pseudotropheus tropheops* photographed off Thumbi Island West, feeding on the green algae carpeting the rocks. *P. tropheops* use their stout teeth to scrape algae off the rock surface. *WORLD WILDLIFE FUND/MALAWI GOVERNMENT*

Male *Pseudotropheus zebra* feeding on algae on rocks off Otter Point. The feeding angle is different to *P. tropheops*; *P. zebra* combs the algae with its long, wider spaced teeth, taking only the looser algae. The markings on the anal fin are the 'egg spots'. *WORLD WILDLIFE FUND/MALAWI GOVERNMENT*

Genyochromis mento which ambushes and attacks other fish to feed on their fins and scales, using its prominent lower jaw. Its colouring provides it with camouflage. *WORLD WILDLIFE FUND/MALAWI GOVERNMENT*

Pseudotropheus livingstonii, which escapes from predators by retreating into a snail shell. *WORLD WILDLIFE FUND/MALAWI GOVERNMENT*

eyes, forceps-like teeth and slender bodies feed on the crustaceans and insect larvae in the algal carpet; many *Cyrtocara* species prey on other fish; and some species feed on crabs. The *mbuna Genyochromis mento* has evolved the habit of feeding on the scales and fins of other fish which it frequently ambushes and attacks; many *mbuna* consequently have pieces missing from their fins. *Melanochromis crabro* steals eggs from the catfish locally known as *kampango*, though it also keeps the body of the catfish clean by removing parasites from it. At times when it cannot obtain sufficient food from the catfish it feeds on algae and plankton.

A high diversity of cichlid species is also found in the sandy shore area. On some parts of the sandy lake floor water-weed grows, its flat leaves encrusted with algae. Among the weed live crustaceans including a species of tiny freshwater prawn, together with insect larvae and nymphs, and several species of snail and other molluscs. Some cichlids browse on the water-weed: *Cyrtocara similis* has specially adapted teeth for this purpose. Others such as *Hemitilapia oxyrhynchus* nibble the algae on the leaves, or take phytoplankton from the water and detritus from the bottom mud.

Docimodus attacking a catfish; it is thought that this fin-biter regularly uses its stout cutting teeth and heavy jaws to sever pieces of fin from other fish.   LIZ and TONY BOMFORD, *SURVIVAL ANGLIA*

A swarm of lakeflies over Lake Malaŵi. Adult flies emerge from the aquatic pupae around the time of new moon when the lake is relatively calm. They form dense swarms, at which time mating occurs.   DAVID WOODFALL

Insectivorous fish include the sand sifters such as some species of *Lethrinops* which take large mouthfuls of sand, sifting it over their gill rakers to retain edible organisms including chironomid larvae. Various species feed on snails, crushing the shell either in powerful jaws (for example, *Chilotilapia rhoadesii*) or more commonly using teeth of the pharynx which have been specially adapted for the purpose, as in *Cyrtocara placodon*. Cichlids which prey upon other fish include *C. livingstonii*, which lies on its side as if dead until an unsuspecting prey comes too close. *C. johnstoni* is camouflaged by vertical barring on its sides, and remains motionless in the forests of water-weed waiting for its prey.

The fish of the sandy areas are also frequently preyed upon by fish coming inshore from deeper waters. In the latter zone the primary producers are phytoplankton, which are consumed by zooplankton along with organic matter in the bottom mud. One organism which feeds on the zooplankton is the larva of the lakefly *Chaoborus*. This organism has a very interesting life cycle, the early larval stage being spent in the water as zooplankton, and the later stage being spent on the bottom mud during the day, swimming up towards the surface at night. Around the time of the new moon when the lake is relatively calm the winged adult flies emerge from the pupae and swarm in large numbers. They form dense reddish-brown clouds, sometimes more than 50 m in height, which can be seen for great distances on the lake. The flies do not bite but swarms are so dense that if they engulf a boat they can be almost suffocating; sometimes they are blown on to the shore by the wind. Only a small proportion of the adults succeeds in mating and laying eggs on the surface of the water to complete the life cycle.

The lakefly is present in vast numbers and constitutes a significant part of the biomass in the lake ecosystem; it is an important food source for many different carnivores. Local people around the lake collect the flies which are known as *nkhungu* by attracting them to lights at night. They are scooped up, boiled and made into cakes. Livingstone partook of them in 1865, considering the taste to be rather like caviare or salted locusts. Many birds also feed on the swarms of adult flies. The larvae, along with other zooplankton in the off-shore zone are consumed by various fish including *usipa* and *utaka*. *Usipa* is a small fish about 10 cm long and is probably the only species which breeds in open water rather than inshore. At certain times large shoals of *usipa* come close to the shore where they are caught in seine nets by fishermen. The largest *usipa* catches are made at night, when teams of fishermen in plank boats and canoes venture far out on the lake and attract them to the surface with flares or paraffin lamps. The *usipa* congregate around the boats and are captured in an intricately constructed purse seine net known as a *chirimila*. *Utaka* are also caught with *chirimila* nets; they comprise a number of closely related cichlid species with protrusible mouths which are found in large shoals in the surface waters, and are particularly abundant in the shallow water above submerged rocks where there is an upwelling of nutrients.

Apart from man the *usipa* and *utaka* have other predators. These include *kampango* and some fast swimming, thin bodied *Rhamphochromis* species, cichlids whose jaws and teeth are well adapted for predation. Another is *binga*, whose numbers are believed to fluctuate in response to the availability of *usipa*. These predators in turn are caught by fishermen, and *binga* is an important sporting fish for anglers.

The largest fish in the lake are the *Bathyclarias* catfish, some of which grow to 50 kg in weight. They occupy a variety of habitats: some live in the surface waters and have developed baleen-like gill sieves enabling them to filter lakefly larvae from the water, while others are entirely predatory and prey upon bottom-dwelling cichlids. Some catfish live at great depths and have been captured from water over 200 m deep. Another fish of deep waters is the elephant-snout fish which sucks lakefly larvae and other food from the bottom mud.

The cichlids have unusual breeding habits. Nearly all are mouthbrooders: the adult female incubates the eggs and then guards the young fry inside her mouth. During the breeding season the males of many species develop a brighter coloration than the females, often blue. They establish territories such as an area of rock or sand or a small cave, depending on habitat. With their bright colours they display vigorously, spreading their fins and swimming in a very characteristic manner to attract available females and warn would-be intruders of their dominance. Any trespasser not heeding the warning is challenged, and if necessary fought. Within his territory, the male usually constructs a nest or clears an area where eggs may eventually be deposited. There is considerable variation in nest shape: *mbuna* species merely guard territories on rock faces or over crevices between rocks, whereas sand-dwelling cichlids often construct large nests by moving sand, a mouthful at a time; the nest may be several times larger than the

Dugout canoe, the traditional boat used by local fishermen on the lake. JUDY CARTER

fish itself. Nests of sand-dwellers range from the dinner-plate sized patch of clean sand of *Cyrtocara kirkii*, through the volcano shaped, 30 cm high sand mound of *C. eucinostomus*, to the complex construction built by *Lethrinops aurita*. The latter consists of a central mound of sand about 20 cm in diameter, surrounded by seven to nine smaller piles arranged in a circle about one metre in diameter.[73]

Once a female in breeding condition has been attracted into a territory the male carries out elaborate courtship rituals, finally stimulating her to lay eggs in the prepared area. The female picks the eggs up in her mouth where they are then fertilised as she mouths the markings on the male's anal fin. She incubates the eggs in her mouth for a period lasting between 22 and 30 days. During this time she does not normally feed, but occasionally moves the eggs around in her mouth with a chewing action to rotate the yolk and ensure normal development. The eggs, and later fry, obtain oxygen from water drawn through the female's mouth and over her gills. Mouthbrooders generally produce fewer eggs than substrate spawners, but the eggs are larger and contain more yolk. The *mbuna* generally produce between six and 150 eggs: it would be difficult for a female to guard larger numbers of fry in her mouth, and with such intensive parental care survival rates are high enough to warrant the relatively small number of eggs.

The female may remain in the territory with the protection of the male during the brooding period, but in some species she is driven away or leaves of her own accord to find a secluded site in which to brood the young. Once the fry have hatched they are released from the female's mouth to feed, keeping

Male *Lethrinops macropthalmus* building a sand nest. When it is completed he will display to attract a female in breeding condition to his territory. LIZ and TONY BOMFORD, *SURVIVAL ANGLIA*

Female *Melanochromis auratus*. The young are guarded in her mouth and released to feed at times when there is no danger; this continues until they are large enough to fend for themselves. LIZ and TONY BOMFORD, *SURVIVAL ANGLIA*

Windsurfing at Cape Maclear in the Lake Malaŵi National Park. Lake Malaŵi is the most important tourist attraction in the country. JUDY CARTER

Fishermen drawing in their net on Chigale Beach near Nkhata Bay. JUDY CARTER

close to her in a tight shoal. They have many predators and the female stays alert for any danger. If a predator comes near she signals to the fry and they disappear rapidly back into the safety of her mouth. The young are cared for in this manner until they are large enough to fend for themselves.

Mbuna are not generally harvested for food, though a limited number are caught under licence by divers and exported for sale to aquarists around the world. In the lake they are an important attraction for visitors who can observe them from rocks and boats or by snorkelling and diving. With its sandy beaches, clear blue waters and tremendous scope for a wide range of water sports, Lake Malaŵi is the greatest tourist attraction in the country. Hotels, inns and camping sites have been developed along the lake, all on a relatively small scale, at Chintheche, Senga Bay, Cape Maclear, and north of Mangochi.

Other fish species are harvested for food, and some 16 000 people living along the lakeshore depend on fishing for their livelihood. Some fish for subsistence, using lines and baited hooks from dugout canoes, their diet supplemented with chickens, home-grown maize and other crops such as vegetables and bananas. Others own or are employed in larger operations, seine netting from beaches, *chirimila* fishing for *utaka* and *usipa*, gill netting from beaches for larger fish, and commercial trawling. Racks covered with *utaka* and *usipa* drying in the sun are a

common sight in the lakeside villages. Larger fish are often smoked over open fires, though in some places shortage of firewood for smoking fish is becoming a severe problem. In one commercial operation fish are frozen. Amongst the larger fish *chambo* is one of the most sought after, and various species of catfish are also caught, including *kampango* which is a delicacy when smoked. Sport angler's quarry includes the *binga*, *ncheni* and *sungwa*, large predatory fish occurring around the rocky areas. Commercial fish catches are transported to the inland towns and cities of Malaŵi, and some fish is also exported to neighbouring countries. In 1979 the yield of Lake Malaŵi was estimated at over 22 000 metric tonnes, nearly half of it from the shallow, productive south-eastern arm of the lake[46]. Fishing is therefore a very important part of the national economy, and fish provides about 70% of the animal protein in the nation's diet[33]. Yields from Lake Malaŵi have been increased in recent years with the expansion of commercial fishing. Fishing effort and catch are being closely monitored to prevent overfishing.

Various other methods of increasing fish catches on a sustained basis have also been considered. One

Fish drying on racks in the sun at Zambo, one of the enclave villages near the Lake Malaŵi National Park.   LIZ and TONY BOMFORD,   *SURVIVAL ANGLIA*

such possibility is the introduction of two clupeid fish species from Lake Tanganyika, *Stolothrissa tanganicae* and *Limnothrissa miodon* (the Lake Tanganyika sardine). The fish productivity of the offshore waters of Lake Tanganyika is much greater than that of Lake Malaŵi due to the presence of the clupeids. In Lake Malaŵi the situation is complicated, but basically the theory for the introduction is that the structure of the food chain in its offshore zone results in a high productivity of lakefly larvae compared to fish. The larvae are not heavily preyed upon by *usipa*, the indigenous zooplankton-feeding fish in that zone. If the clupeids were introduced they would initially prey upon the lakefly larvae and greatly reduce their numbers, and then take over their role in the food chain by preying on other zooplankton, thus increasing the overall fish productivity. *L. miodon* was introduced very successfully to the newly formed Lake Kariba, where the existing riverine Zambezi fish species were unable to exploit the zooplankton of the pelagic zone of the artificial lake.[33]

Many doubts have been expressed about the feasibility of such an introduction to Lake Malaŵi, however. The basic theories of a food source unexploited by fish and the ability of the exotics to use it have been questioned on technical grounds. In more general terms, Lake Malaŵi unlike Lake Kariba

already has a highly developed and extremely complex aquatic system. Fish yields might increase with the introduction of the clupeids, but it is also possible that competition with indigenous species such as *usipa* would cause such severe ecological imbalances that catches would decline permanently. Even with further research it would be very difficult to predict the impact which the exotics would have; the full effect would only be discovered once the clupeids were in the lake. By then, however, it would be impossible to eliminate them should the scheme prove disastrous. The Malaŵi Government is well aware of the possible implications of the introduction and is treating the idea with extreme caution; there are definitely no plans to introduce the exotics at present[74].

The Lake Malaŵi National Park, looking down from the eastern ridge of the Cape Maclear Peninsula across Chembe Village to Thumbi Island West.   JUDY CARTER

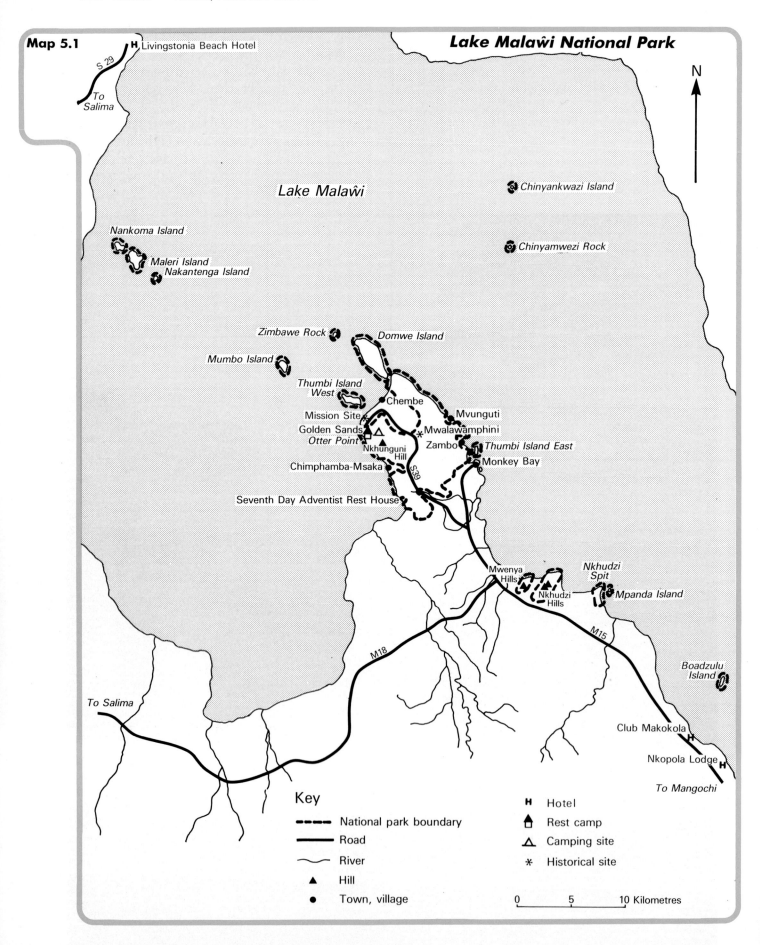

Map 5.1

Lake Malaŵi National Park

N

Livingstonia Beach Hotel

S 29

To Salima

Lake Malaŵi

Chinyankwazi Island

Nankoma Island

Chinyamwezi Rock

Maleri Island
Nakantenga Island

Zimbawe Rock

Domwe Island

Mumbo Island

Thumbi Island West

Chembe

Mission Site

Mvunguti

Golden Sands

Mwalawamphini

Otter Point

Zambo

Thumbi Island East

Nkhunguni Hill

Monkey Bay

Chimphamba-Msaka

S 39

Seventh Day Adventist Rest House

Mwenya Hills

Nkhudzi Spit

Nkhudzi Hills

Mpanda Island

M18

M15

To Salima

Boadzulu Island

Club Makokola

Nkopola Lodge

To Mangochi

Key

```
- - - -  National park boundary
───────  Road
───────  River
   ▲     Hill
   ●     Town, village
```

H Hotel

⌂ Rest camp

△ Camping site

✳ Historical site

0   5   10 Kilometres

Lake Malaŵi National Park[19,31]

Name derivation

From Lake Malaŵi. Various theories exist concerning the derivation of the word *malaŵi* (or *maravi*), which means 'fire flames'. One concerns the (erroneous) belief that the Phiri clan introduced the use of fire into the region. A different tradition is based on the impressions of a band of ancestral immigrants who saw Lake Malaŵi for the first time from the surrounding plateaux, shimmering 'like flames in the sunshine'. Another belief tells of them finding the rich grasslands around the lake on fire; and yet another concerns hot, low-lying land of the southern lakeshore where the 'vibrations of hot air ... "looked like flames of fire"'[8].

Declaration

Many of the larger islands and mainland areas of the present-day park were protected as forest reserves in 1934. The national park was gazetted in 1980.

Present size

About 87 km[2]

Location

Southern end of Lake Malaŵi. The park includes much of the Cape Maclear Peninsula; three small mainland areas to the south-east of it; 12 islands; and lake waters lying within 100 m of these terrestrial areas, as shown on map 5.1.

Landscape type

Inshore waters of Lake Malaŵi; sandy, rocky and marshy shorelines; rocky islands, the largest of which are generally steep-sided and wooded; steep, wooded, rocky mainland hills; and a flat marshy area.

Vegetation

Brachystegia woodland, with some *Combretum/Acacia* woodland and many baobabs in most of the terrestrial areas. Sand-dune and marsh vegetation at Nkhudzi Spit. Filamentous green algae on submerged rocks and various species of water-weed in sandy areas of lake bed; phytoplankton in the waterbody.

Large mammals

Most commonly seen: baboon, vervet monkey, dassie, hippo.

Others: Cape clawless and spotted-necked otters, civet, slender mongoose, leopard, zebra, bushpig, bushbuck, klipspringer, kudu, grey duiker, grysbok, porcupine, blue monkey.

Birds

Water-birds including hamerkop, fish eagle and large colonies of white-breasted cormorant on two islands; birds of *Brachystegia* woodland. Over 100 species of birds have been recorded in the park.

Other animals

A high diversity of fish species, many of them cichlids. Of particular interest are the *mbuna*, small, brightly coloured, highly specialised fish living around the rocks.

A few crocodile occur in the park, and the water monitor, a large *Varanus* lizard, is particularly common on Boadzulu Island.

Sites of special interest

Otter Point, *Mwalawamphini* rock, Old Livingstonia Mission site and graves, the islands of the park.

Access

Road: most areas of the park can be reached from the M15 Monkey Bay — Mangochi road. From Zomba and Blantyre this is reached via the M1 to Liwonde and M3 to Mangochi. There are two alternative routes from Lilongwe, one tarred all the way and one partly on untarred roads. The first is via the single-track M5 to Salima (which can be badly potholed but is due to be upgraded in the near future). This road joins the M17 which should be followed south. Beyond Mtakataka village turn left on to the M18, and follow it to its junction with the M15. The second route from Lilongwe is via the M1 which is followed southward to a point 16 km beyond Dedza where the untarred S22 leads off down the Golomoti Escarpment to the M17, joining the first route. The D81 can provide a short-cut across to the M18 and thence M15, but can become impassable to two-wheel-drive vehicles after heavy rain.

The route to Cape Maclear leads off the M15 5 km south of Monkey Bay, along the S39 for 19 km. This is a scenic, single-track road, extremely steep in places, mostly untarred and can give problems for two-wheel-drive vehicles after heavy rain.

The Mwenya Hills, Nkhudzi Hills and Nkhudzi Spit are reached from turnoffs further south on the M15.

Distances from the main centres to Cape Maclear (Golden Sands):

Lilongwe (via Salima):	245 km
Blantyre:	270 km
Zomba:	204 km

Boat access: the islands, shorelines and aquatic areas are reached by boat. Local launching points for small boats are at Cape Maclear, Monkey Bay, Nkopola Lodge, Club Makokola and Senga Bay.

Continued

Access by air: there is no airstrip within the park, but light aircraft can land on the strip in Monkey Bay.

Visitor facilities

Licensed, catering accommodation is available at Nkopola Lodge and Club Makokola hotels south of Monkey Bay and at the Livingstonia Beach Hotel (formerly Grand Beach Hotel) near Salima. Self-catering camping is also possible at Nkopola Lodge and the Livingstonia Beach Hotel. Within the park, the Golden Sands Holiday Camp at the time of writing offers some basic self-catering accommodation and a camping site. Stephen's Rest House in Chembe village on the Cape Maclear Peninsula offers cheap, clean accommodation and home cooking; it is well known amongst trans-African travellers.

Visitor activities

Beach activities, swimming, snorkelling, scuba-diving (no oxygen tank facilities available), windsurfing, boating, visiting islands, walking, rock climbing, bird-watching, photography.

Administrative arrangements

Enquiries concerning the Golden Sands Holiday Camp should be made to the Department of National Parks and Wildlife, PO Box 30131, Lilongwe 3 (tel 730 853). Details for the hotels are given in Appendix 1. No park fees are charged to visitors at the time of writing.

Best time to visit

Observing *mbuna*:	May to November
Observing other fish:	January to February and August to September
Bird-watching:	May to June and November to December
Swimming:	August to June
Beach activities:	April to November
Walking:	May to August
Boating:	April to May and September to November
Scenery:	November to August

Vehicle access to Cape Maclear can be difficult for saloon cars during the rains (approximately December to April). Temperatures during July and August are usually pleasantly warm for land-based activities, though water temperatures are relatively cold and may necessitate wet-suits for diving. During September to November it is uncomfortably hot for strenuous land-based activities but pleasant for water-based pursuits. The rest of the year is intermediate.

Lake Malaŵi National Park

The Lake Malaŵi National Park contrasts strongly with all the other parks and reserves in the country. It centres around the Cape Maclear Peninsula in the south of the lake and includes twelve islands and four separate areas of mainland as well as 100 m wide zones of water around each terrestrial component, as shown on map 5.1. The inshore waters are perhaps the most important part of the park, harbouring many fish communities. Lake Malaŵi National Park was the first park in the world to be established for the prime purpose of conserving an inland fresh water fish fauna[75], and its international significance was recognised when in 1984 it was declared a World Heritage Site by the United Nations Educational, Scientific and Cultural Organisation (UNESCO).

Animals of the Lake Malaŵi National Park

Mbuna occur in the waters off all the islands and mainland shores of the park, but diversity is highest around the rocky shores of Thumbi Island West which lies off the tip of the Cape Maclear Peninsula. Forty-four different species of fish have been recorded there, although it is known that a number of them were introduced from other parts of the lake in the past. Greatest concentrations of fish occur at the southern and northern ends of the island. Some of the Thumbi West species also occur around the rocks of nearby Otter Point which is easily accessible from Golden Sands. Snorkelling or diving around the rocks off the point and Otter Island reveals a silent world of fascinating and intricate interactions amongst the various forms of life there. Many *mbuna* species may be seen busily feeding on the algae of the rocks, or defending their invisible yet sharply defined territories against intruders. *Mbuna* are so territorial that they are rarely disturbed by divers. Patience is necessary, however, to observe the unusual mouth-brooding habit: a female with a distended looking throat may eventually release young fry to feed if she considers there is no threat to them nearby.

At least five of the *mbuna* species occurring off

Otter Point and Thumbi Island West are believed to be endemic, occurring nowhere else in the lake. Other parts of the park also have their own endemic species. The waters surrounding the small outcrops of Chinyamwezi Rock and Chinyankwazi Island, lying isolated to the north of the peninsula, harbour 17 different species, ten of which are endemic to these outcrops. The nine species recorded off Zimbawe Rock are not endemic to it but all show distinctive colouring in this location, being darker and more sombre than elsewhere. Non-endemic *mbuna* of the Maleri Islands near Senga Bay also display colours unique to the area. Coloration may even differ between these islands: for example, males of *Labeotropheus fuelleborni* occurring near the two larger islands are a uniform powder-blue, whereas off

Hamerkop, a common bird in the Lake Malaŵi National Park, so called because of the hammerhead shape of its large bill and crest. DAVID ELIAS

Nakantenga Island they have a golden flush on the flanks. Thirteen species are known to be endemic to the Maleris. Conditions here are slightly different from the other islands: below a water depth of 12 m the rocks are coated with a firm deposit of mud, presumably deposits from the Linthipe River, and algae grow on this instead of rock.

Many *mbuna* species occur along the rocky shore-line between Monkey Bay and Domwe Island, which lies off the northern end of the Cape Maclear Peninsula. Above this shore is the steep rocky eastern ridge of the peninsula, and in places huge boulders have broken off from the cliffs of the ridge and plunged into the lake. *Pseudotropheus zebra* is very common on this stretch of shoreline, dominant individuals holding territories around the rocks. (Information on the fish of the national park:[4])

The national park protects other fish besides *mbuna*, and many of its rocky shores are important breeding grounds for fish such as *utaka*. The beach off Golden Sands is an important area for sand-breeding species including *chambo*. Many animals of the park are dependent on the fish of the lake. Both the Cape clawless and spotted-necked otter occur in the park; the latter spends much time in the water, well adapted with its streamlined body and webbed feet for swimming and catching fish. The larger Cape clawless otter spends more time on land and includes frogs, crabs and small mammals in its more varied diet. Many species of birds feed on the fish of the lake. These include kingfishers, cormorants, pelicans, darters, herons, egrets, gulls and terns. Hamerkops are particularly common on the shoreline, wading in shallow waters and shuffling and stamping in the mud to stir up their food which includes small fish, insects, worms, crustaceans and frogs. Many trees along the lakeshore bear the huge structures of their nests: massive hollow domes built with sticks, reeds and other materials which take up to six months to complete. The only entrance is from below, inaccessible to would-be marauders. The nests are often inhabited later by barn owls and bees.[60] The fish eagle is another bird commonly seen and heard in the park, catching fish from the water whilst in flight and sometimes following fishing boats. Up to 47 have been counted at once following a trawler into Monkey Bay[73].

Many thousands of white-breasted cormorants live and breed in the park: large colonies occur on Mumbo and Boadzulu Islands where the trees and rocks are stained white with their droppings. Every possible nesting site is occupied by an untidy small

White-breasted cormorants with chicks. Mumbo and Boadzulu Islands in the Lake Malaŵi National Park have large colonies of cormorants. LIZ and TONY BOMFORD, *SURVIVAL ANGLIA*

many of the protected areas are too small for animals which require large home-ranges. The Cape Maclear Peninsula does support a number of species, including leopard, grey duiker, klipspringer, baboon, blue monkey, dassie, bushpig and zebra, though the latter are very elusive. Baboon and klipspringer occur on Domwe Island, and a small population of kudu lives in the area of Nkhudzi Hill. Elephant and lion are occasionally seen in the vicinity of Nkhudzi and Mwenya Hills, coming from the wilderness of the Phirilongwe Forest Reserve to the west. In the past large mammals were much more common: observations made by Faulkner and missionaries of the Livingstonia Mission are outlined later in this chapter.

Mwalawamphini, 'the rock of the tribal face markings'. Despite their man-made appearance these markings were formed naturally. FRANK JOHNSTON

saucer-shaped nest of sticks and twigs, from which in the dry season the ugly grey chicks peer and squawk in perpetual hope of food from their parents. Early in the morning the adults may be seen leaving the roost flying low in long skeins over the lake, heading for the day's fishing grounds. Boadzulu Island also supports a healthy population of large water monitor lizards: they feed on the eggs of the cormorants and on chicks which fall from nests. Basking in the sun on the rocks above the water, they may be viewed from a boat.

Large terrestrial mammals are not common in the park. One reason for this is its fragmented nature:

Components of the park

The scenery of the park is varied and breathtakingly beautiful: islands with rocky shorelines and wooded slopes; the flat sand and marsh area of Nkhudzi Spit; mainland cliffs and hills rising up almost sheer from the sparkling waters of the lake to high ridges and summits; and inland areas of dry bush, with spreading baobabs and huge boulders balanced one on top of another. In the Cape Maclear Peninisula there is a large rock known locally as *Mwalawamphini*: 'the rock of the tribal face markings'. Millions of years ago this rock was formed from molten granite which had been forced upwards into the overlying crust of the earth and as it cooled and solidified it contracted to form a series of parallel cracks. Later more molten rock was forced into the cracks and cooled against the granite, forming a smaller grained rock as it solidified, also contracting and becoming seamed with three sets of parallel, intersecting shrinkage cracks. A boulder containing this interface must have broken away from the main mass of granite and rolled down the hillside, part of it breaking away to expose the face. Weathering by rain and other forces has enlarged the cracks, leaving the rock

Chimphamba-Msaka, one of the enclave villages on the Cape Maclear Peninsula. Houses are built close together because of the shortage of flat ground. JUDY CARTER

with its present carved, man-made appearance.[18] *Mwalawamphini* is now a national monument.

Further inland on the peninsula larger rock faces offer a challenge to the rock climber, and paths along the shoreline and over the hills lead to vantage points with views over much of the park. These paths provide land access to the five fishing villages of the peninsula which nestle in enclaves of flatter land by the lakeshore. Some are so short of space because of the surrounding hills that they have scarcely any cultivable land, and villagers rely largely on fish catches for their subsistence. Chembe, the largest of the enclave villages, has more space and grows maize and other crops. These villages are excluded from the land of the park. Villagers collect firewood in parts of the park under licence, as they have no other supplies for smoking fish and cooking with; long term plans exist to establish fuel-wood plantations elsewhere on the peninsula to alleviate the problem.

The land mass of the peninsula shelters its leeward waters to the north-west from the rough lake conditions generated by the dry season *mwera*, and the sheltered anchorage off the Golden Sands site has been much used during the past 100 years. It is an idyllic spot, calm when storms are blowing past the far end of Domwe Island at the northern end of the peninsula. Captain Lugard, visiting the area in 1888

Thumbi Island West, lying offshore from the Cape Maclear Peninsula. JUDY CARTER

in transit to the northern end of the lake to tackle the private war between the African Lakes Company and Arab traders, wrote of it:

The lake here is so clear that the bottom is visible in comparatively deep water, and the many coloured fishes glide about among the rocks and pebbles like gold-fish in a glass globe. Fairy islands, covered with trees, are studded in the foreground; and giant boulders, which have weathered the storms of years on years, long before the foot of the white man trod these solitudes, rear their

Fish eagle, whose evocative cry is a common sound in the Lake Malaŵi National Park. MICHAEL GORE

craggy peaks from the blue water of the lake. Perched aloft sits the magnificent fish-eagle, and every now and then, his weird cry pierces the stillness, and makes it felt. King-fishers of many kinds, and cormorants, and divers, wait patiently at their chosen posts, till, like a flash, they dart into the water to seize their prey, and returning to their posts, all is once more motionless and still. The waves lap gently on the yellow sand, which glistens with crystals of white quartz and yellow mica ... Behind ... rises a giant mass of rock, crowned with euphorbia and silent cactus growth ... Hard on the left towers a gigantic baobab, that strange tree which possesses no twigs, and rarely leaves, and ... looks like some vegetable remnant of a pre-Adamite age, when giant reptiles and huge saurians roamed on lands where man was not.[27]

History of the Lake Malaŵi National Park

Cape Maclear has a long history of human occupation: quartz artefacts thought to date back to the Middle and Late Stone Ages have been found in the area, along with numerous artefacts and pieces of pottery from the early Iron Age (about 300-600 AD). It is known that by AD 1500 the Mang'anja people had settled on the peninsula[19]. Nkhunguni Hill above the present-day Golden Sands was their rainshrine, and when rain was desired they would lay offerings at the foot of a large rock on the summit beside a spring, kneeling and clapping their hands in respect for the spirits. If the spirits favoured rain either a cloud would appear, or the symbol of lightning: a monitor lizard, with only one eye which was considered a sign of greatness.

These people would have inhabited the relatively flat area of land now occupied by Chembe village and the Golden Sands area below Nkhunguni Hill. When David Livingstone and his brother Charles visited the area in 1861 they commented on the well-kept burial ground of these people, in the shade of a magnificent fig tree. Livingstone was on an expedition to explore Lake Malaŵi and find a site suitable for a trading and missionary centre. He was much impressed with the sheltered anchorage on the north-western side of the peninsula, and named the promontory Cape Maclear (see page 17).

The area was visited six years later by Young and Faulkner on the Livingstone Search Expedition. After discovering that the reports of Livingstone's murder had been false, the expedition sought refuge at Cape Maclear from a storm on the lake. They were much taken with the area, Young considering it a very suitable area for the establishment of a settlement. Faulkner[17] typically records the wildlife of the enclave: 'gazelles' and 'reedbock' (some of which he shot); 'a large quantity of guinea-fowl', 'plenty of old buffalo spoor' (evidently dating from the previous rains) and 'a huge alligator' (crocodile). Wildlife was evidently much more abundant in the Cape Maclear area then than it is now and the antelope were not being heavily hunted as they were not wary of him. Faulkner did, however, encounter two Mang'anja hunters in the area, armed with bows and arrows.

The expedition then sailed down the lake towards the Shire River, anchoring in sheltered bays on the way. Faulkner records the large mammals and spoor he encountered in the vicinity of the southern parts of the present-day park: monkeys, elephant tracks, bushbuck and kudu. Again, wild animals were much more abundant than they are now.

In 1873 Livingstone died at Ilala near the Bangweulu Swamps in present day Zambia. His faithful followers carried his embalmed body over 1000 km to Zanzibar, from where it was taken home by sea and buried in Westminster Abbey. As a result of his work a wave of missionary zeal was inspired in Britain, and the Free Church of Scotland planned

the establishment of a mission in Malaŵi funded by Glasgow businessmen, to be called Livingstonia in memory of the great explorer. Besides its evangelical commitment the mission would work in the fields of education, industry and medicine. In 1875 the mission party travelled to Cape Town, and thence up the Zambezi and Shire Rivers to Lake Malaŵi and, led by Young, selected a site for the mission at the south-west end of the Cape Maclear enclave (page 17). They recorded no people living nearby: the Mang'anja encountered by Livingstone and Faulkner must have undergone some upheaval, perhaps because of pressures from slave traders.

The mission party started on the construction of mission buildings and establishment of gardens for fruit and vegetables. Local people began to appear, willing to work at the mission in exchange for cloth. Dr Robert Laws, a medical missionary, treated several cases of fever on the mission, and eventually started to treat the local people and provide a few of them with elementary education.

Wild animals were still abundant in the area and caused problems for the mission. Hyenas and leopards visited the buildings at night, elephants created havoc in the gardens, and on the beaches there were hippos and crocodiles. A lone bull elephant was discovered to be inhabiting the small Mumbo Island 10 km off-

The Livingstonia Mission at Cape Maclear, as sketched by Captain Elton in 1877. The *Ilala* is anchored offshore.   ELTON

shore: it must have swum out at some time and stayed there. During its period of residence it had uprooted many large trees on the island; when it finally succumbed to the shots of an expedition from the mission it was discovered to have an old injury from a heavy iron bullet. The meat was much appreciated by the local people, and its fat was used to grease the engines of the *Ilala*. There is another remarkable report of four elephants, two bulls and two cows, swimming out to Mumbo Island from Chipole on the west side of the lake, in 1881[76].

Over the years the mission became well established under the leadership of Dr Laws. By the early 1880s it had two schools; was conducting a large amount of medical work; had trained local people in many skills; had baptised its first convert; and stimulated the settlement of a large number of people in the area. The health of those at the mission gave cause for concern, however, and as the graveyard of the mission grew, doubts developed about the suitability of the Cape Maclear site. Apart

Short Solent flying boat anchored at Cape Maclear. The British Overseas Airways Corporation ran a flying boat service between Southampton and Johannesburg which stopped overnight at Cape Maclear on Lake Malaŵi in 1949/50.
COLE-KING

from the incidence of malaria there was inadequate space in the enclave for cultivation and soils were poor. Tsetse fly was another hazard. In 1881 the mission moved further north on the lake to Bandawe, leaving the Cape Maclear site as an outpost. Mission activities continued under the charge of Albert Namalambe, the first convert, until 1896 when the station was abandoned. The natural harbour became a port of call for the *Ilala* on its voyages up and down the lake, and later a refuelling station for other wood-burning lake steamers: a fire-wood plantation was established for this purpose.

At the time of the establishment of the Protectorate the mission placed a claim for the land at Cape Maclear, and obtained a certificate for it from the new Administration. The area was illustrated on a sketch map, and included much of the Chembe enclave as well as Nkhunguni Hill and the western shore at its base. The mission had originally obtained the land from Chief Mponda in 1875 in exchange for a flintlock gun, a tin of gunpowder, a dozen flints, a blanket, a quilt and two shirts. In 1942 it was realised that the land of the mission covered a much larger area than had originally been estimated, and consequently land tax had been greatly underpaid by the mission. The embarrassing situation was resolved by

the transfer of land to the Government in 1943 on the payment of £1500 to the Dutch Reform Church, then responsible for Cape Maclear. The Government guaranteed to maintain the graves and permit access to them; they have since been declared a national monument, as has Otter Point because of its outstanding natural beauty.

A lease of part of the old mission land was granted for the construction of a hotel which was opened, north of the mission site, in 1948. Access was by boat, private aircraft, or road during the dry season. In 1949 the British Overseas Airways Corporation (BOAC)'s flying boat service altered its schedules to include Cape Maclear in some of its flights. This service operated between Southampton and Johannesburg, using inland waters such as the Nile, Lake Victoria and the Zambezi or Lake Malaŵi as stopping places *en route*, the passengers staying overnight in hotels. The service was withdrawn after one year for economic reasons, however, and with road access problems to Cape Maclear the hotel's business declined. It was eventually closed in 1951, dismantled, and the materials shipped to Senga Bay where a new hotel was constructed.

A private house was built at the southern end of the bay near Otter Point in 1949-50. This later became the Glengeary Hotel, and was then incorporated into the Golden Sands camp. There is no longer any sign of the mission apart from five graves, though the mission site is protected as a national monument. (Historical information on Cape Maclear:[18].)

In 1934 various forest reserves were declared in the vicinity of Cape Maclear, including many of the islands and some hilly mainland areas. In 1980 they were redesignated as the Lake Malaŵi National Park, along with a few other areas and the nearby inshore waters of the lake.

Chapter Six

The Shire Valley

South of Lake Malaŵi the rift valley continues on, curving to the west round the Shire Highlands and leading down towards Mozambique. Lying in the rainshadow of the plateaux and mountains to the south and east, most of the valley has a low annual rainfall compared with the rest of the country. Temperatures are high, especially in the southern section where the Mozambique coastal plain extends into the rift valley, and most of the area lies less than 150 m above sea-level. Scenery is very varied: in the upper and lowermost sections of the valley alluvial plains and woodlands line the broad, flat valley trough, the more fertile soils being cultivated

The Shire Valley and Elephant Marsh from the Thyolo Escarpment.   LIZ and TONY BOMFORD,   *SURVIVAL ANGLIA*

for cotton and other crops. The middle section in contrast is narrow, rocky and often infertile, and includes many steep hills and ridges.[5]

Along the rift valley floor the Shire River has carved itself a course. The only outlet from Lake Malaŵi, it is the largest river in the country and carries a substantial volume of water except in very dry years. It flows southward down the valley to its confluence with the Zambezi River and thence the Indian Ocean, a total distance of over 500 km. On its way it passes down some spectacular rapids and falls, as well as flowing through flatter areas where in some places its waters spread across the valley to form large swamps and marshes. One of the few perennial rivers in the region, it exerts a large influence on many plant and animal communities as well as on land-use patterns in the valley.

The Shire leaves Lake Malaŵi to the north of Mangochi and flows past the town in a broad channel for a few kilometres until its waters slow down and spread into the wide, shallow Lake Malombe. An extensive stand of palm trees grows on its northern shore, protected as a forest reserve. In former times when the level of Lake Malaŵi was higher this area and Lake Malombe itself were part of the larger lake, the southern shores of which probably extended as far south as the town of Liwonde[5]. Today, however, the Shire River resumes again at the southern end of Lake Malombe, flowing through Liwonde National Park to the town of Liwonde. Lagoons and reed beds occur along the river margins at the southern end of this stretch and the surrounding area is very flat.

The gradient of the upper Shire is very gentle: between the outlet from Lake Malaŵi and Liwonde town, a distance of more than 70 km, the fall in water level is only two metres. For the next 45 km from Liwonde to Matope the level drops by only another seven metres. The upper Shire therefore restricts the drainage of Lake Malaŵi and enables the lake to rise to high levels in wetter years. During the early 1900s when the lake level dropped the Shire stopped flowing altogether and by 1915 Lake Malombe had virtually dried up. Sediments carried down and deposited on the bed of the Shire by two of its tributaries, the Nkasi and Rivi Rivi, created natural dams so that although the level of Lake Malaŵi started to rise again in 1915 the Shire did not breach these barriers and resume its course downstream for another 18 years.[68] The transport system on the river which had been developed in the late 1800s by the European settlers was seriously disrupted[20].

The flow of the Shire and therefore the level of Lake Malaŵi can now be regulated to a certain degree by a barrage which was constructed in 1965 at Liwonde town. Lowering of the barrage gates restricts excess flow, reducing the flow downstream and keeping the lake level high. This is done to ensure adequate flows throughout the year to operate the hydro-electric schemes downstream. They are on the steep middle section of the Shire at Nkula and Tedzani and supply most of Malaŵi's electrical power. Also on this section, water is extracted from the river at Walker's Ferry and pumped south-eastward up the escarpment to the Shire Highlands, providing most of Blantyre and Limbe's domestic and industrial water supplies.

On the middle section of the Shire the river flows rapidly as it drops nearly 400 m from Matope to Chikwawa, forging its way through rocky gorges and

Mpatamanga Gorge on the middle section of the Shire. The river has carved itself a spectacular course through the rocks of this hilly area. JAMES OGLETHORPE

over waterfalls, scouring and cutting ever deeper into the bedrock. There is often little or no floodplain, and on either side the land rises up into dry, broken, hilly country where soils are thin and infertile except in areas with base-rich rocks associated with geological fault-lines. Series of scarps and ridges give rise to some challenging wilderness areas. At the lower end of this section the river flows along the eastern boundary of Majete Game Reserve to plunge down the spectacular Kapichira Falls. These are the last major falls on the Shire and mark the separation between the fish faunas of the lower Zambezi and Lake Malaŵi. Downstream the diversity of fish species is much poorer although it includes several economically important fish. The Kapichira Falls also mark the first major obstacle to navigation up the Shire from the Zambezi River and the Indian Ocean. Dr David Livingstone first encountered them in 1859, and was forced in subsequent expeditions to proceed overland at this point.

Below the falls the Shire commences a more tranquil passage through the flatter area of the lower Shire Valley. By this stage the river has accumulated a fair amount of silt and the swirling waters are a muddy brown colour. Near Chikwawa the river has cut away its west bank to create high red sand cliffs; during the dry season large colonies of carmine bee-eaters nest in holes in the cliff faces. These highly coloured birds flit over the surrounding area during the day, feeding on beetles, grasshoppers and other insects and swooping low across the river to drink on the wing. South of Chikwawa, stretching from the upper edge of the Shire floodplain across a series of lowlying ridges to the western Mozambique border is

Area in the Shire Valley heavily grazed by livestock. JANET and JOHN HOUGH

Lengwe National Park, protecting a large population of nyala antelope.

On the fertile, alluvial plain between Lengwe National Park and the Shire River lies a large sugar estate, irrigated with water from the Shire. Elsewhere in the fertile parts of the lower Shire Valley cotton and rice are grown, as well as subsistence crops. In less fertile areas cattle and goats graze extensively. Some areas are overgrazed, becoming dusty deserts in the dry season; the problem is exacerbated by frequent outbreaks of foot-and-mouth disease which limit offtake due to meat transport restrictions to the major markets further north.

The Elephant Marsh

East of Nchalo, on the other side of the Shire the land is lowlying, and water leaves the main channel to spread into a huge area of marsh and swamp. About 15 km across at its widest, the marsh continues southwards for over 40 km, a mosaic of islands, lagoons and reedbeds interlinked by deep, tortuous channels of peat-coloured water. The area was named Elephant Marsh by Livingstone's expedition when in 1859 it navigated the main channel *through a vast evil-smelling swamp where hundreds of elephants were moving like grey galleons across the boggy waste*[77].

The significance of the Elephant Marsh was recognised in the early days of the Protectorate when for 14 years it had game reserve status. Although the elephants have now long since gone, the name a nostalgic reminder of another era, other wild animals do still frequent the marsh. Many crocodile inhabit its waters and may occasionally be seen basking on the sandbanks; the marsh has the largest crocodile population in the country[54]. It is also a haven for water birds: egrets and reed cormorants nest in colonies in clumps of tall *Phragmites* and papyrus reed; spoonbills wade in the shallows hunting for small fish and aquatic invertebrates; squacco herons skulk solitarily in the reeds; lines of pelicans glide by in stately fashion; and African jacanas hunt busily for insects and snails, running on their long toes across the waterlily leaves while the call of the fish eagle is all pervasive.

The marsh is a paradise for the bird-watcher and photographer, and one of the best ways of seeing it is from a rowing boat on the lagoons upstream from Chiromo. By punting silently past reedbeds and across lagoons carpeted with waterlilies, the Thyolo Escarpment blue in the distance, it is possible to approach close to the waterbirds and watch them

African spoonbill, which probes the mud with its unusually shaped bill or sweeps it from side to side in the water to obtain food.   MICHAEL GORE

African jacana. Its long toes enable it to move quickly over floating plants on the surface of the water: hence its other name 'lily-trotter'.   MICHAEL GORE

Great white egret, usually a solitary bird which stalks slowly, watching for fish, frogs, insects and small mammals.
MICHAEL GORE

Reed cormorant drying its wings in the Elephant Marsh.
MICHAEL GORE

feeding, preening and looking after their chicks. Also of interest are the traditional fishing techniques used by the local people, mostly from dugout canoes: gill-netting; fishing with hook and line; setting wickerwork traps; and cast-netting. The latter involves throwing a weighted net over the water from a canoe and drawing it in to remove any fish trapped inside. The marsh harbours large populations of fish: along with the Ndinde Marsh in the south, in 1979 the Elephant Marsh yielded an estimated catch of 3361 metric tonnes[46].

Another important animal of the marsh is the hippo. Normally it spends the daytime in the water, playing a significant role in maintaining the network of channels through the marsh by preventing them from becoming choked with silt and reeds. It also augments the productivity of the fishery by stirring

Cast-netting on the Elephant Marsh. The weighted net is swung round and round above the head of the fisherman and released to fall on the water. It is then drawn in, often with fish trapped inside. JUDY CARTER

growth of grass which develops on the newly exposed damp ground. When the waters rise again with the following rains they retreat to higher ground, the dung deposited on the floodplains enhancing the productivity of the system.

Small-scale cultivation occurs on the rich alluvial soils around the margins of the marsh. When the Shire stopped flowing in the early 1900s the Elephant Marsh dried out completely and much of the exposed fertile land was brought under cultivation for cotton and food crops; severe disruptions resulted when the flow of the Shire was resumed and the area was again flooded[3]. Long-term plans have been proposed to drain the marsh for large-scale cultivation, although the technical problems would be great. Should this ever happen, the great wetland wilderness of the Elephant Marsh and its associated wildlife would be lost. Unfortunately the area is no longer legally protected as a reserve.

A more insidious threat is that of agricultural chemicals: a variety of herbicides, insecticides and molluscicides is used to control weeds, insect pests and the bilharzia snail on the sugar and cotton estates of the lower Shire Valley. Some of the chemicals are moderately or very persistent, particularly those applied to cotton which include DDT and the organophosphate dimethoate.[33] Such chemicals remain in the environment for long periods and they could be washed into tributaries of the Shire during the rains, ending up in the Elephant Marsh. There the water movement is very slow and evaporation rate is high, so it is possible that the marsh could be a reservoir for persistent toxic pesticides. It is well known that DDT can become concentrated in food chains, the tissues of carnivorous animals at the top of the chain containing much higher concentrations of chemical than the plants at the bottom. Amongst those at the top of the chain in the Elephant Marsh are predatory fish, birds of prey and man.

At the southern end of the marsh near Chiromo the Shire is joined by its tributary the Ruo, which rises on Mulanje Mountain to the north-east and flows down a steep valley on the eastern border with Mozambique. South of Chiromo the border follows the Shire, and Malaŵi territory narrows to cover only the western side of the valley between the main river channel and the watershed of the Shire and Zambezi basins. Mwabvi Game Reserve lies here, the southernmost protected wildlife area in the country. The Shire eventually leaves Malaŵi as it flows through the Ndinde Marsh east of the Matundu Hills, towards its confluence with the mighty Zambezi.

up the bottom mud and causing the release of nutrients trapped there, as well as further fertilising the water by defecating in it. At night it emerges from the marsh to graze on adjacent floodplains, returning early in the morning before the sun becomes too hot. The floodplains are also grazed by cattle which follow the receding waters of the marsh as the dry season progresses to consume the new

Name derivation

From the chieftainship of Liwonde: the establishment of the park arose from the desire of a former Chief Liwonde to have the area protected. The original derivation of the name is unknown.

Declaration

In 1962 much of the park was declared a controlled hunting area. The national park was gazetted in 1973, and expanded in 1977 to include the northern area.

Present size

548 km^2

Location

Southern Malaŵi on the upper Shire River and south-eastern shore of Lake Malombe, extending mostly eastward but including a northern section connecting with Mangochi Forest Reserve, and a strip 914 m wide on the western bank of the Shire.

Landscape types

Shire River, Lake Malombe and the surrounding alluvial plain which is traversed by drainage lines; and three isolated groups of hills.

Vegetation

Aquatic communities by the river and lake, including extensive reed beds, and water lilies in lagoons; floodplain grassland and riverine thicket above the river, with riverine forest along the major tributaries; palm savanna along the edge of the floodplain in the south; deciduous tree savanna and woodland including many baobabs and stands of mopane on higher ground, with small areas of thicket and dry forest; savanna woodland on hills.

Large mammals

Most commonly seen: elephant, warthog, hippo, sable antelope, waterbuck, kudu, bushbuck and baboon. Also occurring: vervet monkey, pangolin, side-striped jackal, Cape clawless and spotted-necked otters, ratel, civet, various mongoose species, spotted hyena, lion, leopard, wild cat, genet, aardvark, bushpig, grey duiker, reedbuck, impala, klipspringer, oribi, grysbok, porcupine.

Birds

Nearly 300 bird species have been recorded in the park, in the aquatic habitats, floodplain grassland and lowland woodland and thicket. Large colonies of white-breasted cormorants nest by the Shire River and the park has the only population of Lilian's lovebird in the country. The

Liwonde National Park[19,31]

park has the most northerly protected lowland evergreen thicket in Malaŵi, with associated birds such as Livingstone's flycatcher and Böhm's bee-eater.

Other animals

Crocodile are numerous in the Shire River, and water monitor lizard is common. Many fish species occur in the river, including the sporting *sungwa*. African mud turtle occurs in the Shire and Lake Malombe.

Sites of special interest

The Shire River, Lake Malombe, Chiunguni Hill.

Access

Road: the main road access is via the M1 Lilongwe — Blantyre road. Turn off the M1 south of the barrage on the Shire to Liwonde town, following a tarred road for a few hundred metres to crossroads. Turn right here on to the D221 and follow it for about 3 km. Turn left down a signed, untarred road which crosses the railway line and reaches the park entrance after 2.5 km. This last section of road can be inaccessible for saloon cars during the rains.

Distances from the main centres to the entrance gate in the south of the park:

Blantyre:	123 km
Zomba:	57 km
Lilongwe:	236 km

Inside the park there is a network of untarred roads as shown on map 6.1, mostly passable in the dry season only. The park is closed to vehicles during the rains (approximately December to April).

Boat: access by small boat is normally from the launching site just upstream of the barrage on the east bank. An untarred road leads off the M1 just south of the barrage. Follow it upwards to a lefthand turn: this leads to the launching site. Access is also possible from Lake Malaŵi via Lake Malombe, by arrangement with the park management.

By air: there is a grass-surface airstrip suitable for light aircraft at Makanga, near Mvuu Camp.

Visitor facilities

The Kudya Discovery Lodge situated on the west bank of the Shire south of the park offers licensed, catering accommodation. Within the park Mvuu Camp by the Shire River has self-catering accommodation for visitors in eight rondavels, each sleeping two to three people. Cooking is done over open fireplaces or in a communal kitchen: firewood is provided. Running water is being installed to the kitchen and a new ablution block; it is pumped from the Shire and all drinking water must be boiled. There is no electricity at the camp. At the time of writing all bedding, food, cooking and eating utensils, etc. must be brought by visitors.

Continued

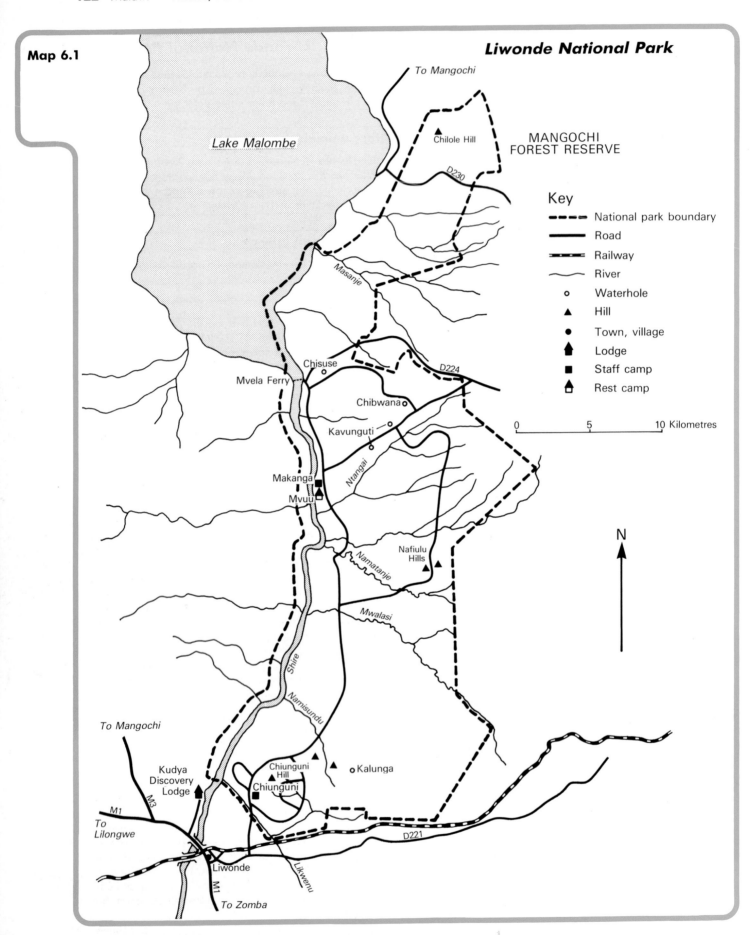

Map 6.1

Liwonde National Park

Lake Malombe

To Mangochi

Chilole Hill

MANGOCHI
FOREST RESERVE

D230

Masanje

D224

Chisuse

Mvela Ferry

Chibwana

Kavunguti

Ntangai

Makanga

Mvuu

Nafiulu
Hills

Namatanje

Mwalasi

Shire

Namisundu

To Mangochi

Kudya
Discovery
Lodge

Chiunguni
Hill

Chiunguni

Kalunga

M3

M1

To
Lilongwe

D221

Liwonde

Likwenu

M1

To Zomba

N

Key

- - - National park boundary
——— Road
—·—·— Railway
——— River
○ Waterhole
▲ Hill
● Town, village
⬟ Lodge
■ Staff camp
⌂ Rest camp

0   5   10 Kilometres

The service of a game-scout guide may be arranged with the park management. If not in use for management purposes, it is possible to hire the park boat.

Visitor activities

Game-viewing, bird-watching, walking, boat trips, photography.

Administrative arrangements

Reservations for the Kudya Discovery Lodge should be made through Budget Travel and Safaris, PO Box 2839, Blantyre, tel. 634 666, telex 4168 MI.

Reservations for accommodation and the hire of the boat should be made to the Parks and Wildlife Officer, Box 41, Liwonde (tel 532 308). Requests for a game-scout guide can be made at the park.

Park fees are charged for visitors, their vehicles and boats, and for accommodation.

Best time to visit

Game-viewing: August to November
Bird-watching: November to December
Walking: July to September
Photography: throughout the year
Scenery: throughout the year

Note that the internal roads are closed during the rains (approximately December to April) but access by boat is possible throughout the year. From June to August inclusive temperatures in the park are pleasantly warm. They can be uncomfortably hot from September to November; the rest of the year is intermediate.

Liwonde National Park

At the upper end of the Shire Valley lies Liwonde National Park, a flat, fertile area dominated by the Shire River. One of the most centrally located parks, it is close enough to Blantyre and Zomba for a day visit and even on a short game-viewing drive in the dry season through the woodland to the river it is possible to see waterbuck, sable antelope, elephant and hippo. An overnight stay at Mvuu (Hippo) Camp by the Shire River gives more time to appreciate the park's outstanding scenery and great abundance of wild animals. After cooking supper in the twilight over an open fireplace to a chorus of hippo in the river, darkness sets in beyond the glow of the campfire, broken only by regular pinpoint flashes of light from fireflies. As the white-breasted cormorants in the nearby trees finally settle to roost for the night other sounds become suddenly apparent: the incessant croaking of frogs and chirring of cicadas and perhaps the cough of a leopard. Early in the morning mist rises from the river and cormorants fly low over the water. A late hippo plods ponderously back to the river, creating a bow-wave which stirs the reeds as he plunges into the water.

This is a good hour for a game-viewing drive, as many animals will be feeding in the open or returning from drinking at the river during the cooler hours. A short walk with a guide from Mvuu Camp in the woodland or by the river may provide views of elephant, waterbuck, bushbuck and crocodile, and perhaps impala grazing on the short grass of the airstrip at Makanga. For the more energetic, a long walk by the edge of the Lake Malombe floodplain

The Shire River in Liwonde National Park, with white-breasted cormorants roosting in the dead trees along the riverbank.
DAVE WOODFALL

and the woodland behind provides a taste of the true wilderness of Liwonde National Park: here there are no roads or people, and herds of sable graze undisturbed in the mopane while elephant browse in the shade of riverine woodland. The park has a great

Mvuu Camp on the Shire River, Liwonde National Park.
JUDY CARTER

diversity of habitat types, from the Shire River with its reed beds and lagoons, and the floodplains which flank it on higher ground, to the woodlands and isolated hills beyond. Much of the area has fertile alluvial soils and the carrying capacity of the park is high.

History of Liwonde National Park

The exceptional wildlife of the area has long been documented: Faulkner commented on the abundance and diversity of game animals in 1867 *from the elephant to the smallest antelope* which he saw from the vessel *Search* whilst sailing up the Shire through the present-day park area. He deeply regretted that he had no chance to hunt because the expedition was favoured with a good wind and consequently did not stop there during the day[17]. Many of the early European explorers and missionaries used the Shire

River as their main access route to Lake Malaŵi from the Indian Ocean and Livingstone sailed through the area of the present-day park on his way to explore Lake Malaŵi in 1861, having marched by it on foot two years earlier when he first set eyes on 'the lake of stars'[77].

In the past there was little human settlement in the park area, except on the raised land between Mvela Ferry and Mvuu Camp[54]. The rest of the area was probably unattractive because of seasonal flooding in lowlying areas and the difficulty of cultivating the heavy black cotton soils which occur in much of the woodland. Tsetse fly, still present today, would have precluded the keeping of cattle because of the fatal *ngana* disease they transmit. It is likely that the present park area was however used by people from settlements outside, visiting the area temporarily to hunt, fish, and gather fruits[19]; their subsistence hunting activities are likely to have had relatively little impact on the wild animal populations.

With the establishment of the Protectorate and the creation of the capital town at nearby Zomba, however, European hunters started to frequent the area and by the 1920s the animal populations were becoming severely depleted. Hippo were considered a threat to boats on the river and were being heavily shot, and eland were eliminated completely. In 1949 efforts were made to exterminate the Liwonde elephants, fortunately unsuccessful. Eventually concern about the status of the remaining wildlife led to the declaration of a controlled hunting area in 1962, followed by the gazettement of the park in 1973 and its extension in 1977; Chief Liwonde was largely responsible for initiating the protection of the area. Unfortunately in the meantime buffalo, zebra and hartebeest had disappeared.[19] The park now covers an area adequate for the ranges of most species, and Lake Malombe and the Shire River provide perennial water. Under protection the populations of wild animals are again abundant, albeit with a lower diversity than in Faulkner's day. Zebra and buffalo were reintroduced in 1985, though the success of the operation is not yet certain.

Vegetation and animals of Liwonde National Park

The Shire River is the most impressive feature of the park, flowing slowly past reed- and palm-lined banks,

Hippo fighting. Male hippo defend their aquatic territories fiercely, often inflicting deep wounds on their opponents.
MICHAEL GORE

carrying with it large rafts of papyrus reed and pale green water lettuce. As it passes Chiunguni Hill in the south of the park it is flanked by extensive water-lilied lagoons, completely screened from the outside by almost impenetrable reedbeds and harbouring many aquatic birds: a miniature Elephant Marsh. Hippo abound, both here and along the main channel where schools of them may be observed resting on sandbanks or submerged with only the tops of their heads above the water, interrupted occasionally as a territorial male threatens a potential rival with a huge gaping mouth and challenging bellow.

Further upstream the river broadens out until the opposite banks are far apart, becoming shimmering mirages on bright, hot days above the shallow waters of Lake Malombe. Here there is very little current, and the heads of African mud turtles may be seen above the water on calm days, swimming hastily away if disturbed. The lake and river have large fish populations including *sungwa*, a fish much sought after by anglers outside the boundaries of the park. The fish support many species of birds, one of the most numerous being the white-breasted cormorant which roosts and nests in large colonies in trees along the river bank. Ospreys are a common sight on the river, poised on a dead tree by the water's edge or flying over the river watching for fish, hovering for a moment before dropping to the water with a splash to grab the prey in their talons: fish eagles

sometimes persecute them for their catches. Less common is Pel's fishing owl, though sometimes a pair may be seen in the late afternoon, hunting from perches on the river bank. Their featherless legs, long claws and horny scales on the underside of the feet equip them well for fishing, though they may also feed on small animals and even guineafowl[60].

Another important predator of the river is the crocodile: the park has a large population which has greatly increased in size during the past ten years with protection from hunting. A favourite daytime haunt in the dry season is the sandbanks downstream from Mvuu Camp, where they may be seen from a boat basking in the sun, especially early in the morning and late in the afternoon. During the hottest part of the day they may return to the water or retreat to the shade by the reeds, their jaws open to allow evaporation of water from the mouth which helps to cool them. At night they return to the water, often floating in the current with only their eyes and nostrils above the surface. A spotlight shone from a boat reveals hundreds of pairs of hungry yellow eyes on the dark water: nowhere is it safe to swim in the park, despite the temptation of the rippled blue waters on a hot sunny day.

Animals drinking from the river bank risk attack by crocodile, the hunting technique being to grab an animal unawares from the water and pull it under, holding it there until it drowns. The reptile can then consume its prey at leisure. An adult crocodile is able to take a large mammal such as a sable antelope despite the considerable size of the latter: the crocodile is thought to be aided in the struggle by the curious presence of stones in its stomach which provide extra weight. The stones also act as ballast, enabling the crocodile to lie submerged on the river bottom and lowering its centre of gravity to increase its stability whilst swimming due to the ventral location of the stomach and stones. The stones consistently comprise one per cent of the adult crocodiles' body weight; they are not found in young animals.

Crocodiles play a complicated role in the food web. The young hatchlings, only 30 cm long, feed entirely on insects such as mosquito larvae, water-bugs, dragonfly nymphs and beetles. As they grow larger their diet changes to include snails, frogs, toads, rodents and small birds until fish becomes a major component; older animals concentrate increasingly on large mammals and reptiles. Crocodiles themselves have many enemies, especially when young. Eggs buried in nests in the sandbanks are

Large crocodile can often be seen on sandbanks by the side of the Shire. The number of crocodile has increased dramatically since 1973 when the park was declared and they were protected from hunting. DENIS TWEDDLE

often raided by monitor lizards, baboons and mongooses, if they can get past the guard of the female crocodile. Hatchlings often suffer high mortality from predators such as the monitor lizard, marabou and saddlebill stork, great white egret and fish eagle, despite the fact that the female guards them for the first three months or so in a nursery area of slack water. (Information on crocodiles:[78].)

The Shire River therefore supports a very intricate and productive system with a high diversity of animals. It does not function in isolation from the surrounding areas, however. Many of its animals rely on food from the terrestrial areas of the park: the hippo and adult crocodile, for example. The floodplains on either side of the river are traversed by distinctive, broad, double-grooved tracks leading from the river to the hippos' grazing grounds, used regularly on their nocturnal forays. Narrower tracks indicate where elephant and various antelope species venture to the river bank and lakeshore to drink. As the dry season progresses these tracks become more heavily used, and at this time of year game-viewing from a boat on the river is excellent. Many of the animals return east and northwards when the next rains start and water is again available in temporary pools and streams on the other side of the park.

As the rains fall the Shire River rises, covering all or part of the low-lying floodplains and depositing silt on them which enhances the fertility of the grassland in the following growing season. Reedbuck and waterbuck remain in this area throughout the year, following the receding water of the Shire for the grass which grows on the damp soil of newly exposed areas. The oribi antelope is more sedentary than the reedbuck and waterbuck as it holds small territories, usually in pairs. Warthog frequent the higher margins of the floodplain, feeding on grasses and roots. There is a wide floodplain north-west of Chiunguni Hill and another by the shores of Lake Malombe; elsewhere the floodplain is narrower, giving way to savanna and woodland on higher ground.

In places the floodplains are fringed with fan palms, tall trees with a strange swelling on the upper

part of the trunk and crowned with grey-green fronds which rustle in the breeze. They produce spherical fruits with a hard brown shell and a thin, edible layer of pulp around the large seed. Each fruit takes two years to mature and up to another two to fall; they are a favourite food of elephant and baboon[65]. Before the park was established palms in the area were tapped by local people for their sweet sap[19]: in this activity the very tip of the tree is removed and a container is placed underneath a funnel to catch the sap as it drips out. Left to ferment the sap becomes palm beer, known locally as *nchema*. The practice of tapping destroys the trees, however, and has now been banned by law in Malaŵi.[66]

Some habitat changes have recently occurred in this part of the park. The exceptionally high water levels of Lake Malaŵi in the late 1970s resulted in abnormally high levels of the Shire River, possibly aggravated in 1978 by the experimental closure of the Liwonde Barrage. The extent of flooding increased and the water-table rose, causing a shift to a more water-tolerant vegetation. The effect has now been alleviated as levels of the Shire have again dropped, but dead palms and other trees may still be seen in

Male waterbuck. These selective grazers frequent the floodplains of the park.   DENIS TWEDDLE

Sable antelope which frequent the woodland of the park, grazing in the open glades.   DENIS TWEDDLE

places on the margins of the floodplain.

Occasionally there is no floodplain at all by the Shire, the river being flanked by dense thicket. Another palm occurs here, the wild date palm, with dark green feather-like fronds and edible fruits similar to commercial dates. Small fever trees and other thorny *Acacias* make the thickets difficult to penetrate. Along the main tributaries of the Shire there is a narrow ribbon of riverine forest, including fig trees and tall specimens of the Natal mahogany tree. Its dense, dark, evergreen canopy provides considerable shade, and elephant often frequent the waterless sandy riverbeds during the middle of the day in the dry season, escaping from the shimmering heat outside. Bushbuck live in these forests, and may often be seen watching warily from the shadows.

To either side of the tributaries, beyond the floodplains, lie extensive savannas and woodlands. On areas of poorly drained black cotton soils much of the woodland comprises almost pure stands of mopane. Some of the individual trees reach a great height for the species, and the area is much used by sable antelope which graze the short grass in the glades of the woodland. There are estimated to be over 1000 sable altogether in the park, sometimes occurring in herds of up to 100 animals: perhaps one of the highest densities in Africa. During the dry season they are often seen crossing the floodplain below Chiunguni Hill early in the morning and late in the afternoon, moving between the woodland and the Shire River.

Woodland elsewhere in the park is more varied,

A strangler vine entwined around a mopane tree. These vines are very common in the woodland.   MICHAEL GORE

often including the striking, white-barked *Sterculia africana*. In the dry season the Sabi star adds a splash of colour to the dry, brown landscape: sometimes also known as the impala lily, this low bush produces showy pink flowers on its leafless, smooth grey stems. Strangler vines are much in evidence, entwined around the trunks of trees, looped and dangling from the canopy, giving the woodland a somewhat sinister air. Another conspicuous plant in the woodlands and savannas is the candelabra tree, its thick, evergreen winged branches bearing sharp spines. It also grows in Namalombo Thicket, an area of dry forest on the eastern boundary. Baobabs are scattered throughout the woodland, and there is one magnificent speci-

men at Mvela Ferry. It is entwined by a strangler fig, with a hollow space inside which is used for shelter by local people when waiting for the ferry. There is a right of way across the park at this point, from the north-west bank of the Shire to villages east of the park.

Although much of the park is lowlying and flat, three groups of hills rise above the surrounding plains. The highest is Chiunguni Hill, an interesting horseshoe-shaped ridge rising more than 400 m above the Shire River, formed by intrusion of igneous rock. On its steep rocky slopes baboons are common, their calls echoing through the open woodland. Leopard also occur, and kudu frequent the wooded areas at the base of the hill. Chiunguni is a rain-shrine, and it is believed locally that the vegetation on the hill must be burnt each dry season to ensure good rains

Böhm's bee-eater, which frequents the thickets and riverine forests of the park.   MICHAEL GORE

for the following year's crops. Consequently, despite its national park status, local people venture in most years to set fire to the vegetation on the hill.[79] After the fires walking on the hill is easier and it is possible to clamber up the steep rocky slope from Chiunguni airstrip, or have a longer but less strenuous walk along the ridge from either end of the horseshoe.

Views from the summit of the ridge are spectacular on a clear day. Lake Malombe shimmers in the distance, light reflecting off the Shire River as it flows southwards, winding through the reedbeds and past the lagoons which lie close to Chiunguni. Away from the river the twin peaks of the smaller Nafiulu Hills protrude from the woodland. Outside the park to the south-east lie the hills of Liwonde Forest Reserve, and to the west in the blue distance is the massive Kirk Range. North-east of Lake Malombe the hills of Mangochi Forest Reserve rise up from the surrounding plains: these are used during the wet season by some of the park's elephant (page 52). In 1977 the national park was extended to include a northern section east of Lake Malombe, connecting with the forest reserve to ensure a migration corridor for these animals. As the water sources in the forest reserve and eastern areas of the park dry out after the end of the rains the elephant concentrate near the Shire River, where they feed in the swamps and nearby woodland, bathing and drinking in the river. They exert a significant impact on the vegetation, and in a few isolated locations have damaged and destroyed trees. A few elephants sometimes behave aggressively towards vehicles and should be treated with respect by visitors driving in the park.

Not all the animals of the woodland are large. Packs of banded mongooses are a common sight, foraging busily in the undergrowth and calling noisily to one another. Each pack has within its territory a series of warrens excavated in old termite mounds or hollow trees. When they are on the move the mongooses follow one another closely, winding through the bush like a huge snake. Their diet is varied and includes insects, amphibians, reptiles, birds and birds' eggs, as well as fruits and bulbs[53]. Overhead the occasional flock of Lilian's lovebird may be seen, the birds chattering shrilly to one another as they fly through the canopy with a flash of green and pink. The park is the only place in Malaŵi where this brightly coloured bird occurs.

Development threats

Liwonde National Park is one of the richest wildlife areas in the country, and it attracts many visitors each year. There are, however, various existing and proposed developments which could potentially disrupt the system as it is today[31]. The Liwonde Barrage has already been mentioned: its present operating regime probably has relatively little effect on the park, but should it be changed for any reason in the future the park could undergo further habitat changes. More serious is the possibility of the construction of a dam for a new hydro-electric plant at Kholombidzo Falls downstream from the barrage: this and the Kapichira Falls in Majete Game Reserve are two sites short-listed for the next power station on the Shire. The reservoir which would be created by a dam at Kholombidzo would probably flood back into the park, altering the water regime and habitats of all the lower-lying areas. Certain animal species could lose their favoured habitats and might disappear completely from the area. If the system were allowed to stabilise with the development of new habitats, however, other animals would eventually move in and exploit them. The nature of the water level fluctuations could be a critical factor in determining the degree of stability of the system.

Another potential threat to the area is the possible development of a water transport system on the Shire between Lake Malaŵi and Liwonde town where there is an existing railhead and favourable conditions for industrial development. The route could be used to transport imported goods to the north of the country, and agricultural produce and fish south to the railhead. Forest products could be shipped down from the plantations on the Viphya Plateau. Such a scheme would involve dredging a navigable channel in the river and through Lake Malombe, affecting aquatic habitats and animals. The wash from cargo boats could cause erosion of the river banks, and the noise of engines and people could seriously disturb the wild animals in the vicinity; the wilderness atmosphere of the Shire would be lost.

Lake Malombe is partly floored by argillaceous limestones which are a potential source of natural cement[6]. Should they ever be commercially exploited there could be serious environmental consequences for the park.

So far these schemes are only ideas on paper. Should they ever be considered seriously, it is to be hoped that adequate environmental impact assessments would be made and if any developments did take place, they should be designed and operated in such a way as to have minimal adverse impact on the park.

Map 6.2   *Majete Game Reserve*

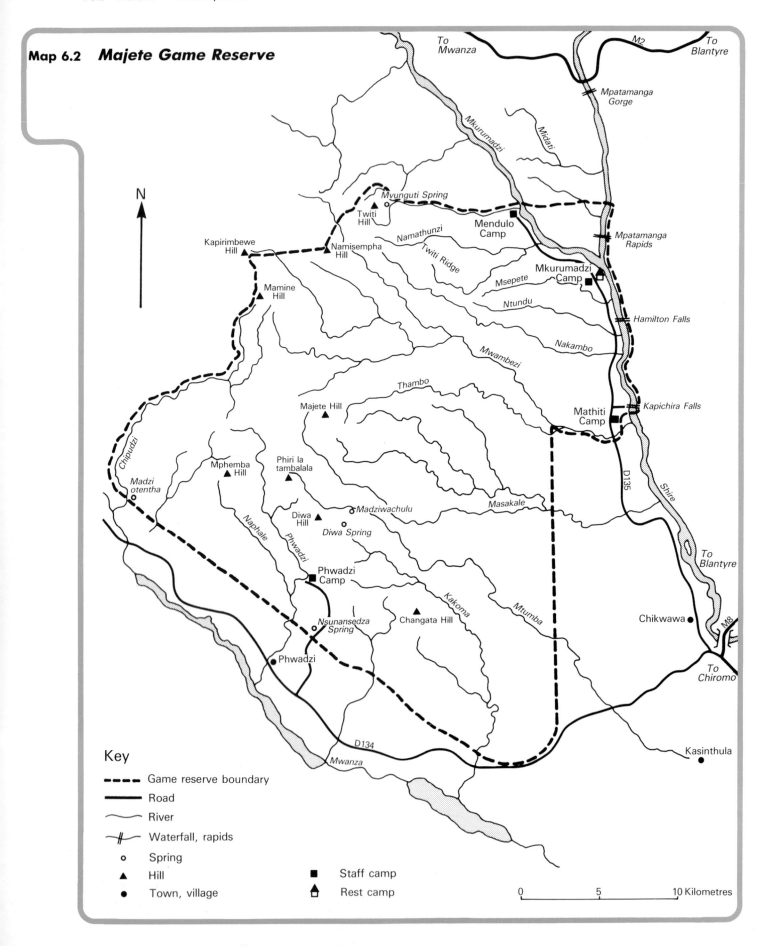

Key

- - - -   Game reserve boundary
──────   Road
~~~~~~   River
─╫─╫─   Waterfall, rapids
○   Spring
▲   Hill
●   Town, village
■   Staff camp
⌂   Rest camp

0   5   10 Kilometres

Majete Game Reserve[19,31,80]

Name derivation

From Majete Hill, a very conspicuous hill in the centre of the reserve. The original derivation of the name is unknown.

Declaration

In 1951 the area around Majete Hill was gazetted as a non-hunting controlled area, and in 1955 a game reserve was gazetted which included this area. Further extensions occurred in 1969 to include dry season water sources, and 1976 to include the full width of the Shire River.

Present size

691 km^2

Location

Southern Malaŵi, on the west side of the southern middle Shire Valley.

Landscape type

Rugged, sloping terrain consisting of a series of faults and ridges, with isolated hills in the centre and west; narrow valleys, including those of the Shire and Mkurumadzi Rivers.

Vegetation

Brachystegia woodland in the west with isolated clumps of bamboo; *Combretum/Terminalia* woodland and a small area of thicket in the east; narrow floodplains in places along the major rivers.

Large mammals

Most commonly seen: kudu, waterbuck, bushbuck, grey duiker, warthog, baboon. Also occurring: vervet monkey, ratel, civet, various species of mongoose, spotted hyena, leopard, aardvark, elephant, dassie, zebra, bushpig, hippo, buffalo, reedbuck, sable antelope, klipspringer, Livingstone's suni, grysbok, porcupine.

Birds

Birds of *Brachystegia* and *Combretum/Terminalia* woodland, and riverine birds by the Shire and Mkurumadzi Rivers. The reserve harbours some of the few rock pratincoles known to breed in Malaŵi. Over 140 species have been recorded so far.

Other animals

Crocodile occur in the Shire River. The reserve contains fish species of both the Lake Malaŵi and Lower Zambezi faunas, separated by the Kapichira Falls. The latter includes tigerfish.

Sites of special interest

Kapichira Falls, Mpatamanga Rapids and the rest of the Shire River; the Mkurumadzi River; perennial waterholes and a hot spring in the west; and Majete, Mphemba, Diwa, Phiri la tambalala, Twiti, Dam and Changata Hills.

Access

The M8 Blantyre — Chiromo road should be followed to the turnoff to Chikwawa, west of the Shire River. This is the untarred D135 which leads through Chikwawa to Kapichira Falls, a distance of 19 km. It is passable for saloon cars in the dry season and for four-wheel-drive vehicles throughout the year, except immediately after heavy rain. A left-hand turn off this road at the barrier near the game-scout camp just before Kapichira Falls leads further into the reserve, following the Shire River to Mkurumadzi Camp and then along the Mkurumadzi River to the game-scout camp at Mendulo as shown on Map 6.2. These roads are passable during the dry season for saloon cars with high clearance, if driven with care.

Another track leads into the reserve on the west side, from the D134 Chikwawa — Mwanza Road: it goes to Phwadzi game-scout camp. At the time of writing, however, it was in very bad condition. There are no other internal roads open to visitors at the time of writing.

Distances from the main centres to Kapichira Falls:

Blantyre: 67 km
Zomba: 133 km
Lilongwe: 414 km

There is no airstrip in the reserve.

It is possible to enter the reserve by boat on the Shire River from downstream, as far as the foot of Kapichira Falls, or to walk in from the M2 in the north down the side of the Shire River, by prior arrangement with the Parks and Wildlife Officer, Lengwe.

Visitor facilities

Mkurumadzi Camp has one chalet with two double rooms and a separate kitchen/ablution block nearby. It is self-catering and visitors must take their own bedding, cooking and eating utensils. Camping is also possible in the grounds. Water is drawn from the river, and should be boiled before drinking. There is no electric power supply at Mkurumadzi Camp. Game-scout guides are available to accompany visitors in the reserve, by vehicle or on foot, if requested well in advance.

Visitor activities

Viewing Kapichira Falls, walking, bird-watching, game-

Continued

viewing, photography, fishing for tigerfish below Kapichira Falls.

Administrative arrangements

Reservations for accommodation and a game-scout guide should be made to the Parks and Wildlife Officer, Lengwe National Park, Box 25, Chikwawa (tel. Chikwawa 0 1203). It is necessary to be accompanied by a guide when walking in the reserve.

Reserve fees at the time of writing: no fees are charged to visitors going only to Kapichira Falls, but are charged to day and overnight visitors who go further into the reserve; no permits are necessary for tigerfishing.

Best time to visit

Game-viewing:	June to October
Bird-watching:	November to December
Walking:	June to September
Viewing falls:	February to July
Photography:	all year
Angling:	October to November

Note that the internal roads are closed during the rains (approximately December to April). During June to August inclusive temperatures are pleasantly warm. September to November can be uncomfortably hot in the reserve. The rest of the year is intermediate.

Majete Game Reserve

Just before the Shire pounds down the Mpatamanga Rapids, creating standing waves and rainbows of spray, it enters Majete Game Reserve. Although close to Blantyre this reserve is little known apart from the Kapichira Falls, and the interior remains a true wilderness. It lies between the Shire River and the Mwanza Valley, a triangle of land sloping down to the south-east. The terrain is much dissected by a series of faults and ridges, and isolated hills rise from the main ridges in the west. Majete Game Reserve is part of the rugged middle Shire Valley and is a dry area whose broken topography gives rise to wild, spectacular scenery, enhanced by the rapids and falls of the Shire itself. The carrying capacity of the reserve for wild animals has not yet been studied in detail: some areas have soils with relatively high

Mpatamanga Rapids on the Shire River, Majete Game Reserve. JUDY CARTER

fertility, and the presence of perennial water in the Shire and Mkurumadzi Rivers on the east side and springs in the west ensures the survival of many water-dependent species including elephant, waterbuck and sable antelope.

History of Majete Game Reserve

These water sources were probably also responsible for the surprisingly high use made of the area by local people before the declaration of the reserve. Livingstone's expedition recorded a group of Maravi people occupying the land in the triangle formed by the west bank of the Shire and the south bank of the Mkurumadzi under the leadership of Chief Kaphwiti, whose capital was near Kapichira Falls[8]. Pottery fragments found in the reserve indicate earlier human presence and it has been suggested that the banks of the Shire and Mkurumadzi were settled for some time, the hinterland being used perhaps for temporary settlements in the wet season with permanent camps near springs. These people would have cultivated the land and hunted wild animals for meat and skins. Their impact on the wildlife was probably very significant, not only through the loss of habitat to cultivation and the effects of hunting, but through loss of access to water in the dry season.[80]

Livingstone saw the area on various occasions during his expeditions to present-day Malaŵi. In 1859 he reached Kapichira Falls for the first time from the Zambezi in the steamer *Ma Robert*: he painted a large VR and the date in red on a prominent rock at the bottom of the cataracts and

The wilderness of western Majete Game Reserve, looking towards the lower Shire River.   JUDY CARTER

named them after his influential friend Murchison[77]. The name was later changed to Livingstone and then Kapichira Falls, one possible derivation of the latter being from the Chichewa *ku pachira*, meaning 'to load up'[80]. While the Shire was being used as an access route to the north by the early missionaries and explorers, porterage was neccessary along the west bank to pass the rapids of the middle Shire. A well-trodden path already existed around them, and Livingstone planned to widen it into a road, along which the dismantled sections of a steamer could be carried on wagons, to be reassembled at the top of the rapids and sailed to Lake Malaŵi. In 1863 he started work on the road and succeeded in driving a mule cart through the present-day reserve as far as the Mkurumadzi River[8].

He had established a camp at Matitu by the confluence of the Mwambezi and Shire Rivers just south of the present-day reserve boundary, and laid out a vegetable garden to supply labourers working on the road in which he planted *English peas, beans, lettuces and Kuruman parsnips, water melons ... Nasturtium seed, spinach and cabbage, and put up a box for bees*[77]. At this time he was rejoined by Richard Thornton who had been the geologist on the 1859 expedition until he was dismissed by Livingstone. Sadly Thornton died that year from malaria, and was buried in the shade of a large baobab by the Mwambezi: his grave today is a national monument. Livingstone's expedition was recalled by the British Government shortly afterwards, before the completion of the road and transportation of the specially commissioned sectional boat *Lady Nyassa* up the Shire. The recall may in fact have come as a relief to Livingstone, who was worried that the new access route to the interior would be used by the Portuguese to expand their slave trading activities as they had done in the lower Shire.[77]

The route was, however, used later to transport two sectional boats: the *Search* which conveyed Young and Faulkner on the Livingstone Search Expedition in 1867; and the *Ilala* which carried the party of missionaries who founded the Cape Maclear Mission in 1875. It might well have been developed as a major trading and transport link to the north if the Established Church of Scotland missionaries had not founded a mission at Blantyre in the Shire Highlands in 1876. Blantyre was soon recognised as a convenient staging post on a more feasible loop-road passing the cataracts to the east, and both missions joined forces to construct a road running from near modern-day Chikwawa up the escarpment to Blantyre, and on to Matope on the upper Shire.[8] Had Livingstone's road been developed and still been in use, Majete Game Reserve would not have become the quiet wilderness by the Shire which it is today.

When Faulkner travelled up by the Shire through the present-day reserve he recorded a 'large herd of hippopotami' in a pool just below Kapichira Falls, three of which he dispatched. A couple of miles further up the Shire he encountered a herd of buffalo: he shot two bulls, one of which charged him when he initially wounded it. Whilst camped by the Mkurumadzi River he shot a hippo cow and wounded a bushbuck[17], before continuing northwards on his trigger-happy way. Buffalo today are almost non-existent in the reserve, and it is likely that pressures of human settlement which continued along the Shire up until 1969, along with the introduction of more efficient hunting weapons, accounted for many more animals.

Before the Second World War conflict between animals from the present-day reserve area and people settled in the Mwanza Valley was causing serious problems. For example, elephant used to migrate to the Lengwe thickets during the rains, from where they would raid nearby crops. The problem was aggravated by poachers who were closing the water holes on the western side of the present-day reserve area to facilitate hunting, forcing the animals to leave this uninhabited area and move to areas more convenient for the poachers; unfortunately this included cultivated areas.[81] In the late 1930s a lone bull elephant who had been raiding crops in the Mwanza valley was hunted and led his pursuers into the heart of the hills on a hot November day. It was then realised for the first time that this wild, uninhabited area would make an excellent game reserve if the animals could be kept inside the boundary away from the crops of the Mwanza Valley. After the war the newly formed Nyasaland Fauna Preservation Society (NFPS) investigated the area and campaigned for its protection.[82]

In 1951 the area around Majete Hill was declared a non-hunting controlled area, primarily to keep the elephant and other animals away from the Mwanza Plain[81]. The following year the NFPS constructed a sub-surface dam to create a permanent water hole in the Phwadzi River[13], increasing the carrying capacity of the western area for wildlife. In 1955 a game reserve was declared, which was extended in 1969 as far as the Shire and Mkurumadzi Rivers to allow animals access to these water sources. In 1976 the reserve was again slightly extended to cover the full width of the Shire River.[19]

Kapichira Falls

The Kapichira Falls which have been protected as a national monument for some time are now included in the reserve. They are a magnificent sight, a huge volume of water plunging down this last of a long series of cataracts to reach the calmer, slower reaches of the lower Shire. At the top of the falls the Shire widens and divides around luxuriantly vegetated islands frequented by hippo and birds. Much of the water is channelled round the far side of the islands, emerging into view again down a broad waterfall which is the main part of the falls. It is joined at the bottom in a cloud of spray by water from a smaller channel near the west bank: here the water thunders and pounds down a deep, narrow gorge. Lined with huge boulders broken off by the force of water the

Kapichira Falls, first seen by Livingstone in 1859. JUDY CARTER

river continues down more rapids for another 300 m, broadening as it curves round a double bend before slowing and deepening into a more sedate course.

Here the tigerfish lurks, sought after by anglers who fish their way downstream from the foot of the falls. This is the upper distribution limit on the Shire for most of the fish typical of the lower Zambezi. A notable exception is the mottled eel: thought to spawn in the Indian Ocean north-east of Madagascar, this species finds its way from the coast up the Zambezi and lower Shire Rivers, continuing overland round the Kapichira Falls and other cataracts and rapids of the middle Shire, swimming up the rest of the Shire and into Lake Malaŵi.[83] Adults return by this route to spawn in the Indian Ocean, a remarkable migration.

Vegetation and animals of Majete Game Reserve

In the reserve the Shire and Mkurumadzi Rivers are ribbons of oases traversing the brown and often charred landscape of the dry season. Walking quietly along the bank of the Shire, following elephant paths through the tall reedbeds and emerging on to the closely cropped green grass of the narrow floodplain or the rockstrewn riverside itself, many different animals may be seen. Small herds of waterbuck graze the finer grasses and drink at the water's edge, and tall, graceful kudu browse in the shadows of nearby thickets. The snort of a hippo in a quiet inlet may be heard above the roar of the Shire. Crocodile bask on sandbanks by the side of the river, sliding quickly away into the glinting waters if disturbed.

It is possible to ford the Mkurumadzi River in the dry season and continue upstream by the side of the Shire, passing the roar of the Mpatamanga Rapids and crossing the reserve boundary into the unpopulated area beyond. A well-used elephant path leads to Mpatamanga Gorge near the M2 road, where the Shire has gouged itself a spectacular course through the bedrock between two hills. Elephant move freely between the reserve and the uninhabited land to the north, crossing the M2 and continuing upstream to the west bank of the Lisungwe River. About 225 elephant are thought to use this area and the reserve. In the dry season many of them frequent an extensive wilderness area of thicket in the Masatwe Valley, between Mpatamanga Gorge and the confluence of the Shire and Lisungwe Rivers. In addition to herds which have always used these parts, others may have moved south into the area comparatively recently due to pressure from expansion of human activity in the Lisungwe Valley and Matope area. Smaller dry season concentrations occur in patches of thicket in the north-east of the reserve, including the Mkurumadzi area.[84]

The Mkurumadzi is a relatively small river, flowing down a narrow valley much frequented by bushbuck and warthog. Water-sculpted rock formations line its bed, and there are some deep, quiet pools as well as faster stretches where the water drops down to the confluence with the Shire. In this peaceful and attractive location stands Mkurumadzi Camp, surrounded by large trees on the river bank. Birds are plentiful in the valleys of both rivers, including the area around Kapichira Falls. Of all the national parks and game reserves Majete is the only one known to harbour the rock pratincole, a small, sooty-brown bird with a white collar and coral-red legs. It may be seen flitting from rock to rock or flying in small flocks over the rapids and rough water, catching insects on the wing. The eggs are laid in rough cracks or depressions in the bare rock with no nesting material; the downy chicks are very difficult to see, so well are they camouflaged against the stone.

Six different species of kingfisher have been recorded in the reserve, all specialised in their feeding habits. The largest is the giant kingfisher, a striking crested bird with a large black bill. It may be seen perched immobile on branches overhanging the river watching for fish and crabs, and its loud, characteristic call is often heard towards dusk. The smaller pied kingfisher is more common, perching on a favourite branch or hovering over a quiet stretch of water, looking for fish which it catches by plummeting head first into the water. In the reeds on the edge of the river the small, brightly coloured malachite kingfisher perches low, a flash of irridescent blue as it repeatedly dives into the water to catch little fish, tadpoles, frogs and insects. It looks very similar to the pygmy kingfisher, but the latter is smaller and has a blue rather than a green crown, with no apparent crest. The smallest of all the kingfishers, the pygmy frequents areas of dry bush sometimes far from the river, perching above the grass and diving into it to catch insects, spiders and frogs. Other kingfishers which may be seen in the woodland away from the river are the migratory chestnut-bellied kingfisher and striped kingfisher, the latter feeding on insects and small lizards, the bush echoing with its characteristic call just before sunset.[60,85]

Away from the rivers the land rises in a series of rolling ridges covered with open *Terminalia*, *Sclerocarya caffra* and *Combretum* woodland. Scattered

Hovering pied kingfisher watching for fish.   MICHAEL GORE

Sabi star flowering in western Majete in the dry season after its leaves have fallen. The swollen-looking trunk acts as a storage organ.   JUDY CARTER

baobabs occur, particularly at lower altitudes: one tree growing south of the Ntundu River is hollow inside to a height of about three metres, and bats roost in the roof of the cavity. North-west of Kapichira Falls is a dense thicket, *Nkhalangowanjobvu*, much frequented by elephant and kudu.

In the west of the reserve the scenery becomes much wilder, with isolated hills overlooking ridges and steep-sided valleys. Much of the vegetation is *Brachystegia* woodland, with isolated clumps of bamboo. In the centre of this roadless wilderness stands Majete Hill, looking across to the twin peaks of Mphemba and the long ridge of Phiri la tambalala. Other hills mark the north-western boundary, facing down the Majete Escarpment to the Mwanza Valley. A walk along the bank of the Shire now seems a mere stroll in comparison with the strenuous but rewarding challenge of this vast, remote wilderness. It is a place of contrasts: just as the closed woodland seems to become endless it is suddenly interrupted by the lower slopes of a rocky-sided hill and a vista opens above the blanket of trees, once more giving perspective. With altitude, the woodland gives way to tufted grass and aloes, and the Sabi star grows from crevices in the rock. From the summits of even the smaller hills views are impressive, looking west beyond the Mwanza Valley to the rolling expanse of Lengwe National Park and the hills of Mozambique, and across the rest of the reserve to its other hills, blue and hazy in the distance.

Animals such as klipspringer, baboon and dassie frequent the rocky slopes, sable antelope, kudu, grey duiker and bushpig occurring in the woodland below. Elephant occasionally cross to this side of the reserve during the rains, returning to the vicinity of the Shire when the temporary water sources dry up again. The few perennial springs and waterholes in some of the riverbeds enable animals such as sable to remain in the area throughout the year; these water sources are also much used by smaller animals including birds and insects. On the western boundary near the foot of the Majete Escarpment there is a hot spring which produces a strong flow of warm water. Known locally as *Madzi otentha* (literally 'hot water'), it is a reminder of the reserve's location in the great rift valley.

Threats to the reserve

The dry season water sources are also well known by poachers. To the west, north-west and south of the reserve there is heavy human settlement, and despite anti-poaching patrols illegal hunting continues to be one of the main reasons for the paucity of large mammals in the reserve. The poachers lie in wait near springs for unsuspecting animals coming to drink. They sometimes cover up water held in potholes in rock outcrops with flat stones to keep it clean for their own consumption[54], hence enabling them to stay longer in the remote dry areas. Poaching, however, is not the only threat to the conservation of the reserve: its main attraction, the Kapichira Falls, have been earmarked as one of the most suitable sites on the Shire for a new hydro-electric power station[31] (see page 131). This would probably involve the construction of a dam above the falls and the installation of a large pipe which would carry water from the dam to a power station lower down, bypassing the falls. Even if the engineering works were implemented in such a way as to have minimal visual impact on the landscape, the amount of water coming over the falls would be greatly reduced. In the dry season the flow could be reduced by as much as 40% below normal, and the spectacle of the falls would be severely affected. However, Malaŵi requires additional power for its expanding industrial and urban developments: it remains to be seen whether this project is implemented.

Lengwe National Park [19,31,86]

Name derivation

From the Mang'anja word for a thicket of thorny plants difficult to penetrate: this is one of the main vegetation types in the east of the park.

Declaration

Lengwe Game Reserve was first proclaimed in 1928, but it was reduced in size in 1934 and again after the Second World War, still, however, protecting the main nyala habitat. In 1970 the reserve became a national park, and in 1975 it was greatly expanded to include a large area adjacent to the Mozambique border.

Present size

887 km²

Location

Southern Malaŵi on the west side of the lower Shire Valley, adjacent to the Mozambique border.

Landscape types

Flat, alluvial area in the east and rolling terrain with sandstone outcrops in the west, drained by seasonal rivers. Small, isolated hills in the south.

Vegetation

Dry forest; thicket; and *Acacia*, palm and *Combretum* savanna in the east. Mopane woodland in the south-west and *Brachystegia/Combretum* in the north-west. *Dambos* and riverine woodland in places along the rivers.

Large mammals

Most commonly seen: nyala, bushbuck, Livingstone's suni, kudu, grey duiker, buffalo, warthog, baboon. Also occurring: blue monkey, vervet monkey, civet, genet, ratel, various species of mongoose, spotted hyena, side-striped jackal, leopard, caracal, serval, wild-cat, aardvark, dassie, bushpig, reedbuck, sable antelope, impala, grysbok, porcupine.

Birds

About 300 species have been recorded in the park, in the wide diversity of habitats. The evergreen thickets support the most northerly occurring populations of essentially coastal species such as Rudd's apalis, Woodward's batis and grey sunbird.

Other animals

Hinged tortoise, terrapin, various snakes, frogs and toads including the large bullfrog.

Sites of special interest

Artificial waterholes and hides; sandstone outcrops; parts of the Nkombedzi wa Fodya River; southern hills; Cape-to-Cairo telegraph line.

Access

The M8 Blantyre — Chiromo road should be followed for about 20 km south of Chikwawa. A signed, untarred road leads off to the west through fields of sugar-cane. Follow it for 9 km, turning left at a T junction and right almost immediately afterwards, passing a tsetse barrier before reaching the park entrance gate. The road is normally passable for saloon cars, but can give problems immediately after heavy rain or overhead irrigation of the sugar. It gives access to the rest camp and the network of dry season game-viewing roads on the east side of the park shown on Map 6.3.

Access to the northern part of the park is normally via the D140 (north). An unsigned and badly overgrown track leaves this road at Suweni: it is advisable to take a guide from the park headquarters as it is very difficult to find. The track leads into the park for about 25 km; it is not maintained so is not recommended for saloon cars, and it

Continued

Map 6.3 *Lengwe National Park*

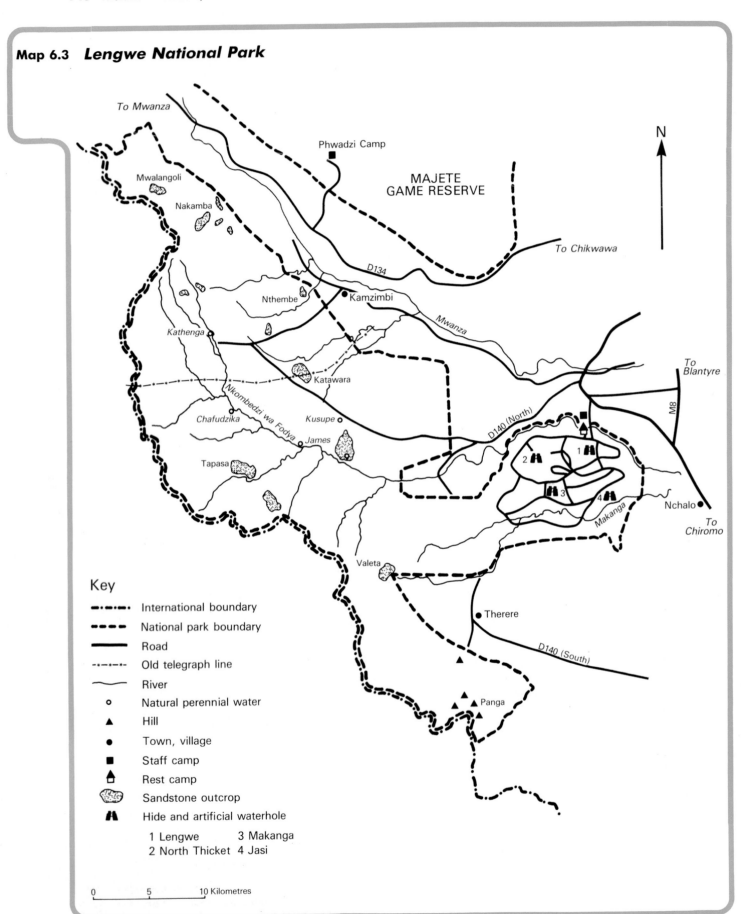

Key

- ·—··—··— International boundary
- ――― National park boundary
- ——— Road
- -·-·-·- Old telegraph line
- ∿∿∿ River
- ○ Natural perennial water
- ▲ Hill
- ● Town, village
- ■ Staff camp
- ⌂ Rest camp
- ⬡ Sandstone outcrop
- ꜰꜰ Hide and artificial waterhole

    1 Lengwe   3 Makanga
    2 North Thicket 4 Jasi

0   5   10 Kilometres

is impassable even for four-wheel-drive vehicles during the rains. Another track leading into the park from Kamzimbi village on the west side of the Mwanza Valley was virtually impassable for visitors' vehicles at the time of writing.

Access to the southern part of the park is via the D140 (south). About 1.5 km south of Therere village a more or less disused track leads off south to the boundary of the park. Again, a guide is recommended.

Distances from the main centres to the entrance gate are:

Blantyre: 77 km
Zomba: 143 km
Lilongwe: 424 km

There is no airstrip in the park.

Visitor facilities

There is a self-catering rest camp inside the entrance gate with four chalets, each with two double bedrooms and a large sitting/dining room. Kitchen/ablution facilities are located in separate buildings, and cooks are available. The camp has running water and mains electricity. An open shelter on a raised area nearby overlooks a bird-bath, and is popular with bird-watchers and photographers. To the east of the rest camp is a picnic site, with trestle tables and seats under shade. A hostel provides accommodation for school parties and other large groups of visitors.

Four wooden game-viewing hides overlooking artificial waterholes offer excellent opportunites for game-viewing and photography in the dry season. There is a nature trail running from near the camp to one of the hides.

Game-scout guides are available to accompany visitors in the park, by vehicle or on foot.

Visitor activities

Game-viewing and bird-watching by vehicle, on foot or from hides; walking; photography; visits to the west of the park by arrangement with the park management.

Administrative arrangements

Reservations for accommodation should be made to the Department of National Parks and Wildlife booking office: Box 30131, Lilongwe 3 (tel. 730 853). Guides should be arranged with the park management, in advance if possible.

Park fees are charged for day and overnight visitors and their vehicles, and for the service of a game-scout guide.

Best time to visit

Game-viewing: August to November
Bird-watching: November to December
Walking: July to August
Photography: July to November

Note: the road network is closed during the rains (approximately December to April), though walking is possible at this time. From June to August inclusive the climate in the park is pleasantly warm. At other times of the year it can be uncomfortably hot, especially in the middle of the day.

Lengwe National Park

In the dense thickets and forest patches of Lengwe the nyala antelope rest like grey shadows during the heat of day, browsing delicately on twigs and leaves and venturing out to drink at tree encircled waterholes during the cooler hours. Thought to be one of the most northerly occurring nyala populations in Africa now, they were the initial reason for protecting the area and are the park's big success story. They are found mainly in the eastern section of the park, a flat, fertile area on the upper edge of the Shire floodplain where the thicket and forest are interspersed with savannas and *dambos*. A few nyala also occur further west as the floodplain gives way to less fertile, undulating terrain, extending in a series of shallow-soiled, wooded ridges to cover a vast wilderness along the Mozambique border. A great contrast to the eastern section with its excellent game-viewing and development of visitor facilities, the west of the park has few roads and animals but does have some spectacular scenery, with great outcrops of sandstone rock, isolated hills and the valley of the Nkombedzi wa Fodya River.

History of Lengwe National Park

Little is known of the early history of the park area. The lower Shire Valley is thought to have been inhabited by man for at least 10 000 years and was an important part of the old Maravi Empire. The park area itself is thought to have been inhabited by the sixteenth century though it is likely that man had an impact there much earlier through hunting, gathering and burning. Human activity was not intense enough to eliminate the wild animals, however, and in 1907 the occurrence of nyala in what is now the eastern section of the park was recorded for the Protectorate.

The north-western section of the present-day park was affected early in the days of the Protectorate by one of its communications developments. A telegraph line was planned to link Blantyre with Salisbury (now Harare); Cecil Rhodes had earlier conceived the idea of a telegraph line running the length of the African continent from the Cape to Cairo, and Salisbury was already linked to Cape Town. In 1894 a section of line was completed from Blantyre to Chikwawa and shortly afterwards it was extended to Tete in the neighbouring Portuguese territory, crossing the north of the present-day park. Difficulties with the Portuguese and the Mashonaland Rising then caused delays, but Blantyre was finally connected to Cape Town by an alternative line through Umtali (now Mutare). Although long since replaced by more modern tele-communication systems, the cutline of the old telegraph route can still be traced as it crosses the park into Mozambique.

In the early 1920s Rodney Wood, a cotton planter and keen naturalist/hunter, spent two years trying to obtain a good nyala trophy in the Chikwawa district. He eventually observed that the nyala were attracted to the fallen flowers of a certain tree species in the Lengwe thicket, and one morning he lay in wait before dawn near one of these trees, hoping for a shot. At daylight he fired twice, and by a quirk of fate killed three bulls with two shots. Overcome with remorse at destroying such magnificent animals, he set about influencing the Government to proclaim the area as a game reserve: this eventually happened in 1928, along with the declaration of the Thangadzi Stream Reserve (now Mwabvi Game Reserve) where nyala also bred.

During the next few years, however, the reserve did not fare well. Management and therefore protection were minimal and a large area was excised in 1934 for agriculture. During the Second World War when there was virtually no government supervision many people moved into the area from nearby Mozambique, clearing patches of land in the reserve for cultivation, and poaching on a large scale. By the end of the war animal numbers had declined considerably. More land was excised, and though the area remaining in the reserve included the main nyala habitat, the wild animal populations continued to decline slowly. One of the major problems was the absence of permanent water. Towards the end of the dry season when all the temporary water sources had

Adult nyala bull, Lengwe National Park. There is a distinctive browse-line on the tree to the left. FRANK JOHNSTON

dried out, the water-dependent animals used to migrate to the Mwanza and Shire Rivers. Heavy human settlement between the reserve and perennial water, however, now created an obstacle which few animals managed to overcome. In 1963 it seemed that the continued existence of the reserve was doomed, especially as plans were being made to establish extensive sugar-cane plantations between the reserve and the Mwanza and Shire Rivers.

Proposals were made to capture the remaining nyala and translocate them to Mwabvi Game Reserve before the protected area was deproclaimed. However, many more nyala than had originally been estimated were discovered hiding in the dense thickets. The Life President Dr Banda (then Prime Minister) himself intervened, ordering not only the retention of the reserve but also the provision of permanent water supplies for the wild animals. In 1964 a borehole was sunk and water was piped to a nearby pan; by 1970 four such waterholes had been developed. To prevent animals causing damage in the neighbouring sugar estate game-proof fencing was erected along that part of the reserve boundary.

In the following years the population of nyala flourished, along with others such as buffalo, warthog,

A rainbow illumines the savanna and woodland of eastern Lengwe National Park. LIZ and TONY BOMFORD, *SURVIVAL ANGLIA*

impala and suni. For some species, however, the provision of water and protection from hunting came too late; for others the park area was not large enough to cover all of their extensive home-range, and they still came into conflict with human settlement when they moved outside the protected area. Species which have disappeared over the years include elephant, zebra, eland, hartebeest, roan, lion, wild dog and possibly black rhino.

In 1970 the area was granted national park status, and in 1975 it was expanded to include a vast new area in the west along the Mozambique border. This area had been classified as having a very low agricultural potential but was of great value to the park as it included parts of the original ranges of some of its large mammal species. New landscapes and vegetation types were encompassed in the park, increasing habitat diversity and adding a huge new wilderness area. Finally, the new boundaries ensured the protection of the catchment areas of several tributaries of the Mwanza and Shire Rivers. (Historical information on the reserve:[13,19,86,87]; information on the Cape to Cairo telegraph line:[8].)

Ecology of Lengwe National Park

The park today covers a large tract of land with a great variety of landscapes, habitat types and animals. At present most management resources are still concentrated in the east, with the waterholes, roads, park headquarters and visitor facilities. Anti-poaching patrols are intensive here, and much research and monitoring of the wild animal populations and their habitats have been carried out in recent years. So successful has the conservation of the nyala been that with the provision of water the population has exploded dramatically from about 350 animals thought to be remaining in the desperate days of 1963, to an estimated 4300 in 1982[54,88]. Distinctive browse-lines are apparent in the thickets and forests especially in the dry season, where the nyala have consumed all the edible leaves and twigs within reach of their long necks. In recent years these vegetation types have become more open as a result of pressure from the nyala. Grass is starting to grow in the thickets where before there was not enough light

Nyala male and females drinking at one of the artificial waterholes. The females have chestnut coloured coats and the males are slaty-brown coloured; only the males have horns.
JUDY CARTER

Suni, the second smallest antelope in Malaŵi, which lives in the Lengwe thickets. Its habitat is being altered by the large numbers of nyala. FRANK JOHNSTON

for it under the dense canopy. The fires which burn the adjacent savanna grasses previously could not penetrate the thickets because there was no fuel for them at ground level; with the development of a grass layer, however, the fire risk has greatly increased. Some of the thickets are regressing, and if this trend continues they may revert to more open woodland on a large scale.[37]

Modification of this habitat must in turn be affecting other species: the little suni antelope, for example, which depends on dense thicket for cover and food. Second only to the blue duiker as the smallest antelope in the country, Livingstone's suni lives alone or with a mate in a territory which it marks with a musky scent excreted from glands on the face. It feeds mainly on leaves and young shoots of shrubs, though it may also consume a very limited amount of grass; it can survive without water though suni with territories adjacent to waterholes do drink. Intense browsing by the nyala has reduced the amount of food and cover available for the suni.

Bushbuck must also be affected as they browse to almost the same height as nyala. Kudu are perhaps more fortunate as they are taller and can therefore browse on a narrow band of vegetation which the nyala cannot reach; they can also survive without water for long periods and therefore have a wider range at least in the dry season. The exact dietary requirements of these four species are not fully understood: each will have some degree of specialisation but there is probably still a large overlap[86]; and the high numbers of nyala are probably having an adverse effect on the populations of suni and bushbuck.

Various bird species which inhabit the forests and thickets are also being affected by the habitat changes. The brightly coloured gorgeous bush shrike was common in many of the thickets until the early 1980s when it suddenly became much rarer: it has not been seen or heard there now since 1983. Woodward's batis has also become increasingly rare in Lengwe, and the barred long-tailed cuckoo has not been seen there for several years. Rudd's apalis was only discovered in the locality in the late 1970s, a number of birds ironically being seen in a garden near the park where they were probably vagrants displaced by the clearance of the last natural thickets on the sugar estate. The apalis has since been recorded in the park and has been found to be an endemic subspecies. Its future in the area is also uncertain with the opening up of the Lengwe thickets. The problem is particularly serious as Lengwe contains much of the last remaining natural thicket and forest of the lower Shire plains: if it is destroyed many essentially lowland and coastal forest bird species will probably disappear completely from Malaŵi.[37]

In 1981 action was taken to avoid further habitat alteration with its consequent impact on other animal species and, ultimately, a probable population crash of the nyala. Culling was initiated by the Department of National Parks and Wildlife with a view to reducing the nyala population to a level which the habitat could support in the longterm without adverse effect. A very efficient and humane technique was implemented, shooting at night from an open vehicle by spotlight using a rifle with telescopic sights. Culling continued in 1983 and 1984. Meat from the cull was sold locally at low prices, a tangible benefit of the park for the local people living nearby. Some meat was bought by hotels and restaurants in the major towns of Malaŵi and served in their dining rooms as a delicacy. The skins were tanned and the horns of the males preserved, these trophies being sold to visitors. Revenue generated from the cull enabled some important work to be carried out in the parks and reserves which would otherwise have been impossible. In 1985, however, culling was not feasible because of foot-and-mouth disease restrictions in the lower Shire Valley. It remains to be seen whether it is resumed in the future. In addition to culling, a few nyala are removed live from the park. They are captured in a permanent enclosure and transferred to a small game farm established on the nearby sugar estate.

To provide the visitor with an understanding of the ecology of the park, including the impact of the nyala, there is a nature trail near the park entrance. It starts in a savanna area interspersed with clumps of thicket, many of which have developed on large termite mounds. Thicket clumps on the lower ground near the Nkombedzi wa Fodya River contain fan palms, and around them the grass is tall. As the trail leads on to higher ground the grass becomes shorter and knobthorn acacia appears in the thicket clumps, a very distinctive tree with large knobbly spines protruding from the trunk. Warthog are often seen in the more open areas, kneeling to graze or busily digging for roots; nyala, bushbuck and suni also frequent the thicket clump savanna.

The trail wends its way to a large area of dry deciduous thicket, a dense growth of trees and shrubs whose trunks and canopies are entwined by climbing creepers and vines. One of the more common trees of the thicket is *Pterocarpus antunesii*, whose tall trunk has a very characteristic pale grey, smooth, sometimes flaky bark. The red-flowered euphorbia also grows here in small colonies: a rare species in southern Africa, it has a distinctive red flower and a candelabra of much divided, slender, spiny branches. As the nature trail leads through the thicket suni can

Warthog wallowing in a waterhole. The coating of wet mud helps to cool the warthog and smother parasites clinging to the skin. JUDY CARTER

sometimes be seen wandering in and out of the undergrowth nibbling at tender shoots and leaves, running away fast like hares if disturbed.

Deep in the thicket the trail ends at one of the artificial waterholes, which is overlooked by a large wooden hide. From the hide animals can be observed and photographed coming to drink, mainly early in the morning. Nyala advance cautiously into the open area, pausing to listen and scent for potential danger. The females are lightly built, with delicate legs and long, slender necks; their coats are chestnut coloured with conspicuous white stripes. Males are

One of the game-viewing hides in the park, which overlooks an artificial waterhole. The grass screen enables observers to approach the hide unseen by animals at the water. JUDY CARTER

Baboons are gregarious, living in troops of up to 40 or more in the park. They mainly feed at ground level, foraging for plants and occasionally animals such as insects and small birds. MICHAEL GORE

larger and appear much heavier bodied, this being accentuated by their shaggy, dark slaty-brown coats: they are very handsome animals, with curved horns and white markings on the face and body. During the height of the dry season up to 200 nyala may be seen at the waterhole at any one time. Always alert, they are often startled by noisy groups of warthog which trot purposefully out of the thicket straight to the water. Once their thirst is assuaged the warthog may wallow in a favourite mud bath, coating their bristly-haired skin with mud to cool themselves and smother any ticks which may be clinging in folds of hide. Afterwards they may have a good scratch on the bank of the waterhole or a convenient fallen log.

Less commonly, bushpig may also be seen, and occasionally small herds of up to 50 buffalo come to drink. Baboons are frequent visitors to the waterhole, stooping low to drink, moving away slowly as they forage on the ground for fruits and seeds and dig up succulent roots. Young baboons provide excellent entertainment as they chase one another around the clearing, over fallen trees and sometimes high into the overhead branches. A rarer visitor to the waterhole is the blue monkey which usually disappears quickly back into the canopy of the thicket. Small troops of vervet monkeys may also be seen in the clearing, foraging on the ground and in the canopy for insects and plants, their young also playing games with each other. Lengwe is one of the few places where all three species may be seen together.

At times there may be no large mammals to watch at the waterhole but there are often smaller animals such as packs of banded mongoose, chattering noisily as they forage around the clearing. Small flocks of crested guineafowl often follow troops of vervet monkeys, feeding on fruits and seeds which the monkeys drop. They also consume insects and snails and may spend some time around the waterhole, scratching in the soil and taking dust baths. The crested guineafowl is another uncommon bird species in Malaŵi whose survival in Lengwe is threatened by the opening up of the thickets. Much more numerous is the helmeted guineafowl which visits the waterhole in large noisy flocks to drink during the late afternoon. Waterbirds such as saddlebill and openbill storks and sacred ibis may be seen feeding amongst the waterplants, and occasionally fish eagles and crowned eagles perch on prominent branches near the hide.

The two southerly hides are located by waterholes in extensive areas of tree savanna, and consequently supply a different community of animals.

Blue monkey. Less common than the baboon, the blue monkey spends most of its time in the forest and thicket canopy but small troops may be seen coming to the waterholes to drink. JANET and JOHN HOUGH

Species occurring in this habitat include buffalo, impala, kudu, grey duiker and reedbuck. The latter also frequents the *dambos* along the major watercourses. In this area of the park game-viewing by car is often better than in the north as the area is more open, especially after the grass has been burnt in the dry season.

During the rains the artificial waterholes are much less heavily used as temporary surface water is widely available in streams and pans throughout the area. These pans have formed from natural depressions in the terrain, deepening as animals such as buffalo wallow in them and leave with their hides coated in clinging mud. Many 'animals, large and small, make use of these temporary waterholes. An interesting one is the great grey tree frog, the adults of which ironically do not like water and avoid it if possible. Their breeding habits are extremely unusual: after rain the female deposits a large quantity of eggs on a branch overhanging a waterhole, sometimes a metre or more above the water surface. The male deposits sperm fluid over the eggs, and then both frogs beat the jelly into a white froth with their hind legs, mixing the eggs and sperm at the same time. The froth of each nest has a diameter of about 20 cm and may contain up to 150 eggs. The surface of the froth hardens and the interior liquifies to maintain

Froth nest of the great grey tree frog. The eggs develop inside the froth nest which is always located above water; when the tadpoles hatch they drop into the water below.   JANET and JOHN HOUGH

moist conditions for the developing eggs. After about five days the eggs hatch and the tadpoles drop to the water below the nest; they then live in the water until metamorphosis, when they leave it for good.[89]

Western Lengwe

The main river of the park is the Nkombedzi wa Fodya whose name means literally 'gathering of tobacco'. In the past tobacco was grown in the upper catchment of the river, and people used to travel from many other parts of the Shire Valley to obtain tobacco there for sale or for domestic use.[90] The river rises in the north near the Mozambique border and flows southward between remote ridges clad with *Brachystegia* woodland. In places deep sand lines the riverbed, interrupted occasionally as it crosses sills of

Sandstone outcrop in the west of Lengwe National Park.
JUDY CARTER

rock, and the banks are flanked by tall riverine trees. Elsewhere the river spreads out into marsh with dense, almost impenetrable reedbeds. As the boundaries are such an irregular shape the river actually leaves the park at one point, to meet the eastern boundary further downstream: here it is flanked in places by evergreen woodland.

The Nkombedzi wa Fodya stops flowing in the dry season but a few permanent pools of water are held behind rock sills in the north-west. When this area was inhabited before the extension of the park local people obtained water from these pools and by digging in certain spots in the sand of the riverbed; there are also a few permanent springs in some of the sandstone outcrops of this region, often in obscure crevices or below overhangs. Limited water is therefore available in the dry season for the wild animals of this great wilderness area and species such as sable, grey duiker and grysbok occur. They are extremely wary of man, however, and their low numbers are due to pressures of illegal hunting as well as the inherently low carrying capacity of the area. At present the resources of the park management are insufficient to patrol this area adequately as well as the eastern area. Game-viewing is therefore not a major attraction, but for anyone who wants to escape from civilisation, camping out under the brilliant stars of the southern hemisphere night and exploring on foot the dry river-courses, woodlands, hills and fascinating sandstone outcrops, this immense wilderness has much to offer.

In the south are the only hills of the park. They stand isolated, most of them close to the Mozambique border. Panga Hill is the park's highest point, and from its rocky summit there are extensive views across the rolling landscape, over the mopane woodland of the southern end of the park towards the floodplains of the Shire, and west to the hills of Mozambique.

Further north the sandstone outcrops are extensive and weathering by the elements has produced some spectacular rock formations: pillars, free-standing arches and curved domes, sheer cliffs and deep caves. In places the outcrops cover vast slopes, and seasonal streams have formed deep gullies and waterfalls as they drain down through the rock. On the smoother rock floors on east-facing slopes amazing waterworn patterns and striations weave and flow across the surface, and in steps and crevices succulent plants struggle for a root-hold. In the midst of the African bush, this striking and unexpected landscape could have come straight from J.R.R. Tolkein's Kingdom of Middle Earth.

Mwabvi Game Reserve[19,31]

Name derivation

The name of the reserve comes from the Mwabvi River which runs through the reserve. *Mwabvi* is the Chichewa name for the tree *Erythrophleum suaveolens* which grows along the river: it has many medicinal properties and was also used extensively as a poison in 'trials by ordeal' before these were banned in Malaŵi[66].

Declaration

The Thangadzi Stream Reserve was gazetted in 1928, and reduced in status to a restricted hunting area in 1951[13]. In 1953 the Mwabvi Game Reserve was declared which included the area of the original reserve. It was extended in 1975 to the Mozambique border, but following a Presidential Order in 1982 is likely to be reduced again to approximately the pre-1975 boundaries. The following information is based on this reduced size.

Present size.

135 km^2 (reduced from 340 km^2)

Location

Southern Malaŵi, on the west side of the southern lower Shire Valley.

Landscape types

Broken terrain with ridges, sandstone outcrops, small hills, gullies and narrow valleys between flatter areas. A range of hills on the eastern boundary.

Vegetation

Mosaic of *dambo*, thicket, *Julbernardia*, *Brachystegia*, mopane and *Acacia/Combretum* woodland, with riverine forest along the watercourses.

Large mammals

Most commonly seen: sable antelope, kudu, warthog, dassie. Also occurring: blue monkey, vervet monkey, baboon, pangolin, wild dog, side-striped jackal, ratel, civet, various species of mongoose, spotted hyena, lion, leopard, wild cat, serval, aardvark, black rhino, bushpig, buffalo, bushbuck, nyala, grey duiker, red duiker, impala, klipspringer, Livingstone's suni, grysbok, porcupine[19,47].

Birds

Nearly 200 species of birds have been recorded in the wide diversity of habitat types. This may be the only national park or game reserve in the country protecting the double-banded sandgrouse and black-tailed grey waxbill.

Other animals

These include monitor lizard, Bell's hinged tortoise, the fish *Barbus choloensis* and an isolated crocodile living in a large pool[34,57].

Sites of special interest

Mulaka Hills, Mwabvi Gorge, sandstone outcrops, Mwabvi and Thangadzi Rivers, various permanent waterholes, Nyantoko Hill (just outside the probable new boundary).

Access

The M8 Blantyre — Chiromo road should be followed south of the village of Sorgin. After crossing the bridge over the Thangadzi River the road curves to the left and the outskirts of Bangula come into sight. A clear turning to the right at this point leads on to the old untarred Blantyre — Chiromo road, doubling back and crossing a drift on the Thangadzi. Shortly after the drift there is a tsetse control barrier; take the left hand fork in the track and follow it for about 6 km, when it reaches the reserve entrance. This road is passable for saloon cars with high clearance during the dry season. It gives access to the roads of the reserve, leading to Mwabvi Camp and Matope game-scout camp as shown on Map 6.4. The Matope road crosses the Thangadzi River by a very rough drift unsuitable for saloon cars; Mwabvi Camp is accessible to saloon cars with good clearance during the dry season if driven with care.

Distances from the main centres to the entrance barrier are:

Blantyre:	138 km
Zomba:	204 km
Lilongwe:	485 km

There is no airstrip in the reserve; the nearest is at Bangula, about 16 km away.

Visitor facilities

Visitors can stay overnight at Mwabvi Camp, either in the two twin-bedded tin rondavels which have basic furnishings, or camping. Water is drawn from a borehole; the camp has a washing shelter and pit latrine; there is no electricity and cooking is done over a wood fire. Visitors should take all their own food, cooking and eating utensils, bedding and any camping equipment needed.

The services of a game-scout guide may be hired if requested well in advance.

Visitor activities

Walking, bird-watching, game-viewing

Continued

Map 6.4 *Mwabvi Game Reserve*

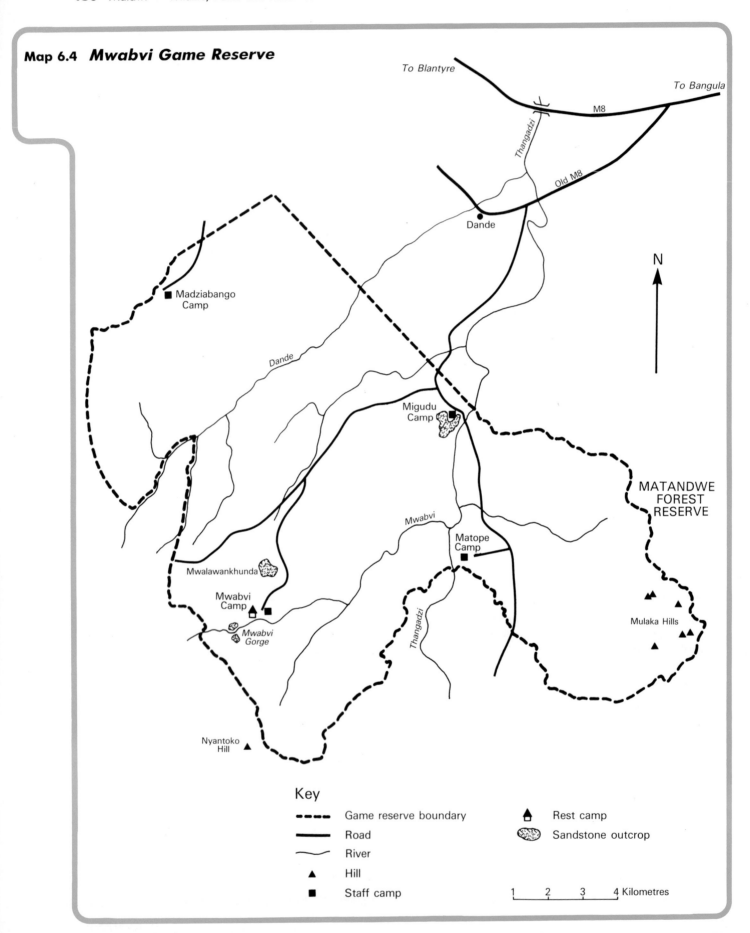

Key

▪ ▪ ▪ ▪ Game reserve boundary	▲ Rest camp
———— Road	⬬ Sandstone outcrop
—— River	
▲ Hill	
▪ Staff camp	1 2 3 4 Kilometres

Administrative arrangements

Reservations for Mwabvi Camp and a game-scout guide should be made with the Parks and Wildlife Officer, Lengwe National Park, Box 25, Chikwawa (tel. Chikwawa 0 1203).

Reserve fees are charged for visitors and their vehicles; accommodation/camping fees are charged for overnight stays.

Best time to visit

Game-viewing: August to November
Bird-watching: November to December
Walking: May to August

Note that the internal roads are closed during the rains (approximately December to April). From May to September inclusive the climate is pleasantly warm. At other times of the year it can be uncomfortably hot, especially in the middle of the day.

Mwabvi Game Reserve

Located away from the large towns and off the main tourist routes, Mwabvi Game Reserve in the far south of the hot lower Shire Valley is little known or visited. It is a surprisingly interesting and diverse reserve, with special appeal for those who like to

Mwabvi Game Reserve.   JANET and JOHN HOUGH

explore wild areas on foot, and perhaps sit patiently by a solitary waterhole on the off-chance of seeing a black rhino or buffalo coming to drink. Part of the area was originally protected as the Thangadzi Stream Game Reserve because of the nyala which occurred there[13], but now the reserve's main function is the protection of a black rhinoceros population.

The terrain is broken, with ridges of sandstone somewhat reminiscent on a smaller scale of western Lengwe. Between the ridges are flatter *dambo* areas draining to the main rivers, the largest of which are the Thangadzi and its tributary the Mwabvi. Although the rivers stop flowing in the dry season there are several permanent waterholes, enabling the survival of water-dependent animals in the reserve throughout the year. Much of the reserve is covered in a mosaic of dense thicket and more open *Julbernardia*, *Brachystegia*, mopane and *Acacia/Combretum* woodland, with small open glades of tall grass. Along the rivers narrow ribbons of riverine forest occur. The area has a fairly low carrying capacity for large mammals, probably limited mainly by the scarcity of perennial water, the presence of rock outcrops and the impacts of nearby human settlements.[54]

History of Mwabvi Game Reserve

Little is known of the early history of the reserve area. There is not much evidence of human settlement until comparatively recent times when the Maravi people occupied the area. It is likely that

Mwalawankhunda (literally 'the rock of doves'), so called because doves are said to nest in the holes. JUDY CARTER

they cultivated crops but did not keep livestock because of tsetse fly which is still present today. Several historical features in the sandstone outcrops around Mwabvi Camp bear testimony to their culture, including various burial sites. One is a large hole in a rock: known as *Mutuwamunthu* (literally 'head of a person'), a burial pot and bones which are reputedly human can still be seen there today. Another rockface known as *Mabokosi* (literally 'the coffin') has a series of large holes, in one of which lies the coffin of a child. Also nearby is *Mwalawankhunda* (literally 'rock of doves'), a large, round, isolated rock about four metres high. Several of its faces have rows of small holes where doves are said to nest. The origin of the holes is uncertain: they could have resulted from weathering, though according to oral tradition they were excavated by people to obtain mineral components for gunpowder[19].

Mwabvi Cave was the scene of many poison ordeals, a form of traditional justice which used to be widely practised in southern Africa. Most often used in cases of suspected witchcraft, the trials were also held for crimes such as theft and adultery. All the local people would gather in the cave and the witchdoctor would pound up dried bark of the *mwabvi* tree, mixing it with water to produce a red-coloured liquid. (The *mwabvi* tree grows along the Mwabvi

River, and the reserve is named after it.) The accused person or people would then be given the poison to drink. If vomiting occurred the person would survive and was deemed to have been innocent; if not, death from poisoning was almost certain to follow and the person was assumed to have been guilty. The poison is the alkaloid erythrophlein which causes severe gastro-intestinal irritation and cardiac failure. It has been suggested that to a certain extent the poison ordeals may indeed have had a judicial element. Excess adrenalin secreted by a guilty and frightened person could prevent the muscles of the stomach from contracting to cause vomiting and rejection of the poison. A person who knew he was innocent, on the other hand, should have produced less adrenalin and therefore vomited. The size of the dose is very significant, however, as a large enough amount will almost certainly cause vomiting whatever the psychological state of the accused, and a very small amount will not. The outcome of the trial was therefore very much in the hands of the witch-doctor. Poison ordeals have been banned in Malaŵi for some time now.[65,66]

The human settlement in the reserve area was never heavy enough to eliminate the wild animals completely, though it must have had severe impacts. Localised clearing of land for cultivation would have destroyed some of the natural vegetation, and on a wider scale seasonal fires would have greatly reduced the amount of dry season forage available. The presence of people may have limited the animals' access to dry season waterholes, and hunting would have reduced their numbers and caused disturbance to the remainder.

In 1928 part of the area was declared the Thangadzi Stream Game Reserve, largely as a result of the efforts of Rodney Wood to have nyala protected (page 143). Management was minimal and in 1951 the reserve was reduced in status to a restricted hunting area. However, during a tsetse survey up the valley of the Thangadzi River around that time nyala and black rhino were discovered in the forests, and the Mwabvi Game Reserve was declared to protect them in 1953, including the area of the degazetted Thangadzi Stream Reserve. The new reserve covered an area of 125 km², lying across the Thangadzi, Mwabvi and Dande catchments, leaving a strip of inhabited land to the south between the reserve and the Mozambique border.[13,19,81]

During the independence war in Mozambique many people living between the reserve and the international boundary moved out as they were being affected by the unrest across the border: Frelimo soliders opposing the Portuguese rule were taking refuge in Malaŵi territory, and a group was even discovered camped on nearby Nyantoko Hill.[91] The abandoned area, which has low agricultural potential, was included in the reserve in 1975 for national security purposes[54]. From an ecological viewpoint, the new extention would ensure the conservation of the water catchments as well as making the reserve a more viable unit. The range of the black rhino was known to extend into Mozambique and the new boundaries ensured protection of the migration route through Malaŵi territory, as well as incorporating some important new thickets, woodlands and water points in the reserve.

In 1982 the people who had moved out of the area made a request for permission to return, and this was granted by Presidential Order that year. It was therefore decided to reduce the area of the reserve again to approximately its former boundaries though at the time of writing this had yet to be legally proclaimed. Many people have since moved back into the area near the border.

Ecology of Mwabvi Game Reserve

These recent developments are serious for the rhino which now have to pass close to villages and areas of cultivation when moving between the reserve and the rest of their range in eastern Tete Province of Mozambique. About six or seven individuals are currently thought to use the reserve, part of a larger population occupying the mainly uninhabited lands across the border to the west. In the reserve they are confined to the central and southern area, using the thickets, riverine vegetation and a large tract of open woodland around Mwabvi Camp. The woodland is sometimes frequented by rhino at night, though most of their time is spent in the dense thickets which provide them with refuge from poachers and with browse throughout the year. Fire does not penetrate the thickets, unlike the open woodland where early dry season fires cause a shortage of edible browse for several months. As the dry season progresses and temporary water sources dry up the rhino tend to concentrate near perennial waterholes. Another source of water for them at this time of year is, surprisingly, the candelabra tree. This *Euphorbia* is common in parts of the reserve and rhino browse the tops of young trees, particularly in the Nyantoko area. The milky white latex of the plants is toxic to man and causes intense irritation and blistering if it comes into contact with the skin; in cattle it can cause severe burns to the face, eyes and lips[65]. Rhino are presumably protected from the latex by their thick hides, and their digestive systems must be able to cope with those chemicals which are toxic to man.

The continued survival of the Mwabvi rhino is particularly important as the species is internationally endangered: its numbers in Africa have been greatly reduced in recent years by illegal hunting. There is an extremely lucrative market for rhino horn, which is used in the Far East for medicinal purposes and in the Middle East for making ceremonial dagger handles, and the species has become eliminated from many areas as a result of intensive poaching[47]. The only other place where it is still known to occur in Malaŵi is Kasungu National Park (page 62). However, without the protection of the migration corridor and adequate control of illegal activities in the reserve, the future of the Mwabvi rhino is uncertain. Continued survival of the larger population of rhino in the neighbouring area of Mozambique is another prerequisite for the survival of the Mwabvi rhino. (Information on Mwabvi rhino:[92,93])

Other species besides rhino have been affected by the reduction of the reserve area, through loss of range and access to dry season waterholes in the south and west and possibly through increased poaching. It remains to be seen whether the reserve will be viable in the longterm: in the 1970s before the expansion of the reserve, elephant, zebra, reedbuck and hartebeest all disappeared[19]. Even so, Mwabvi does still have a reasonable diversity of large mammals. These include many predators such as lion, leopard, side-striped jackal, serval and wild dog; the latter periodically move across the reserve boundaries, covering a very large home-range. In the dry thickets nyala and Livingstone's suni occur, and bushbuck and blue monkey are common in the riverine thickets. Kudu are widespread and in the open woodland impala and sable antelope may be seen, particularly in the mopane. A few buffalo occur in the *dambos*, and dassie and klipspringer are common on the rock outcrops.[34]

Mwabvi Gorge from above. A large, solitary crocodile lives in the pool at the bottom of the gorge.   DENIS TWEDDLE

Euphorbia growing on the rocky slope of Nyantoko Hill.
JUDY CARTER

Birdlife is diverse in the mosaic of habitats in the reserve. Two species are protected in no other national park or game reserve in the country: the black-tailed grey waxbill and the double-banded sandgrouse. The former is a shy, unobtrusive little bird of the woodland which builds a retort-shaped nest with a short, tubular entrance sloping downward to a chamber lined with soft seed heads. The double-banded sandgrouse is a handsome bird, the male having a yellow-tinted throat below which are striking white and black bands, and the female being barred black, tawny and white. They nest on bare ground, sometimes preparing a thin lining of grass. Male sandgrouse in Africa are known to carry water to their young, retained in the feathers of their breasts as they fly from the waterhole back to the nest.[60,85,94]

In the dry terrain of the reserve a large solitary crocodile surprisingly inhabits a long, deep, murky pool in the Mwabvi Gorge. Also in the pool is an isolated population of a barbel fish species, *Barbus choloensis*. This fish has been found nowhere else in the lower Shire Valley apart from the Mwabvi Gorge, and the only other population known in Malaŵi is in the upper Ruo River which rises on Mount Mulanje. As the two populations have slight morphological differences they must have been genetically isolated for a long time.[57] The pool of the Mwabvi Gorge remains deep throughout the year, the tall, water-sculpted walls of the gorge and tangled vegetation above excluding direct sunlight. Ferns and other water- and shade-loving plants grow above the riverbed, clinging from cracks in the rock. As one proceeds up the gorge it narrows, the opposite walls become closer and more vertical, the pool occupying the bottom of the cleft. The gorge here is well named in Chichewa — *Ndipitakuti* — which means literally 'where do I go (from here)?'.

To the southern side of the Mwabvi Gorge there are ridges with fantastic natural rock sculptures: caves, bridges, tunnels, overhangs, cliffs and arches, made more surreal by the presence of twisted *Euphorbia* trees and stark, white-barked *Sterculias*. Other interesting rock formations can be seen on an exploration of the lower reaches of the Thangadzi River as it leaves the reserve, channelling its way through another sandstone outcrop.

To the east, across the Thangadzi River and the open mopane woodland much frequented by sable antelope, are the Mulaka Hills. Steep sided and rocky, the reserve covers only the very western portion of the hills, the rest being protected by the Matandwe Forest Reserve. They are the highest area within the new boundary of the game reserve and a scramble to the top gives a bird's eye view across the southern part of the reserve. In the distance the green ribbon of the Shire River and Elephant Marsh shimmers in the haze; to the west are the slopes of Nyaatoko Hill. This is a large sandstone outcrop rising 100 m above the surrounding area, just outside the new reserve boundary. From its summit on a clear day it is possible to see across the southernmost tip of Malaŵi, to the Shire River in the east and the mighty Zambezi River over the border to the west.

Glossary

Acacia woodland   deciduous woodland where the dominant trees are of the *Acacia* genus

aerobic   using free oxygen for respiration

algae   simple photosynthetic plants, single or multi-celled, occurring in water or damp places

alkaline   having more hydroxyl than hydrogen ions (in an aqueous solution), and strong basic properties

alluvial   (soils) formed from material deposited by rivers or floods

argillaceous   clayey

artefact   object made by human workmanship

barrage   man-made barrier across a river to control water flow

base-rich   containing a high concentration of electro-positive elements or compounds; base-rich rock normally gives rise to fertile soil

bauxite   clay compound containing aluminium

boma   administrative centre

bovid   animal of the Bovidae family of ruminants which includes buffalo, cattle, sheep, goats and many antelope species

***Brachystegia* woodland**   A type of deciduous woodland in which species of the *Brachystegia* genus are dominant

browser   animal which feeds on broadleaved plants such as herbs, shrubs and trees

buffer zone   land separating two areas with different land-uses which would potentially be in conflict if they were adjacent to one another

bulk feeder   animal which feeds non-selectively, consuming a large quantity of forage

canopy   upper, leafy parts of trees

carnivore   meat-eating animal

carrying capacity   number of animals which a given area can support on a sustained basis without environmental damage. Sometimes expressed in terms of biomass rather than numbers of a given species

catchment area   area from which water drains into a particular watercourse

chiperoni   cold, drizzly weather in southern Malaŵi caused by the movement of cool moist air up the Zambezi and lower Shire Valleys, leading to condensation and cloud formation over higher ground

chironomid   member of the Chironomidae family of flies which has aquatic larvae; members of the family include midges

cichlid   member of the Cichlidae family of fish

clupeid   member of the fish family Clupeidae which includes the herring

***Combretum* woodland**   deciduous woodland where the dominant trees are of the *Combretum* genus

confluence   the place where two or more rivers unite

continental drift   movement of continental sections of the earth's crust: it is thought that many of the continents were once joined together, but have since separated

convection (climatic)   spread of heat by the mixing of large masses of air, either because the heated masses move upwards due to their reduced density, or because a wind brings hot and cold air together and thus causes mixing on a large scale

convergent evolution   evolution which produces an increasing similarity in some characteristic(s) between groups of organisms which were initially different

coppice   woodland in which the trees have been broken off near their bases (often by elephant), resulting in a dense, short growth of stems

cotton soil   dark clay soil prone to seasonal waterlogging, and cracking when dry

crustacean   animal belonging to the class Crustacea which includes shrimps, crabs and waterfleas

culling controlled removal of part of a population, usually because animals are considered to be too numerous for the objectives of management

cyprinid fish belonging to the family Cyprinidae

dambo strip of grassland along a drainage line

detritus organic debris from decomposing plants and animals

endemic confined to a given region

epiphytic plant attached to another plant for support only, not parasitic

fault (geological): fracture surface along which rocks have been relatively displaced

filamentous green algae multicellular green algae in which the cells are joined together in filaments

flagellate protozoan belonging to the class Flagellata, having one or more flagella

floodplain relatively flat area near a waterbody which is seasonally flooded; usually with a grass cover

flue-cured tobacco tobacco which is dried and cured in heated tobacco barns

fry newly hatched fish

game pit pit dug by local people and concealed on top, for the purpose of catching animals which fall into it

game reserve area established under the Game Act where vertebrates and vegetation are protected

gill net fishing net which catches fish by the gills when they put their heads through the mesh holes

grazer animal which feeds on grass

green flush growth of new grass stimulated by fire in the dry season

ground water water held in underground masses of rock and sediment

habitat the place in which a plant or animal lives

headload load of goods which a person can carry on his/her head

herbivore animal which eats plants

home-range total area used by an individual animal or population

hunter-gatherers people living by hunting with primitive weapons and collecting edible parts of plants

igneous rock rock formed from magma by volcanic action or intrusions

incisor chisel-shaped tooth in front of the mouth in mammals

indigenous native to a particular area; not introduced

initiation rite ceremony to introduce an individual into a specific role in society

inselberg steep-sided hill rising sharply from the surrounding area, formed by residual intrusive rock

inter-tropical convergence zone climatic zone where south-east trade winds meet moist Zaïre air masses from the north-west, and north-east monsoon air masses

intrusive rock rock formed from magma which did not reach the earth's surface but which solidified underground

Julbernardia **woodland** type of deciduous woodland in which species of the genus *Julbernardia* are dominant

leaching removal of soluble soil nutrients through downward movement of water through soil

levee low embankment formed on either side of a drainage channel by the deposition of coarse material during flooding

magma molten material giving rise to igneous rock

mbuna highly coloured, territorial fish belonging to ten cichlid genera

metabolic rate rate of energy expenditure of an animal

metamorphic rock rock formed from another type of rock under extreme heat and/or pressure

milt spawn of male fish

mollusc animal of the phyllum Mollusca, which includes snails, mussels and octopuses; mostly aquatic with a soft body, often with a hard shell

monocline geological feature formed by the bending of rock beds from one level to another

monocropping the cultivation of a single crop, often over a large area or for a long period of time

montane grassland grassland occurring at high altitude

national park area declared under the National Parks Act for the conservation and study of its animals in their natural habitat, its vegetation, and objects or places of geological, ethnological, historical, scientific and educational interest, for the benefit of the country's inhabitants and visitors

ngana trypanosomiasis disease transmitted by tsetse fly to certain domestic animals

niche   role of an organism in the environment

non-selective feeder   animal which is comparatively unselective in the food which it eats

orographic precipitation   precipitation resulting from the upward movement of air over high ground, when cooling causes condensation of water vapour, and cloud formation

pandemic   large-scale epidemic, for example affecting a whole continent

pediment   sloping surface leading up to a scarp or inselberg

perennial river   river which flows throughout the year

pheromone   chemical substance released by an animal to affect the behaviour or development of other individuals of the same species, for example sexual attractants

phytoplankton   plankton composed of plant organisms

plankton   small organisms which float or drift passively in a waterbody

population   a group of organisms of the same species occupying a particular space at a particular time

Pre-Cambrian   early geological era which occurred more than 600 million year ago

predator   animal which catches and eats other animals

prehensile   capable of taking hold of something

prey   animal which is killed and eaten by a predator

primary producer   organism which produces organic material from inorganic substances through the process of photosynthesis: i.e. plants

protozoan   organism belonging to the phyllum Protozoa which comprises single-celled animals with at least one well defined nucleus

rain shrine   sacred place where local people worship the spirits and take them offerings, praying for rain

rain shadow   occurrence of low rainfall in certain areas due to their location relative to slopes and mountains. Orographic lift over the latter causes high levels of precipitation there, and consequently much less rainfall in the leeward rain shadow areas beyond

raptor   bird of prey

rinderpest   virus disease affecting bovids; a great pandemic occurred at the end of the last century in Africa, decimating livestock, certain antelope and buffalo

river capture   diversion of a river to join another watercourse, leaving its old drainage line dry, often as a result of geomorphological changes

riverine vegetation   vegetation growing along the line of a river, often dependent on the relatively high water-table there

ruminant   group of mammals including antelope, buffalo, deer, cattle, sheep and goats whose complicated stomach has a rumen and other compartments. Ruminants have no upper incisors, and chew cud

saline seepage   slow flow of water with a high salt content from underground

salinity   salt content

salmonid   fish belonging to the family Salmonidae

savanna   vegetation type comprising grass and scattered trees

sedimentation   deposition of sediments

seine net   wide fishing net which hangs vertically, the ends being drawn together to enclose the fish

seismological   pertaining to earthquakes

selective feeder   animal which feeds selectively on the most nutritious species of plants and parts of plants

shifting cultivation   rotational system of cultivation whereby the natural vegetation is cleared and crops grown for one or more years until the soil loses fertility; the area is then abandoned and a new area cleared. The original area may be recleared and used some years later

sleeping sickness   trypanosomiasis, a disease occurring in man, transmitted by the tsetse fly in certain areas; potentially fatal if not treated

sounder   family group of warthog or bushpig

speciation   the evolution of new species

spoor   track or sign of an animal (hoof-prints, droppings, etc)

subcutaneous   immediately below the dermis of the skin of a vertebrate

subsistence hunting   hunting for food, as opposed to hunting for commercial gain

subsistence agriculture   growing of crops (and possibly rearing of livestock) to provide food for the family group, as opposed to commercial production

succession (plant)   progressive change in the composition of a plant community during the development of vegetation, normally from initial colonisation to climax

symbiotic   type of relationship between two individuals of different species which is to their mutual advantage

tectonic   concerning the structure of the earth's crust, or changes affecting it

termitarium   nest of termites

terrestrial   land (as opposed to water)

territory   an area inhabited by an individual or group of animals which is defended against intruders of the same species

thicket   dense, woody vegetation type

translocate   transport to another area

tributary   stream or river which flows into a larger river or lake

tsetse fly   fly of the genus *Glossina* which in some locations transmits sleeping sickness to man and *ngana* to certain animals

tuyère   nozzle through which the blast is forced into a furnace

understorey   lower layer of vegetation

ventral   situated at that side of the animal which normally faces downwards

watershed   narrow elevated tract of land separating adjacent catchment areas

water-table   upper level at which the soil is saturated with water

weathering   natural production of rock wastes by mechanical and chemical means

zoogeographical region   geographical region which has its own distinct fauna

zooplankton   plankton composed of small animals

References

1 *Principles of Physical Geology.*   A. Holmes. Nelson. 1978

2 Richard White: personal communication

3 *The Inland Waters of Tropical Africa.*   L.C. Beadle. Longman. 1974

4 A preliminary survey of the cichlid fishes of rocky habitats in Lake Malaŵi. A.J. Ribbinck, B.A. Marsh, A.C. Marsh, A.C. Ribbinck and B.J. Sharp. *South African Journal of Zoology.*   18 (3): 149–310. 1983

5 *Malaŵi: a Geographical Study.*   J.G. Pike and G.T. Rimmington. Oxford University Press. 1965

6 *The National Atlas of Malaŵi.*   Department of Surveys, Blantyre. 1985

7 Silver Jubilee Journal, Mulanje Mountain Club. Edited by R. Rainbow. Blantyre. 1978

8 *The Early History of Malaŵi.*   Edited by B. Pachai. Longman. 1972

9 *Malaŵi, the Warm Heart of Africa.*   H. Reich and J. Clough. Hanns Reich Verlag. 1984

10 *Guide to Places of Interest around Lilongwe.* J.M. Carter. National Fauna Preservation Society. In press

11 Staple subsistence crops of Africa. G.P. Murdock. *Geographical Review*, 50: 523–540. 1960

12 Miss D.D. Kaspin, Department of Anthropology, University of Chicago: personal communication

13 *A Guide to Malaŵi's National Parks and Game Reserves.*   G.D. Hayes. Montfort Press, Limbe. Undated

14 The introduction and spread of maize in Africa. M.P. Miracle. *Journal of African History*, 6 (1): 39–55. 1965

15 David Livingstone Centre Exhibition, Blantyre, Scotland

16 *Lilongwe: a Historical Study.* P.A. Cole-King. Department of Antiquities Publication no. 10, Zomba. 1971

17 *Elephant Haunts — being a Sportsman's Narrative of the Search for Livingstone.* H. Faulkner. 1868, republished in 1984 by the Society of Malaŵi and the Royal Geographical Society

18 *Cape Maclear.* P.A. Cole-King. Department of Antiquities Publication no. 4, Zomba. 1968

19 Masterplans for national parks and wildlife management. J.E. Clarke. Department of National Parks and Wildlife, Lilongwe. 1983

20 *Alfred Sharpe of Nyasaland — Builder of Empire.* R.B. Boeder. R.B. Boeder. 1980

21 The great Ethiopian famine of 1888–1892: a new assessment. R. Pankhurst. *Journal of the History of Medicine and Allied Sciences*, 21: 96–124. 1966

22 *Animal Life in Africa.* J. Stevenson-Hamilton. Heinemann. 1912

23 *British Central Africa.* H.H. Johnston. Edward Arnold. 1897

24 Report of the first three years' administration of the eastern portion of British Central Africa. H.H. Johnston. 31 March, 1894.

25 Big Game. A. Sharpe. Appendix 1 in: Report on the Trade and General Condition of the British Central Africa Protectorate, 1895–1896. H.H. Johnston.

26 *Wild Game in Zambezia.* R.C.F. Maugham. John Murray. 1914

27 *The Rise of our East African Empire.* F.D. Lugard. William Blackwood and Sons. 1893

28 Representation of biotic communities in protected areas: a Malaŵian case study. J.E. Clarke and R.H.V. Bell. *Biological Conservation,* 35: 293–311. 1986

29 *Malaŵi Monthly Statistical Bulletin: June 1984.*   National Statistical Office, Zomba. 1984

30 various articles, *Daily Times.* 1986

31 Tourism masterplans for national parks and game reserves

in Malaŵi. J.M. Carter. Department of National Parks and Wildlife, Lilongwe. 1985

32 Malaŵi: fuelwood and pole forestry component. Forestry section background. Lilongwe. 1978

33 Environmental effects of development on Malaŵi: Phase II Report. M.A. Brunt, A.J.B. Mitchell and R.C. Zimmermann. AG:/DP/MLW/81.001 Consultant Report. Food and Agriculture Organisation, Rome. 1984

34 *Malaŵi's National Parks and Game Reserves.* John Hough. National Fauna Preservation Society. In press.

35 *Guide to the Mulanje Massif.* F. Eastwood. Lorton Publications, South Africa. 1979

36 *Venture to the Interior.* L. van der Post. The Hogarth Press. 1961

37 Dr. F. Dowsett-Lemaire and Mr. R.J. Dowsett: personal communication

38 *Fingira Preliminary Report.* B.H. Sandelowsky and K.R. Robinson. Department of Antiquities Publication no. 3, Zomba. 1968

39 The Nyika Plateau, Nyasaland. J.C. Cater. *Oryx,* 2: 298–302. 1953

40 Prof. N.J. van der Merwe, Department of Archaeology, University of Cape Town and Prof. D.H. Avery, Department of Engineering, Brown University, Rhode Island: various papers in preparation

41 *The Land of the Lake — a Guide to Malaŵi.* D. Tattersall. Blantyre Periodicals Ltd. 1982

42 Homing ability and territorial replacement in some forest birds in south-central Africa. R.J. Dowsett and F. Dowsett-Lemaire. *Ostrich,* 57: 25–31. 1986

43 *Zovo Chipolo Forest Nature Trail.* D.O. Elias. Department of National Parks and Wildlife, Lilongwe. 1984

44 *Bird-watching in Malaŵi.* R.J. Dowsett. Department of National Parks and Wildlife, Lilongwe. 1982

45 Mr. K. Bota, Game-scout, Department of National Parks and Wildlife, Malaŵi: personal communication

46 Republic of Malaŵi, maps illustrating development projects 1983/4 — 1985/6. Department of Surveys, Blantyre. 1983

47 *Kasungu National Park — an introduction to the ecology, history and management of the park.* R.H.V. Bell. Department of National Parks and Wildlife, Kasungu. 1984

48 Traditions of power and politics in early Malaŵi; a case study of Kasungu District from about 1750 to 1933. K.M. Phiri. *Society of Malaŵi Journal,* 35 (2): 24–40. 1982

49 The social organisation of antelope in relation to their ecology. P.J. Jarman. *Behaviour,* 48: 215–267. 1974

50 *Wild Dogs of the World.* L.E. Bueler. Constable. 1974

51 *Serengeti: Dynamics of an Ecosystem.* Edited by A.R.E. Sinclair and M. Norton-Griffiths. University of Chicago Press. 1979

52 *The Serengeti Lion.* G.B. Schaller. University of Chicago Press. 1972

53 *A Field Guide to the Larger Mammals of Africa.* J. Dorst and P. Dandelot. Collins. 1970

54 Dr. R.H.V. Bell, Senior Parks and Wildlife Officer (Research), Department of National Parks and Wildlife, Malaŵi: personal communication

55 Vwaza Marsh Game Reserve. R.H.V. Bell and J.N.B. Mphande. Department of National Parks and Wildlife, Kasungu. 1980

56 Mr. T. McShane, Parks and Wildlife Officer (Research), Department of National Parks and Wildlife, Malaŵi and Mrs. E. McShane-Caluzi: personal communication

57 The value of Malaŵi's national parks, game and forest reserves to fish conservation and fisheries management. D. Tweddle. *Nyala,* 11 (1): 5–11. 1985

58 *African Insect Life.* S.H. Skaife, revised by J. Ledger. Struik. 1979

59 The biology of aardvark (Tubulidentata — Orycteropodidae). D.A. Melton. *Mammal Review,* 6(2): 75–88. 1976

60 *Roberts Birds of South Africa.* Revised by G.R. McLachlan and R. Liversidge. John Voelcker Bird Book Fund. 1978

61 Dr. P. Mundy, Ornithologist, Department of National Parks and Wildlife Management, Zimbabwe: personal communication

62 Convergent evolution between the Lake Malaŵi *mpasa* (Cyprinidae) and the Atlantic salmon (Salmonidae). D. Tweddle and D.S.C. Lewis. *Luso: Journal of Science and Technology (Malaŵi),* 4 (1): 11–20. 1983

63 Breeding behaviour of the *mpasa, Opsaridium microlepis* (Gunther) (Pisces: Cyprinidae) in Lake Malaŵi. D. Tweddle. *Journal of the Limnological Society of Southern Africa,* 9 (1): 23–28. 1983

64 Angling on the Bua River, Nkhotakota Game Reserve, Malaŵi. D.S.C. Lewis. Department of National Parks and Wildlife, Lilongwe. 1984

65 *Trees of Southern Africa.* K.C. Palgrave. Struik. 1977

66 *Useful Plants of Malaŵi.* J. Williamson. Montfort Press, Limbe. 1974

67 *Trees of Malaŵi.* J.S. Pullinger and A.M. Kitchin. Blantyre Print and Publishing, Blantyre. 1982

68 Development of Lake Malaŵi and the Shire River: identification of the constraints imposed by water level fluctuations. R. Crossley. In: *Proceedings of the Southern Africa Conference of the Commonwealth Geographical Bureau,* Lusaka; edited by G. Williams. 1986

69 On the recent high levels of Lake Malaŵi. D.H. Eccles. *South African Journal of Science,* 80: 461–468. 1984

70 *African Cichlids of Lakes Malaŵi and Tanganyika.* H.R. Axelrod and W.E. Burgess. T.F.H. Publications Inc., Neptune, New Jersey. 1981

71 *Ecology of Fresh Waters.* B. Moss. Blackwell Scientific Publications. 1980

72 Dr. D.S.C. Lewis, Fisheries Research Officer, Department of Fisheries, Malaŵi: personal communication

73 Mr. D. Tweddle, Fisheries Research Officer, Department of Fisheries, Malaŵi: personal communication

74 No plan for exotic fish in Lake Malaŵi. *Daily Times.* 23 April 1986

75 Dr. K.R. McKaye, Duke University: personal communication

76 'Elephant' Island on Lake Nyasa. R.C. Wood. *Nyasaland Journal,* 11 (1): 23–24. 1958

77 *David Livingstone: the Dark Interior.* O. Ransford. John Murray. 1978

78 *Looking at Animals.* H.B. Cott. Collins. 1975

79 Mr. A.M. Morgan-Davies, Parks and Wildlife Officer, Department of National Parks and Wildlife, Malaŵi: personal communication

80 Majete Game Reserve. R.H.V. Bell. Department of National Parks and Wildlife, Kasungu. 1984

81 Game preservation in Nyasaland. B.L. Mitchell. *Oryx,* 2: 98–110. 1954

82 The Mijeti. G.D. Hayes. *Oryx,* 2: 294–298. 1954

83 *The Eel.* F.–W. Tesch. Chapman and Hall. 1977

84 MSc project progress report. B.Y. Sherry. University of Malaŵi, 1986

85 *Birds of Eastern and North Eastern Africa. (African Handbook of Birds; series 1).* C.W. Mackworth-Praed and C.H.B. Grant. Longman Group. 1980

86 *A Field Guide to Lengwe National Park.* B.Y. Sherry and A.J. Ridgeway. Montfort Press, Limbe. 1984

87 How Independence saved an African reserve. G.D. Hayes. *Oryx,* 9: 24–27. 1967

88 Estimate of nyala numbers, Lengwe National Park, August-October 1982. R.H.V. Bell and H.M. Banda. Department of National Parks and Wildlife, Kasungu. 1983

89 *Amphibians of Malaŵi.* M.M. Stewart. State University of New York Press. 1967

90 Mr. F.X. Mkanda, Parks and Wildlife Officer, and Mr. L.D. Sefu, Parks and Wildlife Officer, Department of National Parks and Wildlife, Malaŵi: personal communication

91 Mr. M.M. Sakala, Parks and Wildlife Assistant, Department of National Parks and Wildlife, Malaŵi: personal communication

92 *Status of the Mwabvi rhino (Diceros bicornis).* H. Jachmann. *Nyala,* 10 (2): 77–90. 1984

93 *Black rhinoceros and other large mammals in the Mwabvi Game Reserve.* I.S.C. Parker. Wildlife Services Ltd, Nairobi. 1976

94 *Birds of the World.* O.L. Austin. Paul Hamlyn, London. 1961

Note that where a reference number appears inside a full-stop in the text it refers only to information contained in that sentence. Where it appears outside a full-stop it also refers to information in the previous sentence or sentences.

General information for visitors

Note that this information was collected in 1985/6, and some changes in the future are inevitable.

Transport to Malaŵi

Air: there are international flights to Lilongwe from Zimbabwe, South Africa, Zambia, Tanzania, Kenya, Mauritius, France, Holland and Great Britain.

Road: Malaŵi is accessible from Southern Africa on tarred roads through Zambia to Mchinji, and from East Africa via Tanzania to Karonga (not all sections of this route are tarred). At the time of writing it was unsafe to drive through Mozambique to Malaŵi.

Transport in Malaŵi

Air

Scheduled internal flights are operated between Blantyre, Lilongwe, Mzuzu and Karonga by Air Malaŵi (PO Box 84, Blantyre, tel 620 177, telex 4245 MALAWAIR MI; PO Box 89, Lilongwe, tel 720 966, telex 4762 MALAWAIR MI; PO Box 78, Mzuzu, tel 332 644, telex 4878 MALAWAIR MI).

Air charter services are available from Air Malaŵi (address as above) and from Capital Air Services Ltd. (Box 14, Zomba; tel 522 679).

Road

Car hire: various car-hire companies operate from Lilongwe, Mzuzu, Blantyre, Nkopola Lodge, and Lilongwe and Blantyre airports, offering two-wheel and four-wheel-drive vehicles, self-drive or chauffeur-driven. Companies include:

Halls Car Hire (Hertz licencee), PO Box 368, Blantyre, tel 633 907, telex 4744 HERTZ MI; PO Box 49, Lilongwe, tel 721 977, telex 4787 HERTZ MI; PO Box 229, Mzuzu, tel 332 122

Mandala Motors (Avis), PO Box 467, Blantyre, tel 620 721, telex 4732 AVIS MI; PO Box 218, Lilongwe, tel 721 322, telex 4789 AVIS MI

SS Rent-a-Car, PO Box 2282, Blantyre, tel 635 597, telex 4531 RENTACAR MI; PO Box 997, Lilongwe, tel 733 787/ 721 213

Country Car Hire Services, PO Box 1132, Lilongwe, tel 721 976, telex 4842 COUNTRY MI

Lotus Car Hire, PO Box 5824, Limbe, tel 650 960

There are garages in all the major centres, and petrol stations in many of the smaller towns. Occasional petrol shortages occurred up until 1984 because of logistical supply problems. The situation has improved since then, but should it recur, tourists can obtain special permits for petrol by applying to the local district commissioner. Spare parts for cars are usually but not always available.

Many of the major roads are tarred, but a few major and nearly all secondary and district roads are not. Practically all of the untarred roads are suitable for saloon cars with reasonable ground clearance during the dry season, but many become impassable except to four-wheel-drive vehicles during the rains.

Bus services operate throughout the country. A comfortable coach service runs between Lilongwe and Blantyre, and express buses operate between the main towns. Seats on these two services may be reserved in advance. There is also an extensive network of local bus services; these tend to be slow and very crowded. All bus services are operated by United Transport (Malaŵi) Ltd., PO Box 176, Blantyre, tel 671 388, telex 4152 UNITED MI. Coach reservations only are made through Halls Car Hire, Blantyre (address above) or at the Halls desk in the Capital Hotel, Lilongwe.

Lake

Two steamers each provide a weekly passenger service on Lake Malaŵi between Monkey Bay and Chilumba. The *Ilala* has first class cabins, restaurant and upper deck with bar, as well as second and third class seats. The *Mtendere* has second and third class seats. Advance reservations may be made for cabins on the *Ilala*. The steamer service is operated by Malaŵi Railways Ltd., PO Box 5492, Limbe, tel 640 844, telex 4810 MARLYS MI.

Boats may be hired from many places on Lake Malaŵi, including most of the hotels, the Department of Fisheries, and local fishermen. Boats on the Elephant Marsh may be hired from the Department of Fisheries at Chiromo, or from local fishermen.

Rail

Passenger rail services operate between Lilongwe, Salima, Blantyre and Nsanje. Trains tend to be slow, and the service is not much used by visitors. It is run by Malaŵi Railways, address as above.

Accommodation and food

Hotel accommodation is available in the main cities and at a few centres on Lake Malaŵi. Cheaper accommodation is available in the many forestry, council and government rest houses throughout the country; these provide comfortable, basic accommodation and are often self-catering. The national parks and game reserves have a variety of mostly low-cost accommodation facilities, described in detail in the information box for each park and reserve in the relevant chapters of this book. It is possible to camp in the grounds of many rest houses and in some of the national parks, game reserves and forest reserves, and there are camping sites at Nkopola Leisure Centre, the Livingstonia Beach Hotel, Nkhata Bay and on the Zomba Plateau. Apart from Nkhata Bay, these sites having running water and ablution facilities. Camping is also permitted in the grounds of the Lilongwe Golf Club and the Blantyre Sports Club, with use of the facilities. When camping out in the bush during the dry season, please take special care not to start bush fires.

The main hotels are:

Capital Hotel, PO Box 30018, Lilongwe 3, tel 730 444, telex 4892 CAPHOT MI;

Lilongwe Hotel, PO Box 44, Lilongwe, tel 721 866, telex 4321 LILOTEL MI;

Mount Soche Hotel, PO Box 284, Blantyre, tel 620 588, telex 4235 OVEROTEL MI;

Ryalls Hotel, PO Box 21, Blantyre, tel 620 955, telex 4481 RYLLS MI;

Shire Highlands Hotel, PO Box 5204, Limbe, tel 650 055;

Mzuzu Hotel, PO Box 231, Mzuzu, tel 332 622, telex 4853 MZUTEL MI;

Ku Chawe Inn (Zomba Plateau), PO Box 71, Zomba, tel 522 342;

Kudya Discovery Lodge, Liwonde, c/o PO Box 2839, Blantyre, tel 634 666, telex 4168 MI;

Nkopola Lodge (lakeshore), PO Box 14, Mangochi, tel 584 223 (39 km south of Monkey Bay);

Club Makokola (lakeshore), PO Box 59, Mangochi, tel 584 228 (34 km south of Monkey Bay);

Livingstonia Beach Hotel (lakeshore), PO Box 11, Salima, tel 261 339 (21 km east of Salima);

Chintheche Inn (lakeshore), PO Chintheche, tel Chintheche 11.

Government rest houses are run by the Department of Tourism, PO Box 402, Blantyre, tel 620 300, telex 4645 TOURISM MI. District council rest houses are run by individual councils.

Forestry rest houses are run by the Department of Forestry. They are located in forest reserves, and offer comfortable self-catering accommodation in very pleasant surroundings. Reservations for the two rest houses on the Viphya should be made to PO Chikangawa, tel Mzimba 49 or 332 413; reservations for the Chintheche rest house to PO Box 223, Mzuzu (tel: 332 511); and reservations for Ntchisi and Dzalanyama to PO Box 65, Lilongwe, tel 721 244. When the Dedza forestry rest house opens it will be booked through the latter office. There is also a more expensive rest house at Zomba, below the plateau, run by the sawmill (PO Box 241, Zomba, tel: 522 033). There are six forestry huts on Mulanje Mountain (Chambe, Lichenya, Thuchila, Chinzama, Madzeka and Sombani). They have a few items of furniture (though in many cases no beds), and are supplied with firewood and water. The Mulanje Mountain Club maintains a cupboard in each hut containing cooking and eating utensils, paraffin lamps, campbeds, mattresses, etc, for the use of members only. Accommodation in the huts is booked with the Department of Forestry, PO Box 50, Mulanje, tel Mulanje 218. One hut on Lichenya Plateau, owned by the Church of Central Africa Presbyterian (CCAP), is fully equipped for all visitors, and may

be booked through the CCAP at Likhubula House, PO Box 111, Mulanje, tel Mulanje 262.

It is advisable to reserve accommodation in advance if visiting at peak holiday times: Christmas/New Year, Easter, 14th May (public holiday), July/August and 17th October (public holiday).

For those on a self-catering holiday, all the cities and major towns have well-supplied shops selling a wide variety of perishable and non-perishable food items and alcohol, and colourful markets selling fresh produce. Local produce is usually cheap, but processed and imported commodities tend to be expensive because of external transport costs. Shop hours vary; some shops stay open relatively late and a few are open all day on Sunday.

The major cities have a variety of restaurants offering good food at reasonable prices.

Travel agencies and tour companies

Safari Tours operates exclusive guided tours to national parks, Lake Malaŵi and other places of interest (PO Box 2075, Blantyre, tel 635 057).

Other tour operators which handle reservations for visitors to Malaŵi are: Soche Tours and Travel (PO Box 2225, Blantyre, tel 620 777, telex 4452 SOCTO MI and PO Box 30406, Lilongwe 3, tel 731 477;

Halls (Hertz) Car Hire (addresses on page 163); telex 4725 SOCTO MI);

Budget Travel and Safaris (PO Box 2839, Blantyre);

G and T Tours and Travel (PO Box 30553, Lilongwe, tel 733 895).

Banks and post offices

There are banks in all the main towns of Malaŵi, and mobile banks operate to some of the smaller centres. The main banks are open to the public from 0800 to 1300 hours, Monday to Friday except on public holidays (1st January, 3rd March, Easter, 14th May, 6th July, first Monday in August, 17th October, and 25th and 26th of December). Travellers cheques and Visa, Access, Amex and Diners cards are acceptable, and travellers cheques may be cashed on the *Ilala* and in the main hotels by residents.

Post offices are open from 0730 to 1200 and from 1300 to 1700 hours, Monday to Friday, and the larger ones open from 0900 to 1000 on Sunday. They are closed on Saturday. Conventional poste restante facilities exist at post offices throughout Malaŵi.

Souvenirs and handicrafts

Many attractive handicrafts and souvenirs are available in Malaŵi. They include baskets, mats and other items made from palm leaves, mainly on sale near the lakeshore. Attractive tie-dyed material and clothes are produced by the Malaŵi Council for the Handicapped in Lilongwe, and woven mats, bags, etc are made by the blind in Blantyre. These items are on sale in many shops and at the factories themselves. Lengths of colourful African cloth, manufactured in Malaŵi, are stocked by many shops. Various types of pottery are available, and it is possible to visit the pottery at Malindi on the south-east shore of Lake

Malaŵi. There is a wide range of musical instruments for sale, such as drums, rattles, and xylophones made with gourds.

A wide variety of attractive carvings and jewellery of stone, ivory, bone, ebony and other types of wood can be bought, in the major towns and sometimes by the roadside. Wild animal trophies such as skins and horns are also sometimes available. When purchasing ivory it is essential to check that the vendor has a trophy-dealer's licence to ensure that the purchase is legal, and to obtain an official receipt for the goods. To export ivory it is necessary to obtain an export permit from the Department of National Parks and Wildlife, PO Box 30131, Lilongwe 3, tel 730 944 (the office is in Centre House in City Centre). 'Legal' ivory originates from elephants shot for crop protection and from ivory confiscated by the Government from poachers and illegal traffickers, and has been sold to licensed trophy dealers at government auctions. Revenue generated from these sales benefits conservation (albeit indirectly), as it influences the Department of National Parks and Wildlife's annual budget and hence its effectiveness in combating poaching and ivory smuggling. Illegal ivory in Malaŵi originates both from illegal hunting within the country, and from ivory smuggled in from Zambia and Mozambique for onward dispatch to other continents. Visitors can assist in the control of illegal trafficking, and hence in conservation of the remaining elephant in the region, by refusing to buy ivory from people not in possession of trophy-dealers' licences. This also applies to elephant skin and hair products and products from other endangered species: for example cheetah skins, leopard skins and rhino horn.

Dress

Certain dress restrictions are applied in Malaŵi. Ladies are not permitted to wear short skirts, trousers or shorts in many public places, though they can wear trousers in the national parks, game reserves and some forest reserves, and swimsuits may of course be worn at the main resorts on Lake Malaŵi and hotel swimming pools. Men must not have excessively long hair.

Health

There are few health hazards in Malaŵi. Malaria occurs and prophylactics are strongly advisable, particularly during the rains and near the lakeshore; mosquito nets should be used at night in places where mosquitoes are a problem. There is evidence of some chloroquine-resistant malaria. Bilharzia occurs in some waters and although most of Lake Malaŵi is quite safe, including the areas near to hotels and inns, it is not advisable to bathe in other lakes or rivers with still or slow-flowing water, especially near reeds. Sleeping sickness occurs only in isolated places in the north, and although the chances of catching it are very low, it is advisable to minimise bites from tsetse fly when in Vwaza Marsh Game Reserve. This can be done by wearing long sleeved shirts and long trousers and keeping vehicle windows shut.

All the major towns have well stocked chemist shops. As most drugs and other commodities are imported they tend to be expensive. There are hospitals in all the major towns, and small hospitals or health centres in most other towns and larger villages.

As for travel in all countries, it is advisable to have comprehensive medical insurance cover when visiting Malaŵi. Certain vaccinations are necessary; these vary from time to time and up-to-date information should be sought before travelling to Malaŵi.

Additional information including maps

Further tourist information may be obtained from the organisations listed on page 166. A list of books for further reading on Malaŵi is given on page 171.

There is an excellent map coverage of Malaŵi. For general purposes, the 1:1 000 000 Department of Surveys map of the country is ideal. A series of ten maps at 1:250 000 and another 159 maps at 1:50 000 give more detailed coverage. A special 1:30 000 map of Mulanje Mountain is very useful for visits to that area. All these maps are available from the Department of Surveys. Maps of most of the national parks are available from the Department of National Parks and Wildlife headquarters, or at the parks themselves.

Road distances in kilometres indicating shortest distances between locations on main roads. Those to parks and reserves are to the nearest entrance gate, or to Golden Sands in the case of the Lake Malaŵi National Park.

	Blantyre	Chintheche	Kasungu Town	Lilongwe	Livingstonia	Mulanje	Mzuzu	Nkhata Bay	Salima	Zomba	Kasungu N.P.	Lake Malaŵi N.P.	Lengwe N.P.	Liwonde N.P.	Majete G.R.	Mwabvi G.R.	Nkhotakota G.R.
Chintheche	649																
Kasungu Town	474	273															
Lilongwe	347	327	127														
Livingstonia	861	229	387	514													
Mulanje	81	730	555	428	942												
Mzuzu	725	93	251	378	136	806											
Nkhata Bay	694	45	299	372	184	775	48										
Salima	365	292	233	106	521	446	385	337									
Zomba	66	583	408	281	795	147	659	628	299								
Kasungu N.P.	512	311	38	165	425	593	289	337	271	446							
Lake Malaŵi N.P.	270	431	370	245	660	351	524	476	147	204	410						
Lengwe N.P.	77	726	551	424	938	158	802	771	442	143	589	347					
Liwonde N.P.	123	538	363	236	750	204	614	583	254	57	401	159	200				
Majete G.R.	67	716	541	414	928	148	792	761	432	133	579	337	48	190			
Mwabvi G.R.	138	787	612	485	999	154	863	832	503	204	650	408	79	261	109		
Nkhotakota G.R.	462	175	61	115	404	543	268	220	149	396	99	288	539	351	529	600	
Nyika N.P.	854	222	380	507	141	935	129	177	514	788	418	653	931	743	921	992	397
Vwaza Marsh G.R.	816	184	342	469	103	897	91	139	476	750	380	615	893	705	883	954	359

(Nyika N.P. / Vwaza Marsh G.R. final column: 19)

Appendix 2

Useful addresses

In Malaŵi

Department of National Parks and Wildlife
Headquarters
PO Box 30131
Lilongwe 3
tel 730 944 (general)
    730 853 (accommodation reservations)

Lilongwe Nature Sanctuary
PO Box 30172
Lilongwe 3
tel 730 874

Department of Forestry
PO Box 30048
Lilongwe 3
tel 731 322

Department of Fisheries
PO Box 593
Lilongwe
tel 721 766

Department of Antiquities
PO Box 264
Lilongwe
tel 721 844

Museum of Malaŵi
PO Box 30360
Chichiri
Blantyre 3
tel 672 001

Lake Malaŵi Museum
PO Box 128
Mangochi
tel 584 346

Department of Surveys (map sales offices)
PO Box 120
Lilongwe
tel 720 355

PO Box 349
Blantyre
tel 633 722

Department of Tourism
PO Box 402
Blantyre
tel 620 300; telex 4645 TOURISM MI

Southern Africa Regional Tourism Council
PO Box 564
Blantyre
tel 620 722; telex 4168 SARTOC MI

National Fauna Preservation Society
Blantyre branch
PO Box 1429
Blantyre

Zomba branch
PO Box 321
Zomba

Lilongwe branch
PO Box 30293
Lilongwe 3

Mzuzu branch
PO Box 325
Mzuzu

Society of Malaŵi
PO Box 125
Blantyre

Mulanje Mountain Club
PO Box 240
Blantyre

Angling Society of Malaŵi
PO Box 744
Blantyre

Abroad

Tourism agencies
Air Malaŵi, PO Box 20117, Nairobi, Kenya
Air Malaŵi, PO Box 2752, Harare, Zimbabwe
SARTOC, PO Box 48405, Johannesburg, South Africa
Malaŵi Tourist Office, 33 Grosvenor Street, London W1X 0HS

Areas to visit for special interests

Game-viewing

Nyika, Kasungu, Liwonde and Lengwe National Parks.
Best time of year: see information boxes on individual parks.

Bird-watching

All the national parks; Vwaza Marsh Game Reserve; Dzalanyama, Ntchisi, Dedza, Zomba, Kalwe and Khwazi Forest Reserves; Lilongwe Nature Sanctuary; Salima/Senga Bay; Kasinthula and the Elephant Marsh.
Best time of year: November to December when migrants are present.

Tropical fish

Waters off Cape Maclear and the islands of the Lake Malaŵi National Park; Nkhata Bay area; Likoma Island.
Best time of year: December to April, July to September.

Wild flowers

Orchids: Nyika National Park; Viphya, Zomba and Dzalanyama Forest Reserves.
Best time of year: January to February during the rains.
Aloes: Nyika National Park; Dedza, Zomba and Mulanje Forest Reserves.
Best time of year: June to July.
Other flowers: many areas of grassland, *dambo* and woodland.
Best time of year: December to March during the rains, and September to October after bush fires.

Walking

All the national parks and game reserves; Mulanje, Ndirande, Zomba, Mangochi, Dedza, Dzalanyama, Chongoni, Ntchisi, Ngara, Viphya and many other forest reserves; Michiru Mountain Conservation Area; Ngala, Bunda and Nkhoma Hills.
Best time of year: June to August in low-lying areas; May to October elsewhere. The grass is tall in many areas until it is burnt in July/August; then walking becomes easier but views are more hazy. During the rains (November/December to April) walking can be very pleasant on dry days, though vehicular access to some areas can be problematic.

Horse-riding

Zomba Plateau (dry season only).

Rock climbing

Mulanje Forest Reserve (longest climb in Africa); Ndirande, Zomba, Dedza and Soche Forest Reserves; Lake Malaŵi National Park (Nankumba Peninsula and Nkhudzi); Kirk Range and Midima Hills.

Scenery

Nyika, Lake Malaŵi and Liwonde National Parks; Vwaza Marsh, Nkhotakota and Majete Game Reserves; Mulanje and Zomba Forest Reserves; areas near Lake Malaŵi and the Shire River; Manchewe Falls and the Livingstonia area; many of the major road routes especially those on the rift valley escarpment and the M1 between Lilongwe and Blantyre.

History and antiquities

Kapichira Falls in Majete Game Reserve and missionary graves on the access road; Fort Lister (ruins of fort built to control the pass which was used by slave caravans); Blantyre (historical buildings and museum); Zomba (historical buildings and Botanical Gardens); Magomero (mission); Mangochi (clock-tower and museum); Cape Maclear in the Lake Malaŵi National Park (first Livingstonia mission site; missionary graves; *Mwalawamphini* rock); Chencherere Rocks near Dedza (rock shelters and paintings); Dzalanyama Hills (believed to be site of creation); Kasungu National Park (rock shelters and paintings, fortified villages and iron-smelting kilns); Nkhotakota (old slave-trading centre); Bandawe (site of second Livingstonia Mission); cathedral on Likoma island; present Livingstonia Mission; Fingira Cave in Nyika National Park; Karonga (First World War military cemetery and fortified tree).

Angling

Nyika National Park and Zomba and Mulanje Forest Reserves (rainbow trout: closed May to August inclusive except Nyika streams); Dedza Forest Reserve (*chambo*); Shire River below Kapichira Falls (tigerfish, best in October/November); Upper Shire outside Liwonde National Park (*sungwa*); Lake Malaŵi (*sungwa, binga, ncheni, kampango* and others); northern tributaries of Lake Malaŵi including the Bua River in Nkhotakota Game Reserve (*mpasa, sanjika* and yellowfish, best in the early dry season). Note that fish caught in Nkhotakota Game Reserve must be returned live to the river.

The only permits necessary are for angling in Nkhotakota Game Reserve and for trout fishing. See page 86 for details of the former. Permits for trout fishing are obtainable at Chelinda Camp for Nyika (page 36); Zomba Forestry Office for Zomba (PO Box 29, Zomba, tel: 523 339); Likhubula Forestry Office for Mulanje (PO Box 50, Mulanje, tel: 465 218) and Dedza Forestry Office for Dedza (PO Box 84, Dedza, tel: 220 217). Anglers arriving in the forest reserves outside office hours without a permit may start fishing immediately, and should purchase a permit from the forest guard on duty in the area.

Appendix 4

Scientific names of indigenous animals and plants referred to in the text

Mammals

English name	Scientific name	Local name[13,34,47,90]
aardvark	*Orycteropus afer*	*godi, nkumba-kumba, nsele, uningu*
baboon	*Papio ursinus* and *P. cynocephalus* (the latter in the north only)	*nyani*
buffalo	*Syncerus caffer*	*njati, enari*
bushbuck	*Tragelaphus scriptus*	*mbawala, balala, paala*
bushpig	*Potamochoerus porcus*	*nguluwe*
caracal	*Felis caracal*	
cheetah	*Acinonyx jubatus*	*kakwio, kambulubulu*
civet	*Civettictis civetta*	*fungwe, vungo, chombwe, zungwala*
dassie (hyrax)	*Dendrohyrax* and *Procavia* spp.	*mbila, nkonko, zumba*
duiker, blue	*Cephalophus monticola*	*kaduma*
grey	*Sylvicapra grimmia*	*gwapi, hisa*
red	*Cephalophus natalensis*	*gwapi*
eland	*Tragelaphus oryx*	*nchefu, mpofu*
elephant	*Loxodonta africana*	*njobvu, ndemo*
elephant shrew, chequered	*Rhynchocyon cirnei*	*sakwe*
genet	*Genetta rubiginosa* and *G. mossambica* (the latter in the south only)	*mwili*
grysbok, Sharpe's	*Raphicerus sharpei*	*kasenye, goro, tungwa*
hare, red rock	*Pronolagus rupestris*	*kalulu*
hartebeest, Lichtenstein's	*Alcelaphus lichtensteini*	*nkhozi, ngondo*
hippopotamus	*Hippopotamus amphibius*	*mvuu, bokho, chigwere*
honey badger (ratel)	*Mellivora capensis*	*chiuli, chimbuli*
hyena, spotted	*Crocuta crocuta*	*fisi, chimbwe*
hyrax (see dassie)		
impala	*Aepyceros melampus*	*nswala*
jackal, side-striped	*Canis adustus*	*nkhandwe*
klipspringer	*Oreotragus oreotragus*	*chinkhoma*
kudu, greater	*Tragelaphus strepsiceros*	*ngoma, ndandala*
leopard	*Panthera pardus*	*nyalugwe, kambuku, kimbwe*
lion	*Panthera leo*	*mkango, lisimba*
mongoose, banded	*Mungos mungo*	*msulu*
slender	*Galerella sanguinea*	*nyenga*
monkey, blue	*Cercopithecus albogularis*	*nchima*
vervet	*Cercopithecus pygerythrus*	*pusi*
nyala	*Tragelaphus angasi*	*boo*
oribi	*Ourebia ourebi*	*choe, chosimbi*
otter, Cape clawless	*Aonyx capensis*	*katumbu, katubwi*
spotted-necked	*Hydrictis maculicollis*	*katumbu, kauzi*
pangolin	*Manis temmincki*	*ngaka*
porcupine	*Hystrix africaeaustralis*	*nungu*
puku	*Kobus vardoni*	*nseula*

English name	Scientific name	Local name[13,34,47,90]
ratel (see honey badger)		
reedbuck, Southern	*Redunca arundinum*	*mphoyo, nsengo*
rhinoceros, black	*Diceros bicornis*	*chipembere*
roan	*Hippotragus equinus*	*chilembwe, mpherembe*
sable antelope	*Hippotragus niger*	*mphalapala, mbalapi*
serval	*Felis serval*	*njuzi*
suni, Livingstone's	*Neotragus moschatus*	*kadumba, puru*
warthog	*Phacochoerus aethiopicus*	*njiri, kapulika*
waterbuck	*Kobus ellipsiprymnus*	*chuzu, nakodzwe*
wild cat	*Felis libyca*	*bvumbwe, bonga*
wild dog	*Lycaon pictus*	*mbulu*
wildebeest, Nyasaland	*Connochaetes taurinus johnstoni*	
zebra, Burchell's	*Equus burchelli*	*mbidzi, liduwe, boli*
zorilla	*Ictonyx striatus*	*Kanyimbi*

Birds

English name	Scientific name	English name	Scientific name
akalat, Gunning's	*Sheppardia gunningi*	Swainson's	*Francolinus swainsonii*
Sharpe's	*Sheppardia sharpei*	guineafowl, crested	*Guttera edouardi*
alethe, white-chested	*Alethe fuelleborni*	helmeted	*Numida meleagris*
apalis, Rudd's	*Apalis ruddi caniviridis*	hamerkop	*Scopus umbretta*
batis, Woodwards'	*Batis fratrum*	harrier, African marsh	*Circus ranivorus*
bee-eater, Böhm's	*Merops boehmi*	heron, Goliath	*Ardea goliath*
southern carmine	*Merops nubicoides*	squacco	*Ardeola ralloides*
broadbill, African	*Smithornis capensis*	hobby, European	*Falco subbuteo*
bulbul, grey-olive	*Phyllastrephus cerviniventris*	honeyguide, greater	*Indicator indicator*
olive-breasted		hornbill, ground	*Bucorvus cafer*
mountain	*Andropagus tephrolaemus*	ibis, sacred	*Threskiornis aethiopica*
yellow-streaked	*Phyllastrephus flavostriatus*	jacana, African	*Actophilornis africanus*
bustard, Denham's	*Otis denhami*	kingfisher, chestnut-bellied	*Halcyon leucocephala*
buzzard, augur	*Buteo rufofuscus*	giant	*Ceryle maxima*
lizard	*Kaupifalco monogrammicus*	malachite	*Alcedo cristata*
cormorant, reed	*Phalacrocorax africanus*	pied	*Ceryle rudis*
white-breasted	*Phalacrocorax carbo*	pygmy	*Ispidina picta*
coucal, green	*Ceuthmochares aereus*	striped	*Halcyon chelicuti*
crane, wattled	*Grus carunculatus*	kite, black-shouldered	*Elanus caeruleus*
crimsonwing, red-faced	*Cryptospiza reichenovii*	yellow-billed	*Milvus migrans parasitus*
cuckoo, barred long-tailed	*Cercococcyx montanus*	lanner	*Falco biarmicus*
darter, African	*Anhinga rufa*	loerie, green	*Tauraco persa*
dove, cinnamon	*Aplopelia larvata*	lovebird, Lilian's	*Agapornis lilianae*
duck, white-faced tree	*Dendrocygna viduata*	mannikin, pied	*Lonchura fringilloides*
eagle, bateleur	*Terathopius ecaudatus*	osprey	*Pandion haliaetus*
black-breasted snake	*Circaetus pectoralis*	owl, barn	*Tyto alba*
crowned	*Stephanoaetus coronatus*	Pel's fishing	*Scotopelia peli*
fish	*Haliaeetus vocifer*	parrot, brown-necked	*Poicephalus robustus*
long-crested	*Lophaetus occipitalis*	pelican	*Pelecanus* spp.
martial	*Polemaetus bellicosus*	peregrine	*Falco peregrinus*
egret, great white	*Egretta alba*	pigeon, rameron	*Columba arquatrix*
flamingo	*Phoenicopterus* spp.	pratincole, rock	*Glareola nuchalis*
flufftail, red-tailed	*Sarothrura affinis*	raven, white-necked	*Corvus albicollis*
flycatcher, black-and-white	*Bias musicus*	robin, Heuglin's	*Cossypha heuglini*
blue-mantled		olive-flanked	*Cossypha anomala*
crested	*Trochocercus cyanomelas*	red-capped	*Cossypha natalensis*
Livingstone's	*Erythrocercus livingstonei*	starred	*Pogonocichla stellata*
paradise	*Terpsiphone viridis*	sandgrouse, double-banded	*Pterocles bicinctus*
wattle-eyed	*Platysteira peltata*	shrike, gorgeous bush	*Malaconotus viridis*
francolin, red-winged	*Francolinus levaillantii crawshayi*	spoonbill, African	*Platalea alba*

English name	Scientific name
starling, white-winged	*Neocichla gutturalis*
stork, marabou	*Leptoptilos crumeniferus*
openbill	*Anastomus lamelligerus*
saddlebill	*Ephippiorhynchus senegalensis*
sunbird, greater double-collared	*Nectarinia afra whytei*
grey	*Nectarinia veroxii*
swallow, blue	*Hirundo atrocaerulea*
swift, mottled	*Apus aequatorialis*
scarce	*Schoutedenapus myoptilus*
tinkerbird, moustached green	*Pogoniulus leucomystax*
trogon, bar-tailed	*Apaloderma vittatum*
vulture, hooded	*Necrosyrtes monachus*
lappet-faced	*Aegypius tracheliotus*
palm-nut	*Gypohierax angolensis*
white-backed	*Gyps africanus*
white-headed	*Trigonoceps occipitalis*
warbler, red-winged	*Heliolais erythroptera*
waxbill, black-tailed grey	*Estrilda perreini*
swee	*Estrilda melanotis*
weaver, Baglafecht	*Ploceus baglafecht nyikae*

Reptiles

chameleon, Goetze's Nyika	*Chamaeleo goetzei nyikae*
crocodile	*Crocodylus niloticus*
monitor, water	*Varanus niloticus*
python	*Python sebae*
terrapin	*Pelusios sp.*
tortoise, hinged	*Kinixys sp.*
turtle, African mud	*Cycloderma frenatum*

Amphibians

bullfrog	*Pyxicephalus adspersus*
frog, great grey tree	*Chiromantis xerampelina*
squeaker, Nyika	*Arthroleptis xenodactyloides nyikae*
toad, Nyika dwarf	*Bufo taitanus nyikae*

Fish

binga	*Cyrtocara kiwinge*
catfish (Bua)	*Clarias gariepinus*
chambo	*Oreochromis spp.*
eel, mottled	*Anguilla nebulosa labiata*
elephant-snout fish	*Mormyrus longirostris*
kampango	*Bagrus meridionalis*
lake salmon (see *mpasa*)	
mbuna	*Cyathochromis, Cynotilapia, Genyochromis, Gephyrochromis, Iodotropheus, Labeotropheus, Labidochromis, Melanochromis, Petrotilapia and Pseudotropheus spp.*

English name	Scientific name
minnow (Bua)	*Barbus spp.*
mpasa	*Opsaridium microlepis*
ncheni	*Rhamphochromis spp.*
sanjika	*Opsaridium microcephalus*
sungwa	*Serranochromis robustus*
tigerfish	*Hydrocynus vittatus*
usipa	*Engraulicypris sardella*
utaka	*Cyrtocara spp.*
yellowfish	*Barbus spp.*

Plants

acacia, knobthorn	*Acacia nigrescens*
aloe	*Aloe spp.*
aningeria	*Aningeria adolfi-friedericii*
bamboo	*Oxytenanthera abyssinica*
baobab	*Adansonia digitata*
bracken	*Pteridium aquilinum*
candelabra tree	*Euphorbia ingens*
Cape olive	*Olea capensis*
cycad	*Encephalartos gratus*
dovyalis, shaggy-fruited	*Dovyalis macrocalyx*
elephant's tongue	*Streptocarpus goetzei*
euphorbia, red-flowered	*Euphorbia lividiflora*
everlasting flower	*Helichrysum spp.*
fever tree	*Acacia xanthophloea*
fig, strangler	*Ficus natalensis*
impala lily (see Sabi star)	
juniper	*Juniperus procera*
mahogany, forest Natal	*Trichilia dregeana*
Natal	*Trichilia emetica*
milkwood, brown-berry fluted	*Chrysophyllum gorungosanum*
mopane	*Colophospermum mopane*
Mulanje cedar	*Widdringtonia cupressoides*
mwabvi	*Erythrophleum suaveolens*
palm, borassus	*Borassus aethiopum*
fan	*Hyphaene ventricosa*
raffia	*Raphia farinifera*
wild date	*Phoenix reclinata*
papyrus	*Cyperus papyrus*
protea	*Protea spp.*
reed	*Phragmites spp.*
Sabi star	*Adenium obesum*
stag's horn lily	*Vellozia splendens*
stinkwood, bastard white	*Celtis gomphophylla*
strangler vine	*Fockea multiflora*
tree fern	*Cyathea spp.*
water lettuce	*Pistia stratiotes*
waterlily	*Nymphaea spp.*
wild mango	*Cordylla africana*
winterthorn	*Acacia albida*

Further recommended reading

General

Malaŵi: a Geographical Study. J.G. Pike and
G.T. Rimmington. Oxford University Press. 1965

Malaŵi, the Warm Heart of Africa. H. Reich and J. Clough.
Hanns Reich Verlag. 1984

The Land of the Lake: a Guide to Malaŵi. D. Tattersall. Blantyre
Periodicals Ltd. 1982

The National Atlas of Malaŵi. Department of Surveys, Blantyre.
1985

Guide to Places of Interest around Lilongwe. J.M. Carter.
National Fauna Preservation Society. In press

History

The Early History of Malaŵi. Edited by B. Pachai. Longman.
1972

Fingira Preliminary Report. B.H. Sandelowsky and K.R.
Robinson. Department of Antiquities Publication no. 3, Zomba.
1968

Cape Maclear. P.A. Cole-King. Department of Antiquities
Publication no. 4, Zomba. 1968

Lilongwe: a Historical Study. P.A. Cole-King. Department of
Antiquities Publication no. 10, Zomba. 1971

Livingstone's Lake — the Drama of Nyasa. O. Ransford. John
Murray. 1966

David Livingstone: the Dark Interior. O. Ransford. John Murray.
1978

The Livingstone Search Expedition 1867. P.A. Cole-King.
Department of Antiquities Publication no. 2, 1968, reissued in
1984 by The Society of Malaŵi, Blantyre

The Search after Livingstone. E.D. Young. 1868, republished in
1984 by The Society of Malaŵi and the Royal Geographical
Society

*Elephant Haunts — being a Sportsman's Narrative of the Search for
Livingstone.* H. Faulkner. 1868, republished in 1984 by the
Society of Malaŵi and the Royal Geographical Society

Nyassa — a Journal of Adventures. E.D. Young. 1977,
republished in 1984 by Blantyre Rotary Club

The Shire Highlands. J. Buchanan. 1885, republished in 1982 by
Blantyre Rotary Club

British Central Africa. H.H. Johnston. 1904, republished in
1985 by Blantyre Rotary Club

Alfred Sharpe of Nyasaland — Builder of Empire. R.B. Boeder.
R.B. Boeder. 1980

Central African Planter. reissue of the Protectorate's first
newspaper, 1895–6, by the Society of Malaŵi in 1983

Venture to the Interior. L. van der Post. The Hogarth Press.
1961

Protected areas

A Guide to Malaŵi's National Parks and Game Reserves.
G.D. Hayes. Montfort Press, Limbe. undated

Malaŵi's National Parks and Game Reserves. John Hough.
National Fauna Preservation Society. In press

A Field Guide to Lengwe National Park. B.Y. Sherry and
A.J. Ridgeway. Montfort Press, Limbe. 1984

*Kasungu National Park — an introduction to the ecology, history and
management of the park.* R.H.V. Bell. Department of National
Parks and Wildlife, Kasungu. 1984

Zovo Chipolo Forest Nature Trail. D.O. Elias. Department of
National Parks and Wildlife, Lilongwe. 1984

Zomba Plateau Mulunguzi Nature Trail. J. Alder *et al.* National
Fauna Preservation Society, Malaŵi. 1979

Chingwe's Hole Nature Trail, Zomba Plateau. T. Carter *et al.*
National Fauna Preservation Society, Malaŵi. 1979

Guide to the Mulanje Massif. F. Eastwood. Lorton Publications,
South Africa. 1979

Silver Jubilee Journal, Mulanje Mountain Club. Edited by
R. Rainbow. Blantyre, 1978

Rock climbing in Malaŵi. F. Eastwood. Unpublished

Mammals

A Field Guide to the Larger Mammals of Africa. J. Dorst and
P. Dandelot. Collins. 1970

A Field Guide to the Mammals of Africa including Madagascar.
T. Haltenorth and H. Diller. Collins. 1980

Wild Mammals. D. Kenmuir and R. Williams. Bundu Series,
Longman, Zimbabwe. 1984

Signs of the Wild — a field guide to the spoor and signs of the mammals of southern Africa.   C. Walker. Sable Publishers, South Africa. 1982

Mammals of Malaŵi, an annotated check list and atlas.   W.F.H. Ansell and R.J. Dowsett. Trendrine Press. In preparation

Checklist of the Mammals of Nyasaland.   R.C.H. Sweeney. Society of Malaŵi, Blantyre. 1959

Mammals of Malaŵi.   Department of National Parks and Wildlife, Lilongwe. 1982. (booklet and set of five posters)

Guide to the Rats and Mice of Rhodesia.   R.H.N. Smithers. Trustees of the National Museums and Monuments of Rhodesia. 1975

Birds

Roberts' Birds of Southern Africa.   Fifth edition by G.L. Maclean. Trustees of the John Voelcker Bird Book Fund, Cape Town. 1984

Birds of Eastern and North Eastern Africa. (African Handbook of Birds; series 1).   C.W. Mackworth-Praed and C.H.B. Grant. Longman Group. 1980

A Field Guide to the Birds of East Africa.   J.G. Williams and N. Arlott. Collins. 1980

Field Guide to the Birds of Southern Africa.   I. Sinclair. Struik. 1984

Birds of Southern Africa.   K. Newman. Macmillan. 1983

The Birds of Zambia.   C.W. Benson, R.K. Brooke, R.J. Dowsett and M.P.S. Irwin. Collins. 1971

The Birds of Malaŵi.   C.W. Benson and F.M. Benson. Montfort Press, Limbe. 1977

Bridging the Bird Gap — a field guide to the 64 species in Malaŵi not described in Roberts' Birds of South Africa.   N.G.B. Johnston-Stewart and J.B. Heigham. Montfort Press, Limbe. 1982

Birdwatching in Malaŵi.   R.J. Dowsett. Department of National Parks and Wildlife, Lilongwe. 1982 (poster with photographs and text)

Reptiles

Field Guide to the Snakes of Southern Africa.   V.F.M. Fitzsimons. Collins. 1970

Snakes of Zimbabwe.   D.G. Broadley and E.V. Cock. Bundu Series, Longman. Zimbabwe, 1975

Amphibians

Amphibians of Malaŵi.   M.M. Stewart. State University of New York Press. 1967

Fish

The Inland Waters of Tropical Africa.   L.C. Beadle. Longman. 1974

The Cichlid Fishes of the Great Lakes of Africa: their Biology and Evolution.   G. Fryer and T.D. Iles. Oliver and Boyd. 1972

Mbuna — Rockdwelling Cichlids of Lake Malaŵi, Africa.   P.B.N. Jackson and T. Ribbinck. T.F.H. Publications Inc., Neptune City, New Jersey. 1975

African Cichlids of Lakes Malaŵi and Tanganyika.   H.R. Axelrod and W.E. Burgess. T.F.H. Publications Inc., Neptune, New Jersey. 1981

A Guide to the Fishes of Lake Malaŵi National Park.   D.S. Lewis, P. Reinthal and J. Trendall. Creda Press, Cape Town. In press

Insects

African Insect Life.   S.H. Skaife, revised by J. Ledger. Struik. 1979

Field Guide to the Butterflies of Africa.   J.G. Williams. Collins. 1969

Butterflies of Malaŵi.   D. Gifford. Society of Malaŵi, Blantyre. 1965

A Guide to the Butterflies of Zambia.   E. Pinkey and I. Coe. Anglo American Corporation Ltd, Lusaka. 1977

Butterflies of Rhodesia.   R. Cooper. Bundu Series, Longman. 1973

Plants

Trees of Southern Africa.   K.C. Palgrave. Struik. 1977

A Field Guide to the Trees of Southern Africa.   E. Palmer. Collins. 1977

Common Trees of the Central Watershed Woodlands of Zimbabwe. R.B. Drummond. Natural Resources Board, Zimbabwe. 1981

Evergreen Forests of Malaŵi.   J.D. Chapman and F. White. Commonwealth Forestry Institute, University of Oxford. 1970

The Evergreen Forests of Malaŵi: natural history and conservation status.   R.J. Dowsett and F. Dowsett-Lemaire. In preparation

Trees of Malaŵi.   J.S. Pullinger and A.M. Kitchin. Blantyre Print and Publishing, Blantyre. 1982

Flowers of the Veld.   K. Linley and B. Baker. Bundu Series, Longman, Zimbabwe. 1972

Wild Flowers of Malaŵi.   A. Moriarty. Purnell. 1975

Malaŵi Orchids.   Vol. 1, Epiphytic Orchids. I. la Croix *et al.* Montfort Press, Limbe. 1983

Orchids of Malaŵi.   B. Morris. Society of Malaŵi, Blantyre. 1965

Malaŵi orchid book in preparation (to cover terrestrial and epiphytic orchids) I.F. la Croix. Balkema, Roterdam.

Succulent Flora of Southern Africa.   D. Court. Balkema, Cape Town. 1981

Common Veld Grasses of Rhodesia.   C. Lightfoot. Natural Resources Board, Zimbabwe. 1970

Useful Plants of Malaŵi.   J. Williamson. Montfort Press, Limbe. 1974

Dictionary of Plant Names in Malaŵi.   B. Binns and J.P. Logah. Government Printer, Zomba. 1972

Index